# PROTESTANT FUNDAMENTALISM

## and the

# BORN- AGAIN CATHOLIC

by

Father Robert J. Fox

 **FATIMA FAMILY APOSTOLATE**
Alexandria, South Dakota

Copies of this book
may be obtained from

Fatima Family Apostolate
Box 217, Alexandria, South Dakota, 57311-0217

Single copy: $9.95 plus $2 for postage and handling

Nihil Obstat:

June 9, 1989
Rev. James M. Joyce
Diocese of Sioux Falls

Printed in the United States of America by the
St. Martin de Porres Dominican Community, New Hope, Ky.

# Contents

# U. S. Bishops' Statement On Fundamentalism

*This preface is an excerpt from a pastoral statement
on Fundamentalism issued by a committee of the U.S. Bishops.*

---

... The basic characteristic of Biblical Fundamentalism is that it eliminates from Christianity the Church as the Lord Jesus founded it. That Church is a community of faith, worldwide, with pastoral and teaching authority. This non-church characteristic of Biblical Fundamentalism, which sees the Church as only spiritual, may not at first be clear to some Catholics. From some Fundamentalists they will hear nothing offensive to their beliefs, and much of what they hear seems compatible with Catholic Christianity. The difference is often not in what is said — but in what is not said. There is no mention of the historic, authoritative Church in continuity with Peter and the other Apostles. There is no vision of the Church as our mother — a mother who is not just spiritual, but who is visibly ours to teach and guide us in the way of Christ.

Unfortunately, a minority of fundamentalist churches and sects not only put down the Catholic Church as a "man-made organization" with "man-made rules," but indulge in crude anti-Catholic bigotry with which Catholics have long been familiar.

We believe that no Catholic properly catechized in the faith can long live the Christian life without those elements that are had only in the fullness of Christianity: the Eucharist and the other six Sacraments, the celebration of the Word in the liturgical cycle, the veneration of the Blessed Mother and the saints, teaching authority and history linked to Christ, and the demanding social doctrine of the Church based on the sacredness of all human life.

It is important for every Catholic to realize that the Church produced the New Testament, not vice versa. The Bible did not come down from heaven, whole and intact, given by the Holy Spirit. Just as the experience and faith of Israel developed its sacred books, so was the early Christian Church the matrix of the New Testament. The Catholic Church has authoritatively told us which books are inspired by the Holy Spirit and are therefore canonical. The Bible, then, is the Church's book. The New Testament did not come before the Church, but from the Church. Peter and the other Apostles were given special authority to teach and govern before the New Testament was written. The first generation of Christians had no New Testament at all — but they were the Church then, just as we are the Church today.

A study of the New Testament, in fact, shows that discipleship is to be a community experience with liturgy and headship and demonstrates the importance of belonging to the Church started by Jesus Christ. Christ chose Peter and the other Apostles as foundations of His Church, made Simon Peter its rock foundation and gave a teaching authority to Peter and the other Apostles. This is most clear in the Gospel of Matthew, the only Gospel to use the word *church*. This history of twenty Christian centuries confirms our belief that Peter and the other Apostles have been succeeded by the Bishop of Rome and the other bishops, and that the flock of Christ still has, under Christ, a universal shepherd . . . .

# INTRODUCTION

Fundamentalism is considered one of the greatest dangers today to mainline Protestantism and Roman Catholicism. Scriptural Fundamentalism, in which the Bible is interpreted literally and without regard to scholarship, without regard to the intention of ancient writers or two thousand years of Church history, is generally simplistic. When zeal and enthusiasm is added to the fundamentalist's approach, it disturbs many so that some actually leave their traditions and seek easy answers and solutions, religious-wise, according to Fundamentalism.

This book should be useful, therefore, for the Catholic parent and others suffering because a son or daughter, or perhaps some friend, who has, in today's confusion, fallen into the camp of Fundamentalism. If by prayer and a positive loving approach you can present this book to such a one, he or she may rediscover a lost faith. Such a one may for the first time discover the true face of Catholicism.

The book was not written so much with a view to reaching Fundamentalists and saying, "Look, here is where you are wrong." It was written with a great love for the Catholic Church. It was written to be given to Catholics confused and in danger of leaving the fullness of true faith. It was written to help those who have wandered, to help them find their way back to their Father's House. It was written for practicing Catholics to come to a deeper faith and in the sense used in Chapter 11 to become "born-again Catholics." Hopefully it will assist in the true "renewal" for which Vatican II worked while looking toward a New Pentecost for the Church.

It is not easy to write a book on Fundamentalism. It is said that much of what has sometimes been written on Fundamentalism is really on dispensationalism. The dispensationalists are descended from the Plymouth Brethren and date back to about 1830. They believe

Scripture should be interpreted absolutely literally. This is particularly important with regard to prophecy, as they think all Old Testament prophecies apply to Israel as an earthly nation and not to the Church. They divide God's dealings with man into seven dispensations. We are now in the dispensation of grace, which was preceded by the dispensation of law. The present dispensation, according to this, will last until the millennium, which will be the final one. They use the Scofield Bible, which has notes that explain some of these things.

Fundamentalism began at the end of the last century in opposition to Modernism. This explains why some Catholics today have fallen into Fundamentalism when Modernism, condemned by Pope St. Pius X, has gained prominence in Catholic writings and educational circles, misrepresenting true Catholicism and thereby confusing many from recognizing true Catholicism.

While generally we do not regard fundamentalists as Biblical scholars, there have been among fundamentalists some fine scholars, e.g., Dr. J. Gresham Machen, who wrote *The Virgin Birth of Christ*, regarded as a classic on the subject by many Protestants and Catholics alike. Some fundamentalists are extremely anti-Catholic. On the other hand, many are allies of Catholicism in their insistence on certain basic teachings and on moral issues. On some basic issues they will be closer to Catholicism than modernists who call themselves Catholic but misrepresent the Church. What we are saying here is that it would be a mistake to give one position as representative of all fundamentalists. Protestantism, of whatever variety, is hardly united.

The attacks by what is commonly called Fundamentalism have been answered thousands of times in the past hundred years. Yet, ever new approaches with the same old attacks continue to emerge, as seen even in some television evangelists. Such TV evangelists now reach other countries. They also send thousands of lay-evangelists into Catholic countries suffering from poverty and sometimes provide education in an attempt to lead them out of Catholicism.

For dispensationalists or fundamentalists or anyone else who may firmly believe that Roman Catholicism is against the Bible and that the Catholic faith has no base in Scripture, this book should demonstrate how unfairly and mistakenly the Catholic Church is presented. Inconsistencies and dishonesty in attacks will be shown especially in regard to the Holy Eucharist.

It is claimed that thousands of Roman Catholics have been drawn into fundamentalist camps in the past few decades. That is probably correct. Back in the 1940's and 50's, when Catholics in the United States had greater zeal, *we* were doing the converting. If they are in some cases drawing people away from the Catholic Church, it is because we are not effectively teaching the true Catholic religion. A whole generation of young Catholics grew up after Vatican II without the basics of their faith, without a firmness of Catholicism. The fault was not Vatican II but abuses in interpreting it, just as Scripture itself is misinterpreted.

This book is designed to appeal to Roman Catholics in general. It will serve to explain to young Catholics as well as older Catholics the soundness of their faith in harmony with the Scriptures and two thousand years of tradition. Apologetics is a science that picks the mind and touches the heart. This book will be a challenge to Catholics everywhere to dig deeper into their faith, and as the Apostle St. Paul wrote, "have a reason for the faith that is in you."

This book is not intended to attack Protestantism. It is not against authentic ecumenism. Dialogue between Catholics and mainline Protestant denominations, such as Lutheran, Methodist, and Anglican congregations has been possible. This has not been possible with fundamentalist sects. This book will be a dialogue, to a degree, in presenting words and positions of those who have attacked the Catholic position, regardless of what name we give them. I will give the Catholic response.

Unfortunately, most sincere Catholics are so far removed from these attacks on their faith that they do not understand at times the attacking positions and fail to communicate effectively with them, even when (rarely) the attackers give Catholics the opportunity. These attackers usually do not have an open mind to dialogue in listening as well as speaking. Catholic parents who have too often taken the education and formation of their children in the faith for granted have sometimes awakened too late to discover that their children know not Catholicism, but have discovered Fundamentalism.

Fundamentalists are not bashful. They are often full of zeal. They have even entered our Catholic centers at times at university and college campuses to hand out or leave their pamphlets attacking Catholicism. Not a few conscientious Newman chaplains have had to deal with invasions of their Catholic students by fundamentalists attempting to lead their students out of the Church.

While it is impossible to take up all of the hundreds of attacks directed against the Catholic position, this book handles the major areas of concern and questions which are basic to Catholicism. It deals with areas most frequently under attack. The book will be of great interest to Catholics. It is hoped that it will help them have their faith reaffirmed. In some cases it may well help them to come alive in the fullness of true faith, which they may have taken too much for granted. In that case I will call them "born again" along with those who rediscover a lost faith.

It is hoped that this book will in no way convey the thought that fundamentalists lack all truth. Many of them have a zeal for the Gospel that should be our envy. Many stress the basic morals of the Gospels and faith doctrines regarding Jesus Christ that is sadly in need of witness. While they may not preach the full Gospel they are in fact preaching a fuller Gospel than those tinted with Modernism, who teach while wearing the mask of "Catholicism."

If we speak of the "enthusiasm" of fundamentalists or Pentecostals, it is not intended as a condemnation of their presentation of the Gospel, which is given with a certain emotion. Emotion for emotion's sake without substance, of course, will not long endure. But there is certainly a place in our holy Catholic faith which touches the heart.

It has long been the contention of this author that Jesus Christ Himself made valid use of the emotions. Is not emotion a part of the whole man? Jesus Christ, the perfect Teacher, appealed to the whole man. It can easily be the weakness of conservative Catholic intellectuals to play down emotions so completely that even the valid use of emotions are neglected. In our teaching of the fullness of Catholic faith — the full Gospel — we need to appeal not only to the head, but to the heart as well.

Older readers willl remember well the late Archbishop Fulton J. Sheen, a scholar, a man of God, an intellectual, and one who could preach the Gospel and the doctrines of faith and morals of Catholicism with the fire of an Apostle. The action of the Holy Spirit within him as he spoke as an instrument of Jesus Christ thrilled millions, while he touched both the head and the heart. Would that our younger generation of Catholics could hear the full Gospel, the flaming truths of Catholicism, of Jesus Christ Himself, preached by a thousand, ten thousand Bishop Sheens. Then they could see well the true face of Catholicism and become witnesses to bring about within the Catholic Church that New Pentecost for which Pope John XXIII prayed when he convened the Second Vatican Council.

I have taken thousands of Catholic youth to Europe during the past two decades. With each group, which ranges in age from teenagers to those in their early twenties, I've met people who for the first time discovered the true face of Catholicism. We would spend up to two weeks at the International Shrine of Fatima where the Mother of Jesus Christ appeared at the beginning of this century. Her message has been described by each Pope since 1930 in words such as Pope Piux XVII used, "FATIMA IS A REAFFIRMATION OF THE GOSPELS." Yes, some have thought all this too devotional, too emotional. God help us if the "explosion of the supernatural" is "too emotional."

Sincere and committed Catholics believe they have the fullness of true faith. Not every Catholic lives it and not every "Catholic" preacher preaches it. Jesus Christ may seem, as in the Gospel account, asleep in the boat at times, especially in some areas. It is still the Church of Jesus Christ, however poorly represented at times. When such is the case, the answer is not to abandon ship, "O you of little faith," but to remain with Jesus Christ in the Church He Himself founded, and work to bring that true revival to all Catholics in Jesus Christ.

What a pity it would be if a fundamentalist with an incomplete Gospel and a vibrant faith treasured a part of the Gospel more than the Catholic who was dead to his "pearl of great price." If fundamentalists at times have attacked Catholicism it might well be in part due to our failure to live and communicate the faith as we ought.

The author of this book offers a prayer that each one who reads it will do so in sincerity of heart, and prayerfully seek Jesus Christ in the manner Jesus intended to teach, sanctify and govern our souls upon this earth. Jesus Christ is "the Way, the Truth and the Life." Jesus Christ is our Lord, God and Savior, the one essential Mediator between God the Father and mankind.

— Father Robert J. Fox

# CHAPTER 1

# A History of Fundamentalism

The challenge of fundamentalism has surfaced with great vigor at least once in each generation of religious life in America. We are in such a period. The rest of this century may well witness the resurgence of this phenomenon on the American scene as it reaches from the United States down into Central and South America and beyond. The mass media and modern transportation has made it easy for the fundamentalists to take their teachings of "born again" and certain salvation beyond American shores.

The fundamentalists may be unwittingly doing the Catholic Church in America a favor. There is evidence that their challenge is reawakening more Catholic educators to the fact that we need to return to teaching our youth the fullness of Catholicism and reaffirming for all the faithful the basics of Catholicism. Cardinal Franz Konig of Austria was quoted in *Newsweek* in October of 1986 as saying to a Polish bishop: "Thank God you have communism — that keeps you from sleeping." The famed cardinal reportedly stated: "Europe has lost its Christianity. The Pope believes the future of the Church is in Africa, South America and India." He also was quoted by *Newsweek* as saying:

> ... The Pope is never a pessimist. I often had lunch with him, and I was surprised how he always found a positive outlook everywhere. He speaks about the re-evangelization of Europe. And for us that also means the United States, because it has more or less the same history, although Americans are less pessimistic than Europeans. The Pope feels that the bishops should first take a common position and then find a way to re-evangelize a Europe that has, in a certain way, lost its Christianity.

Young people are hungry for religion. If Catholic educators do not present to youth the true face of Catholicism and the fullness of our holy faith and its practices, our youth will find a substitute some place else. The same is true for adults. If those who claim to be spokesmen, teachers for Catholicism, water down the faith and present another kind of "Catholicism" from that of the One, Holy, Universal and Apostolic Church of Jesus Christ, members of the Church which Jesus Christ Himself founded and promised would exist until the end of the world will become confused and weakened in their faith. They will seek satisfaction and become confused in easy solutions. The fundamentalists, in turn, who speak with "absolute authority" in quoting the Word of God, the Bible, will be giving them private interpretations which do not in fact reflect the authentic revelations of God. In their simplistic enthusiasm the seeming "fire" of the fundamentalist will appear to be "in the Spirit," offering certain salvation through being "born again."

In 1984 a nationally-known evangelist claimed that in America there were already one hundred and ten thousand fundamentalist churches, one thousand-six hundred Christian radio stations and eighty-two Christian television stations. About one-third of all professional athletes were reported as being "born again."

Fundamentalism is defined by the *Oxford English Dictionary* as a

religious movement which became active among various Protestant bodies in the U.S. after the war in 1914-18, based on strict adherence to traditional orthodox tenants (e.g., the literal inerrancy of Scripture) held to be fundamental to the Christian faith; opposed liberalism and modernism.

Fundamentalism makes its main emergence in the early twentieth century. At the same time an earlier movement, originating in the eighteenth century, called Evangelicalism, (not Evangelism) took a new turn. Evangelicalism holds to the doctrine of salvation by faith in Christ alone, as taught by Martin Luther. It also denies the need of good works and the Sacraments. This movement, while stressing the authority and divine inspiration of the Bible, has traditionally claimed that human nature was in itself depraved. It has stressed the necessity of reading the Scriptures and has fostered a zealous preaching that is Gospel-oriented.

The nineteenth century saw the introduction of the Plymouth Brethren which flowed from a movement started by John Darby, a former Church of Ireland clergyman, and which fostered prayer meetings in people's homes and stressed a more fundamentalist doctrine than he was permitted to practice in his church. This movement rejected all creeds and confessions itself. It took a strict literalist approach to the Bible and stressed the imminent Second Coming of Christ. The basic approach was Calvinistic.

While fundamentalism does not make any major impact on the American scene until the early twentieth century, the beginning was present in Evangelicalism, which was invigorated by the introduction of Liberalism and Modernism into mainline Protestant denominations. Modernism was condemned by Pope St. Pius X in two formal documents, *Lamentabili* and *Pascendi,* both published in 1907. Pope Pius X and his successors were able, for the time being, to prevent the theologians and others of the Catholic Church who were tempted by Modernism from having any great impact on the average Catholic. In fact, until the Second Vatican Council those in special positions in the Catholic Church were required to take an *Oath Against Modernism.*

The *Oath Against Modernism* was a solemn declaration issued by Pope St. Pius X, on Sept. 10, 1910, and was required to be taken on oath by all clergy who were to be advanced to major Holy Orders, pastors upon being assigned to a Catholic parish, confessors, preachers, religious superiors, and by professors of philosophy and theology in seminaries. The first part of the *Oath* is a strong affirmation of the principal Catholic truths opposed to Modernism; the demonstrability of God's existence by human reason, the value of miracles and prophecies as criteria of revelation, the historical institution of the Church founded by Christ, the invariable constancy of the essentials of Catholic tradition, and the reasonableness and supernaturalism of the Christian faith. The second part of the Oath is an expression of interior assent to the decree *Lamentabili* and the encyclical *Pascendi.* Particular modernist errors are singled out for censure and rejection. In 1967 the Sacred Congregation for the Doctrine of the Faith in the Vatican issued a new *Profession of the Faith* to replace the longer *Oath against Modernism.* The intention, of course, was not to discount the importance of the condemnation of the errors which were sweeping over the Christian world; it was to retain the obligatory profession of faith — the Nicene Creed — for persons occupying various ecclesiastical offices, along with an affirmation "firmly to accept and hold the doctrine on faith and morals which has been defined by the Church by solemn judgment or which has been affirmed and declared by her ordinary magisterium" (Fr. Umberto Betti, O.F.M., an advisor to the *Congregation for the Doctrine of the Faith*).

More recently, on Feb. 25, 1989, the Vatican published a new *Oath of Fidelity*. Issued by the Congregation for the Doctrine of the Faith, it consisted of two parts:

First, the profession of faith — essentially, the Nicene Creed, with three paragraphs added, which declare adherence to the Church's teaching authority.

Secondly, the *Oath of Fidelity*, in which, among other things, oath-takers pledge to "preserve the deposit of faith in its entirety, hand it on faithfully and make it shine forth."

This latest oath is nothing new in Church history. For centuries, various ecclesiastical officeholders have been required to make a profession of faith. It is an ancient practice rather than a new one.

What is Modernism? It is a theory about the origin and nature of Christianity. It was first developed into a system by George Tyrrell (1861-1909), Lucien Laberthonniere (1860-1932), and Alfred Loisy (1857-1940). According to Modernism, religion is essentially a matter of experience, personal and collective. Modernism teaches that there is no objective revelation from God to the human race, on which Christianity is finally based, nor any reasonable grounds for credibility in the Christian faith, based on miracles or the testimony of history. According to this theory faith is uniquely from within. In fact it is part of human nature, "a kind of motion of the heart," hidden and unconscious. It is, according to Modernism, a natural instinct belonging to the emotions, a "feeling for the divine" that cannot be expressed in words or doctrinal propositions, an attitude of spirit that all people have naturally but that some are more aware of having. According to Modernism the Christ of faith is not the Christ of history. He did not personally found the Church or institute Sacraments; these were merely historical *developments*. Its advocates sought freedom from religious authority and the emancipation of conscience. They assumed that everything modern was more perfect than what had gone before. Modernism denied dogma, the true efficacy of the Sacraments and the authority of Sacred Scripture. Those were the forms in which it attempted to invade Catholicism and which the Popes condemned. But Modernism made immediate inroads into the mainline Protestant Churches.

In reality Modernism goes back further than the eighteenth century; it was present in the thinking which led to the Protestant Revolt at the beginning of the sixteenth century. We see some of its principles even in what is thought of as very conservative fundamentalism today in the denial of any religious authority except the Word of God, which for them means exclusively "the Book." The fundamentalists, as we shall soon see, cannot accept defined doctrines or dogmas of faith. In reality, then, the very spirit against which the fundamentalists turn has victimized themselves in causing them to deny any religious authority in the Church which Jesus Christ Himself established.

As stated earlier, Evangelicalism was actually invigorated in the early twentieth century. Certain members of conventional Protestant churches — Methodist, Episcopal, and Presbyterian, reacted strongly to Liberalism and Modernism. They separated themselves from their churches and became known as fundamentalists. They saw their co-religionists as weakened in doctrine, and as abandoning the authority of Sacred Scripture. These churches responded by criticizing fundamentalists for not having enough regard for social justice, and for their militant separatism from other Christians.

There is some truth in both positions. We've seen the Modernist mentality develop to the extent of denying the historical Resurrection of Jesus Christ, a basic requirement of authentic Christianity and the supreme proof of the divinity of Jesus Christ as Lord, God and Savior. At the same time there has been little regard for helping the poor or the underprivileged among fundamentalists who look to the Bible as the only authority for the Word of God.

The entire historical context for these developments would have to go back to Europe, to the events that led to the Protestant Reformation, but in restricting our study to America we see in the 1700's what is called the "Great Awakening" in the thirteen original colonies. It resulted in "Revivalism" in America, following upon German Pietism and the Puritanism and Evangelicalism of the British Isles. Itinerant preachers became popular in the colonies, stressing a personal and emotional experience of conversion. These traveling preachers in an unorganized fashion held basically to the same tenets of today's fundamentalists. Jonathan Edwards and George Whitefield, the two most famous traveling preachers, covered the entire settled eastern seaboard. This "Awakening" movement achieved respectability when in its context colleges such as Princeton and Dartmouth were established. But not much was heard of the "Awakening" for the next generation because of a crisis in politics, the Revolution.

A second "Awakening" revival was ignited in the early 1800's and proved popular for a generation. The major Protestant churches out of which this movement came and from whom they broke were the Presbyterian, Congregational, and Methodist-Episcopal denominations. People who felt inspired and were disillusioned turned to new independent congregations, such as the Baptist churches, which represented the tenets of Fundamentalism.

While the ramifications of the various fundamentalist revival movements are very complex, even a brief survey reveals the divisions to which Christians turn when they break from the means Jesus Christ gave, namely Peter and his successors under the guidance and protection of the Holy Spirit, to keep the Church in "one Lord, one faith, one Baptism" (Ephesians 4:5).

There was a "holiness revival" movement within the Methodist Church following the Civil War. The "holiness spirit" in Protestantism flows from the emphasis given by John Wesley who taught that there were two stages to attaining holiness: 1) justification, or freedom from sin, and 2) sanctification, or the second blessing. When the strictly Wesleyan principles among American Methodists declined in use, groups of perfectionists were organized to promote holiness as an essential part of the Methodist tradition. About thirty new denominations grew out of this emphasis in the United States.

The religious bodies which grew out of the theology of holiness were fundamentalist in nature. Their theology, even if they say they are simply repeating the Word of God, is based on what they claim is an emotional experience produced in the heart, by a direct action of the Holy Spirit; it stresses the winning of converts and emphasizes the imminent, or soon-approaching, Second Coming of Jesus Christ.

The second blessing is central to the sects. It could require years of preparation but when it comes it is instantaneous. It can be lost and regained or may increase in efficacy. They identify this with the Spirit's coming. Some sects identify that coming of the Spirit with extraordinary gifts such as speaking in tongues or miraculous healing. More moderate sects will speak of the coming as a type of exalted feeling, an inner impression, a bodily emotion, deepened awareness of God's loving presence. In any case these sects became known as "Perfectionist Churches."

After the Civil War, continuing into the twentieth century, the Perfectionist Churches advanced in the westward drive of Methodist circuit travelers. Today their emphasis has evolved into the "Pentecostal" movement and a revolt against Modernism.

The Pentecostal churches today are characterized by an emphasis on sanctification, whereby adults have conversion experiences resulting in justification in the baptism in the Holy Spirit. This, according to them, involves an instantaneous spiritual transformation, separate from and following justification and a reception of the gifts of Pentecost, especially the climactic gift of *glossolalia* (speaking in tongues), and faith healing. The Assemblies of God is the fastest growing of the Pentecostal bodies today.

Annual conventions of the Assemblies and others were a part of the phenomena of Bible Conferences held in America in the "Bible Belt" (South and Midwest) from the late 1800's to the present. These conferences struck out against secularism and the infiltration of liberal theology found in the seminaries and universities. One of the most famous was the Niagara Bible Conference of 1895 where there were drawn up five points of strict conservative belief that became the cardinal tenets of Fundamentalism. The five articles in summary were: 1) the literal inerrancy and infallibility of the Bible, 2) the Virgin birth and full diety of Christ, 3) the physical Resurrection of Christ, 4) The atoning sacrifice of His death for the sins of the world, and 5) Jesus's Second Coming in bodily form to preside at the Last Judgment.

Between 1905 and 1915 these five articles were published and explained in twelve small volumes called, *The Fundamentals: A Testimony to the Truth*. The booklets were subsidized by two wealthy men from Los Angeles, Milton and Lyman Steward. At least three million copies of *The Fundamentals* were mailed free to pastors, missionaries, theology students and church workers throughout the country. This had a tremendous influence at a time which was unacquainted with the mass media.

The five points of the Niagara conference became the five "fundamentals." These booklets, written by different authors, opposed what is known as "higher criticism" as a way of studying the Bible. It also opposed the theory of evolution and the "social Gospel." This decade thus became a time of doctrinal organization and popularization of Fundamentalism.

The sincere and educated Catholic will have no problem accepting the five articles as stated above. The problem is *how* the fundamentalists interpret these articles and what they deny. Any interpretation at variance with their own is a serious threat to them, a sign that others are not and will not be saved as long as they do not accept their interpretations. The unsuspecting Catholic and others, especially if the Catholic is not well grounded in the basics of his or her own faith, may be enticed by these five fundamentals. They are true if properly understood; but they lack much of Catholic orthodoxy, of the *fullness* of faith. And the claim that these are the *absolute* and *only* acceptable test of orthodoxy is one of the reasons why Fundamentalism can have no place in Catholic theology. There is no mention, for example, of the Blessed Trinity, which is essential to the fullness of true faith. There is no mention of the Church of which Jesus spoke and which He founded. There is no mention of the Sacraments and no mention of Tradition in connection with Sacred Scripture. And the fundamentalist's notion of the Bible, which excludes any scholarly or scientific study of the Scriptures characteristic of modern Catholic Biblical scholarship, eliminates the possiblity for ecumenical dialogue, which might lead us to more completely understand the sacred Author's original intent.

While we shall see that Catholicism does not desire to make religion a matter which tends only to social problems, to make better the things on this earth, it is nonetheless sure that concern for our fellow man is very much a part of Christianity. Similarly, the booklets on Fundamentalism hold that the Bible is to be taken in a naive literal sense in the manner in which it reports the creation of the world. Fundamentalism misses the point that Sacred Scripture is not teaching natural science regarding how God created the world, but that He indeed created it out of nothing. If one interprets the Genesis account of the creation of the world literally then God creates light the first day but does not create the sun and moon until a few days later. But the inspired author is using a literary vehicle to teach not scientific truths, but religious truths, and this is not acceptable to fundamentalists. We will return to this matter of Scriptural interpretation in a later chapter. All must be interpreted literally, they say, as God can make no mistake. Yes, it *is* God's Word; but they forget that God is revealing religious truths in man's language and in a human manner and in a way understandable to the mentalities of a time which was not scientifically minded but more poetic in conceptual thinking. The story of the Genesis account of creation is nonetheless the work of a genius, an inspired author who is guided by God to teach only inerrant religious truths. The Genesis account contrasts with the pagan mythologies of the time, which were contrary to the revelation that God made all things out of nothing and that He made them good. Also in Genesis, man, who is made in God's image and likeness, is ordered to adore one true God, not many gods. Genesis answers all the basic questions of human life and its destiny while guiding people away from false beliefs. Fundamentalists, however, will simply interpret everything literally and miss much of the message. The author of Genesis and the creation accounts, in addition to being divinely inspired, knew the errors of the people of the time, the pagan beliefs, and the mode of human thought. God used some secondary author so that he wrote only divine truth on religious matters. Genesis used a literary vehicle to get God's message across. It used a story, but not just any story. As noted, the story was the work of a genius who conveyed the divine truths of God and at the same time corrected the errors that were common at the time. What Genesis reveals is valid and true for all time and for eternity. This is all more fully explained in many other Catholic volumes.

The summary above is only a brief hint at the wisdom of Sacred Scripture and shows that the Bible is not a book of natural science. It tells not how the heavens go but how to go to heaven. It is a book of true religion, not a book of natural science, or secular history. Concepts of history in the minds of the ancients was much different from that of modern mentalities. God spoke through human modes of expression at the time He spoke. If God had revealed Himself thousands of years ago according to present knowledge of the natural sciences, or present modes of expression, His message would have been meaningless for thousands of years.

In 1919 the fundamentalist movement took a major step with the establishment of the militant World's Christian Fundamentals Association. It began publishing a quarterly review and conducted annual rallies in North America for a decade. Around 1920 the title "Fundamentalism" came into common use. It was used as a badge of honor in spreading and defending the "fundamentals" as outlined above.

All this had a tremendous effect on American Protestant churches, especially those claiming to be evangelical. These included the Presbyterians, Methodists, Baptists, Disciples of Christ and various Pentecostal churches. Controversies raged and gave rise to several national and international movements. These include the International Council of Christian Churches, formed in opposition to the Federal Council of the Churches of Christ in the United States. More recently, representatives of these congregations have taken a more sophisticated stance in seeking to shed the Fundamentalist badge by identifying themselves with international conservative Protestant groups, e.g., the World Evangelical Fellowship.

It is helpful to know something of Fundamentalism's historical development. But Fundamentalism remains difficult to define precisely, for it is more than simply a theological or religious phenomenon. It appears to carry all kinds of political and psychological implications as well. The next chapter provides some of the broad characteristics of today's Fundamentalism, including their socio-religious implications.

# CHAPTER 2

# Major Characteristics
# of Fundamentalism Today

Fundamentalism is a dynamic and ever-shifting force, and in our own time it has taken on a number of characteristics which both arise from and go beyond the five "fundamentals." This chapter attempts to identify these characteristics.

First, Fundamentalism is uniquely American, while Anglo-Saxon in origin. It has a missionary thrust that uses the mass media and works to collect millions of dollars in its efforts at world expansion. It is sometimes confused with psychological feelings of patriotism. It has a sense of being specially chosen, a sense of manifest destiny and righteousness. One can detect this in the words of its more public ministers who speak of being anointed, or specially chosen. They will even see the material blessings people of America have received, unparalleled in the world, as proof of being chosen. (The Catholic response, however, would be reflected in Matthew 5:44 where Jesus commands us to pray for and love our enemies. Then we are informed that God withholds His blessings from no one, as Jesus says God's "sun rises on the bad and the good, he rains on the just and the unjust" (NAB).

Secondly, Fundamentalism, as seen in most of its preachers, professes to be non-denominational. It is at pains to show that it is reacting against the cold formalism and bureaucracy of established churches in favor of spontaneous, and often extreme, religious experience. It is often organized around the personality or charisma of a particular preacher. Therefore it is often trans-denominational. It crosses all lines, appealing to individuals to go "back to the basics" which are the "fundamentals" described earlier in this chapter. There will often be criticisms of priests and ministers who have rituals or liturgies and they will be presented as being ignorant of the Scriptures. To Christians whom they consider trapped, even by the devil in these churches, they will cry, "Come out."

Third, there is a basic hostility to Catholicism. How direct this hostility is depends upon the particular preacher. All the while listeners or readers will be repeatedly reassured that the preacher "loves Catholics." It is his very "love" for Catholics that causes him to be so hostile to Catholicism, to its teaching of the spiritual authority of the Pope, of devotion to Mary, of its "pagan belief" and practice of thinking they can eat the Body and drink the Blood of Jesus Christ, etc. There is the constant claim that the Catholic Church replaces the Bible with itself, its Magisterium, Sacraments, etc. These serious accusations, which the fundamentalist preacher says he makes as a duty in love, arises from individual interpretations of the Bible; he claims to speak for God but distorts God's Word by isolating and misrepresenting Scriptural texts. What the preacher believes to be divine inspiration which he has received, is adequate to qualify him to interpret the Bible correctly and without error, independently of any guidance from a faith-community which has two thousand years of faith tradition in its Magisterium (teaching authority) established by Jesus Christ. While he himself claims to be individually divinely guided and inspired, evidences of heaven's favors to Catholicism, such as Lourdes and Fatima, are simply swept aside by the fundamentalist preacher as false and a trick — but he does not give any evidence or proofs for making such statements. These apparitions were approved as worthy of belief after years of careful investigation by many experts and then approved by the Catholic Church only because they are in harmony with the Gospels and the near two thousand years of Christian teachings. These divine favors, which came from heaven to Catholicism and were given to the whole world, are a threat to fundamentalists, so they are simply swept aside as false.

The fundamentalist gives no room for development in the understanding of Divine Revelation. To him the Word of God does not allow for growth in which faith seeks greater understanding of God's revelation. The fundamentalist has it all in the Bible since its meaning jumps from the pages, if one will just read it. For them the meaning is obvious. Just read and believe. But if it were that simple there would not be over eighteen thousand different Christian denominations — each claiming to read and believe correctly.

The fundamentalist position is the result of replacing the Church Jesus founded with a book which was not compiled and approved as divinely inspired until some centuries after the death, resurrection and ascension of Jesus Christ. While fundamentalists accuse the Catholic Church of replacing the Bible with the Church, they replace the

Church with the Bible which in fact, as will be shown in subsequent chapters, could not exist without the Church. Because of their position of accepting only a part of Divine Revelation, God's Word coming to us through Tradition, that is, the Church He Himself established, one can see why they have antipathy toward the ancient Catholic Church and their attempt to deny its historical existence from the time Jesus placed it upon the earth and gave it the Holy Spirit at Pentecost.

Fourth, the fundamentalists have no use for a social gospel. The prophets are interpreted as having two purposes: predictors of the Messiah and predictors of the end times. To interpret the prophets also as persons protesting social situations and announcing the need for peace and justice in the world, presented as ideals of the Bible, are for them abhorrent interpretations. Because of their constant eschatological outlook, (end of the world; coming of Christ), they have a political conservatism often marked by extremes. The end times will be cataclysmic. One should not try to better one's lot — that would be affirming good works. At the same time they oppose Communism (which the Catholic Church also opposes). A government leader who opposes Communism will get support from them, but, not of course, the Catholic Church which has always opposed atheistic Communism and, through its Popes, has been a leader in pointing out its evils.

Because of its simplistic interpretations of the Bible and the times, Fundamentalism can easily appeal to people who find it difficult to contend with our technological, complex world, the immense social problems of a world in revolution, a world in change, while Fundamentalism offers a back-to-something "basic," which in reality is the articles of Fundamentalism outlined earlier and which is a very incomplete Gospel. The fundamentalist closes his mind to a wider view.

Fifth, there is a strong support of Israel. This may seem strange, as there has been a history of strong anti-semitism among fundamentalists. However they see Israel as the location connected with the end times. Israel is the harbinger of the kingdom to come, of the end-time cataclysm, of the final battle at Armageddon (Revelations 16:16) between good and evil before the Day of Judgment. Two important books used in their preaching are Ezekiel from the Old Testament and the Book of Revelation, the last book of the New Testament. Both contain much symbolic language. The veiled symbolic language gives the fundamentalist room for seeing an interpretation that applies literally and historically to present realities in the international scene of nations and religions. This allows them to make exact interpretations of current events and predictions of what will happen in the near future.

Sixth, fundamentalists make a frequent distinction between "real" and "nominal" Christians. The "nominal" Christian is he who follows the Gospel as preached in mainline Christian churches, while the "real" or true Christian is not identified with any membership in those churches, but who accepts the Gospel as preached in terms of Fundamentalism. There is often no hesitation to say that members of the mainline Christian churches, e.g., major Protestant churches, and especially Roman Catholic, will not be saved unless they "come out."

Seventh, fundamentalists deny an ordained ministry. There are leaders among the fundamentalists who have been especially called or chosen usually because of some special religious experience. Fundamentalists accept leaders who manifest some charisma to rise up as preachers and evangelists among them. This amounts to a kind of popularity ordination. There is no need for formal theological training and it is to be avoided as trusting too much in the intelligence. One must live by faith, not by reason. While Biblical studies are encouraged and even required, there is no Biblical theology. (Catholics and other Christians on the other hand hold that reason and faith must exist in harmony, for God is the Author of all truth. Right reason and true faith are never in conflict.)

Eighth, since all material things are corrupt, totally alienated from God due to original sin, the fundamentalists reject the use of the Sacraments established by Christ, and even often slight His humanity. There is a failure to recognize Christ's redeeming power, not only of human persons, but also over created things. The Sacraments involve the use of the things of the world, e.g., water, bread and wine, and oil, as signs in bestowing the powers of Jesus Christ; that is, Christ Himself acts in the Sacraments in the Catholic Church through the one administering the Sacraments in His Name. While the fundamentalists fail to recognize the goodness in created things and the possible use of them on the part of Jesus Christ in His Church, they will make of the Bible what they abhor in Sacraments, namely the material reality of words on paper of the Book which conveys for them the divine reality of God and His will and grace to humans. The Catholic Church, too, regards the Bible as inerrant, the recorded Word of God, but it is the "living Word" of God as believed by the Church and interpreted by the Magisterium (Teaching Church) which the Catholic Church sees, especially when read in the Church, and used in its official teachings, as bringing a living reality of Jesus Christ.

God chose to send His Divine Son in the flesh. "In the beginning was the Word; the Word was with God and the Word was God . . . . The Word became flesh, He lived among us, and we saw His glory, the glory that He has from the Father as only Son of the Father, full of grace and truth" (John 1:1 ff.). God chose to become flesh, to become man, one like us in all things except sin (cf. Hebrews 4:15, Romans 8:3, 2 Corinthians 5:21). God surely honored material reality when to accomplish the redemption He took on human nature from this world through Mary and the overshadowing of the Holy Spirit. Now such is Catholic teaching, but the fundamentalist, emphasizing the divinity of Jesus, often neglects the "in flesh" — the humanness of Jesus Christ, that God became God-Man in order to redeem us. The whole doctrine of what Christ is must involve both God and Man, the God-Man.

We can study the two thousand years of Christianity and see that the same errors have been made by those who have not followed the Church with its teaching authority aided by the Holy Spirit as established by Jesus Christ. What fundamentalists advocate are shades of Gnosticism, a theory of the first century. The Gnostics were disciples of various pantheistic sects that existed before Christ. They borrowed what suited their purpose from the Gospels. Matter was said to be hostile to spirit, and the universe was held to be a depravation of the Deity. Gnosticism disclaimed that Christ established in the Church a teaching authority to interpret decisively the meaning of the revealed word of God.

In the Catholic Church there is an ongoing sanctifying process. One grows in holiness gradually, not simply and automatically by receiving the Sacraments, but by growth in a life of prayer, responding to faith in good works for the love of Christ in neighbor, by worshipping God in His Way by doing as Christ commanded when He established the Holy Eucharist, "Do this in memory of Me. . . ." By approaching the Sacraments to encounter Jesus Christ more and more in faith, love, and growth in grace, the Catholic grows in sanctification as he grows more intimately into the likeness of Jesus Christ, offering all he is and has to Christ in the perpetuation of His Eucharistic Sacrifice. There is required faith, a response of love, and the identification of one's will more and more with the will of God. The fundamentalists, however, will ridicule all this, even using as proofs the claims of fallen-away Catholics, especially rebel "ex-priests" who are disturbed and whom they offer as experts on the teachings of Catholicism. They will use such betrayers to ridicule Catholicism, as when they claim one cannot encounter Jesus Christ in a piece of "bread."

Ninth, fundamentalists tend to avoid the use of the word "church" as a definite organization which Jesus intended as a visible body. They attempt to negate the long history of the Catholic Church reaching back to the days of Jesus and the Apostles. There is some vague realization of Jesus starting a Church and for them it will be revealed only at the end of time. In this way they attempt to discount what even secular historians will note about the ancient Catholic Church which exists to the present moment.

Tenth, the fundamentalists hold the Bible as absolute, a reality in itself whose meaning is clear and evident. It presupposes that the Word can immediately be grasped in meaning by all. Fr. Eugene LaVerdiere has stated:

> ... Fundamentalism is not a kind of interpretation but a denial of the need and legitimacy of interpretation. It presupposes the Word can be immediately grasped by all. Unwittingly, however, the fundamentalist does interpret. Such is the nature of reading and communication. Without realizing it, the fundamentalist equates the Biblical Word with his or her interpretation of it and makes an absolute of that interpretation as the one for all who hear the Word.

One who tries to discuss the meaning of a Biblical text with a fundamentalist can only run into frustration, for discussion is denied from the beginning and no progress can be made at penetrating more deeply into the meaning of Sacred Scripture. One hears the fundamentalist say, "the Bible says" but you will not hear him say, "the Bible means" even though they are anxious to share with everyone who will to listen to their interpretation of what the Bible means. The message contained in their presentation is the divine meaning for salvation and, as already stated, the more forceful personalities among them at times do not hesitate to say that other Christians who do not accept the meaning they give cannot be saved.

For the fundamentalist it is heresy to even consider that the Bible or its inspired writers should err even in their accounts of history, politics, ideas, geography, scientific descriptions of the universe, etc. Now, the Catholic Church also says the Bible does not err, but remember that when the fundamentalist says it he is speaking of a literal interpretation without regard for the genre in which it was written. If science or archeology seems to contradict some of the information given in the Bible, their response will be either that our modern scientific information is wrong or God made it to look that way so that faith would be required on our part. Thus by Biblical dates they see the world as created on some such date as 4,004 B.C. and 1,655 years later the flood occurred, and for them such is held as historical fact regardless of scientific archeology, geology, or anthropology. This is the most literal approach to the Bible.

A limited number of moderate literalists have interpreted the Bible to broaden such an approach. Thus each of the six days of creation may be interpreted as a period of time. But all forget that the Bible is not attempting to give a scientific description of the world but simply to reveal that the one true God made it out of nothing, and made man His crowning achievement in creation, in His own image and likeness, and that man must be obedient to God to have happiness. As soon as we look at the Bible as a book of science of the Old Testament, or as a book of history according to the modern method of recording history, there is a falling away from the intention of the sacred authors and of God Himself, who used the human beings to record divinely inspired religious truths for our salvation.

Since this matter of Scriptural interpretation is central to the problem of Fundamentalism, we will pause to consider it in greater depth here. What will be important for the modern reader is to appreciate the genres in which the sacred writers wrote. Now if one allows of no interpretation of Sacred Scripture, as do fundamentalists, one is going to fall into all kinds of errors by failure to know the genres. Father William G. Most in his splendid book, *Free From All Error* (The Franciscan Marytown Press; Libertyville, Ill.), writes:

> Now it is obvious that Scripture belongs to a very different culture stream from ours, the ancient Semitic. Can we just assume that the ancient Semites used the same genres as we do? Of course not. That would be foolish. In fact, we would not even be faithful to Scripture if we treated it as if it had been written by a modern American. We would not be trying to find out what the ancient inspired author really meant to assert. Instead, we would be imposing our own ideas on his words. To do that is called Fundamentalism. Fundamentalists ignore genre, acting instead as if Scripture had been written by a modern American. For example, they will say that since Genesis says God made the world in six days, that means it was done in six times twenty-four hours.

Before reading any book of Scripture, we need to determine the genre being used. The genre may even vary within a Biblical book. Pius XII put it this way in his great encyclical *Divino Afflante Spiritu* (1943):

> What is the literal sense in the words and writings of the ancient oriental authors is often not obvious as with writers of our time. For what they meant to signify by their words is not determined only by the laws of grammar and philology, nor only by the context; it is altogether necessary that the interpreter mentally

return, as it were, to those remote ages of the East, so that, being rightly helped by ... history, archeology, ethnology, and other fields of knowledge, he may discern... what literary genres ... those writers of the ancient time wished to employ and actually employed.

The original texts which were written under divine inspiration have long ago turned to dust. We rely on copies of copies of copies and translations of translations of copies handed down through the centuries. There was no divine inspiration given to those who copied or translated. Yet, I recently read a popular fundamentalist who claimed that even every comma of the Bible is divinely inspired and that there is a common style throughout both the Old and New Testaments. Every Biblical scholar will agree that each part of the Bible where God used a different human author reflects the style of the human author while through divine inspiration inerrantly preserving the divine truths contained therein. Scholars make use of the piecing together of many scrolls, fragments, codices, etc., preserved and discovered over the centuries. The Catholic Church truly teaches that there was the divine inspiration and guidance of the Holy Spirit in recording the religious truths of the Bible but that the human author did not write as a secretary taking dictation word for word from God. The human author did not necessarily realize at the time that he was being divinely inspired and kept from error.

The fundamentalists who hold to literal interpretations cannot live with any (often only apparent) inconsistencies of the human author and must seek to find ways to harmonize the texts, that is, to explain away the inconsistencies because God could not possibly make a mistake. This is no problem for the Catholic scholar and Protestant scholars of mainline churches because they do not hold that the Bible contains exact descriptions of science, history, and the like according to modern ways of expressing and understanding.

In viewing the Biblical Word, scholars know that these differences are explained as human in style and that they vary according to the individualities of the writers while holding to the divine quality of the Word. To use a very simple example, the Bible speaks of the sun rising. We know that the sun does not rise even though we use the expression yet today. The secondary author of Scripture merely wrote in the way it appears to man. There is no question here of the Bible teaching a science of the manner in which the universe operates.

Absolute harmonization is difficult for the fundamentalist, for the Bible is complex, having been written over hundreds of years. For example, the Bible repeatedly gives different accounts of the same event. There are even several versions of the Ten Commandments. The two most famous are the Ten Commandments of Exodus 20 and Deuteronomy 5. Which is the most real? Which does God more intend? Also, who killed Goliath? 1 Sam. 17:51 has David killing Goliath of Gath. 2 Sam. 21:19 says Elhanan killed Goliath of Gath. It is all part of the inerrancy of the Bible. How do you explain this? There is an explanation but it is not found by literal reading of the Bible.

These problems in accepting the Bible as the only authority in faith are solved for the Catholic who believes in a Church founded by Jesus Christ, divinely guided in its tradition of interpretation, in its teaching, and who believes in the one Church for which it was promised that it would never be destroyed but always have the Holy Spirit to keep it in the truth until the end of the world. That divinely guided Church supports scholarship to research these matters. It also recognizes the human side to the Bible while yet proclaiming its infallible truth.

Interesting situations exist in the New Testament also. In Luke 9:50 Jesus says, "Anyone who is not against you is for you." Luke 11:23 Jesus says: "Anyone who is not with me is against me"; 1 John 3:9 says, "No one who is a child of God sins." (This is sometimes used by fundamentalists to show there is no need for confession if one is saved.) But see 1 John 1:8: "If we say, 'We have no sin,' we are deceiving ourselves and truth has no place in us: if we acknowledge our sins, He is trustworthy and upright so that he will forgive our sins and will cleanse us from evil." Again read Romans 10:9: "If you declare with your mouth that Jesus is Lord, and if you believe with your heart that God raised Him from the dead, then you will be saved." However, in Matthew 7:21 we read: "Not everyone who says to me, 'Lord, Lord,' will enter the kingdom of heaven, but the person who does the will of My Father in heaven."

In John's Gospel Jesus cleanses the Temple at the beginning of His ministry. In the other Gospels he cleanses it during His passion, at the end of His earthly life. Some fundamentalists will attempt to harmonize this by saying that he must have cleansed it twice. They also say that Jesus must have taught two sets of beatitudes since Matthew 5 and Luke 6 vary in presenting the beatitudes.

The above is enough to indicate the complexities of Sacred Scripture, and to show that humility is needed in reading God's Word. It takes hard work, scholarship, humility and faith to believe that God gave us a divinely guided means of preserving ourselves from error in interpretations.

The idea that fundamentalists know the whole of Sacred Scripture better than anyone else is a myth. There must be humility, honesty, openness in inquiry — in short, a great carefulness about God's Word. The Catholic Church does indeed encourage private reading of the Bible but we should do so humbly and with the realization of the totality of how God has given us His revelation in the Church.

The complex modern world has added to the challenge of interpreting and applying God's Word rightly to moral problems that continuously arise. Today, for example, there is a series of complex bioethical issues challenging the Christian. The Church holds that science and medicine exist to serve human beings and ultimately to be used for the glory of God. A fundamentalist who sees the world — all matter — as evil would find easy answers in his simplicity. The Church, however, must distinguish the fine line in concrete situations which separates science serving humanity and science exploiting human beings. A short list of the questions that would have to be answered using God's Word for moral guidance would include *in vitro* fertilization, genetic engineering, experimentation on humans and human embryos, and the double-edged effect of many drugs, to name a few. Yet the Bible does not address these problems. The fundamentalist, in his literal and simple interpretation, simply blanks out of his mind the real world with its complex issues.

A final characteristic of fundamentalists is often their apocalyptic view of history. The world is essentially evil, they believe, with little hope for it, so their focus is on a cataclysmic end of the world culminating in divine judgment. The term "dispensationalism" is used to explain both Scripture and the present times in terms of an unfolding plan of God toward this end time as revealed in the Bible. Its definition comes from the Greek word *oikoneme*, meaning the plan of God.. "Economy" and "order" are rooted in this word as well as the expression, "the divine economy." The world is governed by divine plans.

According to fundamentalists, there are five plans in the Biblical era: 1) the ages or dispensations of innocence, conscience, and human government that existed before the time that God called Abraham, 2) the promise (Covenant through Abraham), 3) the Law (Mosaic Covenant), 4) the Christian age of grace and the Church, and finally 5) the kingdom to come.

This may well explain why there is no emphasis on a social Gospel, to improve the lot of man and his rights and needs here and now, for there is much focus on the kingdom to come and frequently this focus is millennial (*mille* is Latin for one thousand). They speak of the one thousand-year reign of Jesus Christ, taken from a strictly literal interpretation of Revelation 20:1-6.

There were already Christians after the conversion of Constantine in the fourth century A.D. who felt they saw the ushering in of the one thousand-year reign (which would have lasted only until the Middle Ages). Then Christ would appear in His final coming and Last Judgment. Another interpretation was that as the year one thousand approached, the thousand year-reign could be counted from Christ's birth. There was great expectation among some Christians then that the end of the world was about to arrive.

Fundamentalism today emphasizes apocalyptic or dispensational pre-millennialism. The expression "rapture" is used. This view holds that history as we know it will culminate with the sudden descent of Jesus toward earth to bring rapture to His Church. The believers of Jesus will be caught up with Him in heaven and remain there for a seven-year period known as the "tribulation" during which someone known as the anti-Christ will gain world power. This will be a time of the worst suffering ever in the world and will culminate in the Battle of Armageddon near Jerusalem. At a decisive moment in the battle, Jesus and His followers will reappear to vanquish the anti-Christ and to usher in the one thousand-year reign. At the end of all this the old earth will pass away and will be replaced by "a new heaven and a new earth" where the saved will spend eternity. When they speak of "rapture," then, they mean a coming of Christ other than the final coming at the end of the world.

We can anticipate that with the year 2000 approaching, and even for awhile thereafter, there will be much speculation and attention about the "end-times" from the millennialists.

The various imaginative concepts of the one thousand years from that one passage of Revelation are not in agreement with the teaching of the New Testament as a whole concerning the Resurrection, nor with Jesus' words that neither angels nor humans nor Jesus Himself (as man) knew the day or the hour (See Mark 13:32; Matt. 24:42; 25:13-15; Luke 12:38). The message of the New Testament is that we are to be expectant, vigilant, and always ready.

The millennium is symbolic as is the whole book of Revelation. Scriptural scholars see the one thousand years as meaning, as it does in many places in Sacred Scripture, a very long time. The first Resurrection symbolizes Baptism (cf. Rom. 6:1-10). In Revelation, one thousand years is seen as the life span of the Church from Jesus'

Resurrection until the Last Judgment, and three and one-half years symbolizes the Church in its times of persecution (Rev. 11:2-3; 12:14). The chaining of Satan obviously means that his power or influence has been greatly reduced because of the hope of redemption in and through Jesus Christ. There is the constant apocalyptic theme that there will be the struggle of the end times, but fear not, Jesus Christ will be victorious. These are the findings of Catholic Scriptural scholars.

This review of the main characteristics of Fundamentalism, while perhaps not exhaustive, is sufficient to identify Fundamentalism as it exists today.

We conclude this chapter with a summary of how Catholics fall into Fundamentalism. In his booklet, *Catholic Answers to Fundamentalists' Questions* (Liguori Publications), Philip St. Romain relates experiences he had while serving on a campus ministry team at Louisiana State University. He counseled many students there involved in several of the strong fundamentalist communities. His experience is typical of other experiences across the U.S. His explanation confirms my own experiences and studies on the subject with which I conclude this chapter.

The common occurrence is that in which a person falls from a fuller Christian faith into the fundamentalist camp while initially being convinced he has found real Christianity, in its pure, unadulterated form in the Sacred Scriptures. We present here a typical mode of development:

1. One becomes confused when he encounters a fundamentalist who is convinced that a person will not be saved unless he comes into his camp. The fundamentalist comes on with great enthusiasm, an overwhelming conviction which attracts him and makes him think that such a person really knows the Bible and has a deeper, stronger, and admirable faith. The fundamentalist gives witness to faith, to the Bible, to Jesus Christ, in a way never before encountered by the listener.

2. The listener, previously satisfied with his religion (although sometimes not well educated in it), is powerless to contradict the fundamentalist who has deeply ingrained within him certain Biblical references (however, these are out of context and without the meaning of the Biblical author), which seem to contradict the doctrines of faith which the listener has been accepting.

3. The listener agrees to go with the fundamentalist to a Bible

discussion or prayer meeting, but has reservations.

4. The group accepts the newcomer with great enthusiasm and warmth that overwhelms the novice. (This is much like those being introduced to cults.) It appears to be genuine Christian charity such as he has not met in the traditional church which he has been attending. The novice, in response, experiences a warmth which seems to be a deeper personal relationship with Jesus Christ than ever experienced.

5. The novice becomes convinced that he is in serious need of studying the Bible, of which he knows little. (He does not realize that the doctrines of faith which he accepted since childhood are indeed in harmony with the Sacred Scriptures.) The novice goes through an indoctrination in the principles of Fundamentalism as he studies the Bible which in no way seems to contradict the basics of his earlier identification with Christ Jesus in faith. Only now, it seems, he is coming to a deeper and personal relationship with Jesus Christ. He begins to share his newfound enthusiasm with others. As he becomes more deeply entrenched in Fundamentalism, however, he begins to deny many doctrines of his former faith. This stage continues for a considerable length of time. While some adults advanced in age have been known to become confused in the complexities and crises of faith in the modern world, more often one will find good religious parents, who have remained faithful to their Church, become very anxious when they see a son or daughter reject their parents' religious values and doctrines, and seem to become more excited about Jesus Christ and salvation then ever before. The parents are at a great loss as how to handle the situation and find a solution difficult. The young person may even attempt to convert his or her parents to the "Real Jesus, Savior of the Bible," and even state that the parents cannot be saved in the way in which they presently believe. Often, the parents, who still love their child, must proclaim that whereas they do not disown their child they must insist that he not discuss religion in the home or with family members.

6. After being indoctrinated in the Scriptures according to the principles of Fundamentalism, the one who has long left or become inactive in his former church now notices that he is hearing the same things over and over again. Since the emotional high or warmth of his initiation has long waned, he has a steady diet of fear heaped upon him as he hears that most other Christians are doomed to damnation. He begins to *feel* that

he also is not pleasing to God.

7. A realization comes that the group is not going anywhere. There is no growth. Sticking to the limited number of fundamentals, and lacking much in basic Christianity, he has no depth and is without the accumulated fruit of faith seeking understanding through the centuries. The former novice (especially if he has intellectual ability and a mind that seeks depth and width of insight), will began to become disillusioned by the quick and easy answers. The simple black and white answers are not providing faith and moral insights into the many complex issues of today. What seemed like an exciting, new, and deeper faith now appears very shallow.

8. This step can vary. There are former Catholics who have fallen into the fundamentalistic camp, and when arriving at step 7, remain for a while there. But eventually many find their way back to Catholicism. They rejoice in reclaiming a lost faith. Now they experience the depth of Catholic doctrines and realize that these doctrines are truths about the Person they love, namely the God-Man Jesus Christ who is fully their Savior. Now they discover that there is a personal relationship with Jesus Christ to be found in Catholicism that could never be achieved elsewhere. Now they are prepared to probe into deeper waters of Catholicism to appreciate the fullness of true faith and the religious wisdom of the ages. The Mass and Sacraments are especially recognized as personal encounters with Jesus Christ. They find Jesus as Lord, God and Savior in all aspects of official Catholicism. They recognize how their minds had been closed for a time to the truths of Jesus Christ in the Catholic Church.

Others in step 8 may become disillusioned with all religion and fall into agnosticism or even atheism. Such simplistic incorrect reading of the Bible has led the former fundamentalist to lose faith in what he thinks is the Word of God. This step can involve becoming guilt-ridden and seriously neurotic.

There are, of course, many people who remain a part of the fundamentalist movement throughout life. Taking the Bible as the only Word of God, they have doubtlessly never thought through the deeper implications of their position. They find a tremendous security in shutting out involvements in many of the problems and complexities of modern life around them. They are content with God as they perceive Him. It must be recognized that there is a beauty in these souls. Many, perhaps most of them, who accept the approach of

Fundamentalism live good moral lives, which is not seen in the lives of many others who call themselves Christian but whose minds and lives are far from Jesus Christ. We can admire the enthusiasm of those who remain in Fundamentalism. If only they could have not only that enthusiasm, that love, that desire to witness Jesus Christ to all, but also the fullness of faith in Jesus Christ. They would find that witness, that tremendous love, that whole-hearted commitment to Jesus Christ in the lives of countless Catholic apostles, saints and mystics throughout the centuries, right into our own day. Happy with only a part of the truth, how glorious it could be for them to experience a fuller reality of Jesus Christ, Whose generosity, Whose love, is without limit.

# CHAPTER 3

# A Preliminary Word
# About Scripture

Before examining in greater depth the fundamentalist abuse of Scripture, it is important to be sure that the reader understands how Scripture came to be and how we are to approach it to better understand the truths God wishes to teach us. When 1 Timothy 3:16 says, "All Scripture is inspired by God, St. Paul is referring to the Old Testament as inspired. The Old Testament was the Bible of the Apostles and of Jesus. The New Testament was merely in the process of either being written or accepted by the Church, which was not complete for the first Christians. Jesus did not have an official authoritative list of books specifically called the Bible. The accepted Hebrew books of the Old Testament were not standardized until later, around 90 A.D. At that time, the Sacred Scriptures in order of importance were: The Torah (Law), the Nabi'im (Prophets), and the Kethuvim (Writings). There was a collection in Hebrew. There was also the more developed collection in the Greek Septuagint, which Jesus and the early Apostles quoted frequently and which the Catholic Church uses today in presenting its canonical lists of inspired books.

St. Paul, who, under divine inspiration, wrote much of what we have today in the New Testament, possibly never read any of the Gospels in their present form. The faith of the first Christians was not passed on by handing them a New Testament of the Bible. The New Testament was being developed in the early Church which Jesus Christ had founded and to which He had promised the Holy Spirit, the Spirit of Truth to guide and keep it in truth. History attests that there was a hierarchical apostolic leadership in the early Church. Fundamentalists deny any identification of early Christians or the early Church with the Catholic Church. However, there is much evidence in the New Testament as we have it now that the first Christians considered Peter to have received from Jesus Christ special authority. There are abundant historical sources which list the successors of St. Peter.

Concerning the Bible, there were numerous religious writings among the early Christians. A way to determine which ones were divinely inspired was needed. The authority of the Church, which Jesus Christ established with Peter as visible head, enabled the Christians to do so. It was the authority which Jesus gave the Church which presented to the world for the first time the Bible we now have. They had no printing presses to make a Bible availabe to all. Even so, how many could read? God did not present the world the Bible, the book bound together as we have it today. It came forth from the Church, divinely guided by the Holy Spirit.

While the Catholic Church warns against fundamentalist errors, it on the other hand advises us against the abuses of some Scriptural scholars, even some who bear the name Catholic, who adopt theories tainted by Modernism — theories which are increasingly being discarded by Jewish and Protestant scholars. Let us keep in mind that while the Catholic Church encourages Biblical scholarship, these scholars do not represent the official teaching Catholic Church. In fact, all Biblical scholars should take into account not only "recent scholarship" but the testimony of the early Fathers of the Church, statements in the Bible itself, and constant tradition, all recommended to exegetes by the Pontifical Biblical Commission and by the Second Vatican Council in *Dei Verbum** (*The Word of God*). What the Catholic Church teaches in an ecumenical council such as the Second Vatican Council represents its official position.

For the Old Testament, the Catholic Church adopted all the books that were in the Septuagint, the same source from which Jesus quoted, as mentioned earlier. It is the source of most quotations found in the New Testament. For the New Testament, the Catholic Church adopted the books which were known to be of apostolic origin and of unquestioned authenticity, and which were believed to have been written under the guidance of the Holy Spirit, that is, to be inspired. Pope Pius XII wrote the Encyclical *Divino Afflante Spiritu*, in 1943, in which he insisted on the inerrancy of the "entire books with all their parts." One who thinks and believes with the Catholic Church must regard

---

* *Dei Verbum* is the Latin term used to identify the *Dogmatic Constitution on Divine Revelation*, a document issued by the Second Vatican Council. The statements issued in an ecumenical council such as this one reflect the official position of the Catholic Church.

the Gospels as historical, as a record of what Jesus did and taught up to the time of His Ascension. This is what the Council Fathers of Vatican II say explicitly in *Dei Verbum* (n. 19).

Father Eugene A. LaVerdiere, S.S.S. (quoted earlier), writes much about the various types of literature found in the Bible and differentiates between modern historical writing, which is secular in orientation, and the history found in the Bible, which links human events with God's creative and saving presence. Well and good, but he does not make it entirely clear that the teaching of the Church is that the Gospels are *historical*. (See *Dei Verbum*, n. 19 of the Second Vatican Council).

I wish to make the reader of this volume at least aware of the controversies that go on among Biblical scholars, while at the same time point out that even if scholars should bear the name "Catholic" they are not necessarily the Catholic Church speaking. While the Church gives scholars freedom to research and debate, the Magisterium, that is, the teaching authority of the Church vested in the Pope and the bishops united with him have the last say when it comes to an official interpretation of the Church. The Church makes such interpretations officially when a serious need arises.

By the time of Jesus, the rabbis agreed that Moses wrote Genesis and the four books that followed; all five books are collectively called the Pentateuch. It is often held today that there were four sources, J, E, P and D, and that the Pentateuch is the result of the combined insights of many generations of teachings in ancient Israel, and at some time skillfully united by a single author. In saying this, we must recognize that although some twentieth-century scholars disagree with the single-author theory, much has been written in support of the substantially Mosaic authorship of the Pentateuch.

An example of the disputes concerning dates will further show the complexity of Scriptural study. It is held that the most likely time for the writing of St. Matthew's Gospel was between 80 and 90 A.D. But a date as late as 140 A.D., and as early as 50 A.D. has been suggested. It must be added here that what is most important is not who the secondary authors were whom God used to write the various parts of the Bible, nor when they wrote, but that in all cases, in all parts, according to the teaching of the official Catholic Church, *God is the Primary Author.* In no way, however, can it be held that Jesus left the world with a book, or that it was completed with His Ascension or immediately thereafter. He founded a Church on the rock and commanded that Church to "go forth and preach to nations."

A subsequent chapter will return to the official position of the Catholic Church regarding the Bible as explained in *Dei Verbum* but at this point it is important for the reader to appreciate that the following had been pronounced and promulgated by an ecumenical council for the entire Catholic Church. Any other position with regard to the Bible's inspiration and inerrancy is not Catholic, as stated in *Dei Verbum*:

> Holy Mother Church, relying on the faith of the apostolic age, accepts as sacred and canonical the books of the Old and the New Testaments, whole and entire, with all their parts, on the grounds that written under the inspiration of the Holy Spirit (cf. John 20:31; 2 Tim. 3:16; 2 Peter 1:19-21; 3:15-16), they have God as their Author and have been handed on as such to the Church herself. To compose the sacred books, God chose certain men who, all the while He employed them in the task, made full use of their powers and faculties so that, though He acted in them and by them, it was as true authors that they consigned to writing whatever He wanted written, and no more.

> Since, therefore, all that the inspired authors, or sacred writers, affirm should be regarded as affirmed by the Holy Spirit, we must acknowledge that the books of Scripture, firmly, faithfully and without error, teach that truth which God, for the sake of our salvation, wished to see confided to the Sacred Scriptures (n. 11).

Loyal Catholics accept the teaching that there is no error in Sacred Scripture. To explain difficulties where there appears to be error or contradiction requires special research and work. But, in accepting the Bible as free from all error we must keep in mind that there is an answer to the difficulties encountered. With new techniques in the study of Scripture, many problems have already been solved which used to baffle scholars even in the early part of the twentieth century.

Scriptural scholar Fr. William G. Most wrote in his book, quoted above,

> Precisely at the time when new techniques enable us to do what seemed impossible before, so many scholars are not only not solving but even saying that problems are insoluble whose answers have been known for a long time!

Fr. Most takes issue with some scholars who hold that Scripture can be inerrant only on things needed for salvation. According to Pius XII, Vatican I gave a solemn definition of the Church that there is no error in all of Scripture, and Fr. Most notes that Vatican Council II stood with that definition.

It is not the purpose of this book to deal extensively with apparent

Biblical difficulties, which could occupy several volumes. We use but several examples here. According to Mark 2:26, David entered the house of God under the high priest Abiathar. According to 1 Samuel 21:1ff, it was under his father, Ahimelech, not Abiathar.

Fr. Most explains,

> The answer is easily found with the help of Greek grammar. The Greek text here has *epi Abiathar archiereos.* Now Greek *epi* followed by a genitive of the person can readily have a generic time meaning, i.e., "In the days of," according to a standard reference work, *Greek Grammar for Colleges,* by H.W. Smyth, par. 1689. Smyth gives as an example, Thucydides 7:86, *ep'emou,* meaning "in my time." So the expression in Mark 2:26 really means "in the time of Abiathar" and not necessarily "when Abiathar was high priest." Abiathar's name was chosen to designate the period because he was better known to readers of the Old Testament than his father, Ahimelech, and because Abiathar was closely associated with King David.

In the New Testament, our Lord and St. Paul commonly spoke of King David as the author of all the psalms. That was the usual way of speaking. St. Paul may not have known that all psalms were not by David. Jesus surely knew. It was proper for both to speak according to the custom of the time. They did not mean to assert such was the strict authorship in every case.

There is a big question about the historicity of Jonah. When our divine Lord compares Himself to Jonah, can we use Jesus' words as proof that Jonah was historical? While our purpose here is not to settle whether the account of Jonah was an Old Testament parable or a historical event, Jesus' quote here does not assert that Jonah was historical. He made use of the account to illustrate a point. Modern writers use characters from *Alice in Wonderland* to make their points without in any way indicating they consider the story historical.

Another example of claims that error exists in Sacred Scripture concerns Matthew 27:9, where we read that with the fate of Judas, a prophecy of Jeremiah was fulfilled. But it was really Zechariah 11:12f that was quoted. Did the Bible err? The New Jerusalem Bible has a footnote stating:

> Actually this is a free quotation from Zechariah 11:12-13 combined with the idea of the purchase of a field, an idea suggested by Jeremiah 32:6-15. This, plus the fact that Jeremiah speaks of potters (Jer. 18:1 seq.), explains how the whole text could by approximation be attributed to Jeremiah.

Fr. Most says,

> Again, the answer is easy . . . . As to the fact that Matthew puts the
> name Jeremiah on the combined text, it was a rabbinic practice to
> use the name of the best-known author in such combined texts.

For those who would discount the account of Jonah being swal-
lowed by a whale as not historical because it is scientifically or physically impossible for a whale to swallow more than a small object, Fr.
Most answers,

> There is no great difficulty about the great fish that swallowed
> Jonah. God could, by a miracle, have brought that about. In fact,
> some think He could have done it without much of a miracle, ex-
> cept for having the fish at the right place at the right time, and for
> having the fish disgorge Jonah at the right time and place.
> Wallechninsky and Wallace tell us that in February 1891, after
> the ship *Star of the East* had caught an eighty-foot sperm whale, a
> seaman, James Bartley, was missing. After a search, he was pre-
> sumed drowned. But the next day, when the crew was cutting up
> the fish, Bartley was found alive inside the whale.

In the Epilogue of his book, *Free From All Error,* Fr. Most states,

> Early in our study we saw that only six easily observable facts
> are needed to prove that the teaching authority of the Church
> comes from Jesus. That Church, in turn, assures us that there is
> no error at all in Scripture. With the help of the new tech-
> niques, we can see that the Church is completely right. Numer-
> ous problems that early in this century would have seemed in-
> soluble have been solved. In regard to the methods themselves,
> some think that only highly trained specialists can understand
> them. These people are too easily awed. Anyone can grasp at
> least the basics of these two methods, and more too. These
> methods are not mysterious or formidable. They are our
> friends. They help us understand Scripture more fully. They
> make it possible for us to defend its complete inerrancy.

What must be avoided are the two extremes. One extreme is that of
the fundamentalists who ignore the genre in which Sacred Scripture
was written and thereby err in reading it as if written today. The other
extreme is to fall into errors of Modernism. What is needed is the
Church which Jesus founded and promised to abide with and keep
from error through the Spirit of Truth, the Holy Spirit. That Holy Spirit divinely inspired early Churchmen in writing the New Testament
and continues to abide with the Church yet today and until the end of
time in preserving Divine Revelation. We need the Body of Christ, the

Church, which was promised to have the Holy Spirit until the end of time, if we are to be free from error.

Fundamentalists have no appreciation of the development of theology, which is faith seeking understanding. In the Catholic Church, the Word of God has been studied and meditated upon for nearly two thousand years. It is correct that theology is not the faith, and theologians can be wrong. The authority which Christ gave His Church is needed in order to have the development of theology, which becomes part of official Catholic doctrine. There have been great mystics in the two thousand-year history of the Church; there have been great theologians, such as St. Augustine, St. Albert the Great, St. Thomas Aquinas, etc. Great minds and holy souls meditating on Divine Revelation have often given insights into what God has revealed. If the Sacred Scriptures allow of no interpretation, but speak for every century without the guidance of the Church, then each generation starts anew without taking into account of the wealth of understanding and appreciation of God's Word of past centuries. Some fundamentalists go so far as to believe that declared Catholic doctrines belong to the realm of the pagan and non-Christian or even the anti-Christian.

If each generation or individual reader had to start anew to penetrate God's Word without inheriting the fruit of the centuries, they would in reality be two thousand years behind in appreciating God's Revelation. It can be documented that the first Christians respected the authority of the first Apostles and their successors, especially St. Peter. How else did the teaching develop from the first century that Peter always would have a specific successor? Today we call Peter's successor the Pope.

# CHAPTER 4

# Fundamentalists
# And The Scriptures

Only recently have I appreciated the need to write a book of this type. In teaching our holy faith it has always seemed ideal to accent the positive. But lately, Catholicism is increasingly coming under fire by Protestant fundamentalists. The true face of Catholicism is thus being obscured. While I have written thousands of articles, at least twenty books, delivered more than five thousand sermons, conducted retreats and pilgrimages, I've not felt it necessary until now to supply some answers to Fundamentalism.

It has been said that responsible clergy have not spoken about the threat of anti-Catholicism that comes from the extreme variety of fundamentalists. As I was about to begin this book a young Lutheran minister said to me, speaking for his own denomination, "I've said to fellow Lutherans, the threat to us is not Roman Catholicism but fundamentalists." Most lay people are not aware of the scope of the potential problem. Good Catholic parents are heartbroken when they learn that their children have fallen into one of the fundamentalist groups.

What the fundamentalists are saying has been answered thousands of times, and hundreds of years ago. They surface ever more strongly from time to time, and with contemporary twists. We need to answer them, taking these twists into account. We need to offer our people apologetics, not simply to protect them from errors of the fundamentalists, but to instill in them a deeper appreciation of their holy Catholic faith. If we have the fullness of faith, it is worth defending; and more so, it is worth spreading. It offers an opportunity for a more mature faith.

The word "apologetics" comes from the word "apology." It is the science which explains and justifies religious doctrine. It shows the reasonableness of such doctrine while answering objections offered by those who refuse to accept any religion, or by those whose religion is different. Apologetics is called fundamental theology because it is the science that establishes the credibility of Christian Revelation on the evidence of miraculous phenomena and the testimony of unbiased history. At the same time it labors to demonstrate how some abuse the Scriptures by isolating texts or interpreting them apart from the whole.

I have the fundamentalists to thank for the realization that as a Catholic priest I need to teach apologetics. Priests and catechists before my time taught apologetics well. The next chapter will explain how fundamentalists have taken advantage of the many years during which apologetics has become an almost forgotten subject. In fact, it is centuries old. The time for revival of apologetics is long overdo. While a book of this nature does not intend to deal with every possible area in need of attention, it will attempt to take up the more common subjects of Catholic belief under attack.

Many Catholics think that if a fundamentalist comes to the door, or meets them on the street, Bible in hand, ready with a big smile, that to say simply, "I'm a Catholic" will cause the "evangelist" to back off. On the contrary, that statement to a fundamentalist is all the more reason, according to their thinking, why the Catholic needs to be saved. They actually believe that you will be lost if you follow and live by the teachings of Roman Catholicism. They actually want to save you; to have you accept Jesus Christ as your personal Savior.

It is almost impossible to get into a logical discussion with fundamentalists. They may impress you with their knowledge of the Bible. They memorize verses of the Bible. Their training has been to use the Bible against the Catholic Church. The average Catholic does not realize that the very language he uses and that the fundamentalist uses have different meanings. It is almost like talking two different languages whereby one does not understand the language of the other. To be saved or to accept Jesus as your personal Savior will mean something different to these two parties.

As a Catholic you may (or you may not) have a deep understanding of the basics of your faith. But if you don't understand the technique of the fundamentalists, all your knowledge will do little good to convince the fundamentalist that you are right. To put another on the defensive is an easier position. This is what the fundamentalist does. His statements, *seemingly* made with a deep knowledge of Scripture, are direct, brief, but can take you or me much time and many pages to answer. The fundamentalist who is so convinced he is saved, and you are not, is not interested in listening to you even if you are capable of giving, in a logical presentation, a reason for the faith that is in you.

Listening to fundamentalists, Catholics have been known to say, "Well, at least I can say this, they really know their Bible." But the contrary is true. If you pay close attention, you will realize that the average fundamentalist, trained to use the Scriptures in a simplified way, or to isolate texts, is the one leading the conversation. He brings up the subjects. He brings up questions for which he already has memorized stock answers using Sacred Scripture verses which he quotes. He can find just the right place in the Bible to answer his own questions in a matter of seconds while flipping the pages very rapidly. The technique at which the fundamentalist has become a master will make him seem like a master of the Bible and make you feel quite inadequate or foolish. They have a few anti-Catholic source books from which they get their misguided information.

To make an impression on fundamentalists, if one is fortunate to have them open their minds to listen, one must be familiar with Sacred Scripture. Your knowledge of Catholicism, even if only from the simple catechism, is authenticated in all its major areas in the Word of God. Unfortunately, the average Catholic is not well equipped to show reasons for his faith from the Scriptures. He has trusted the Church, and the fundamentalist's task is to break that trust — even to lead you out of the Church so you can be "born again" and "saved."

The New Testament, which means covenant, is rooted or contained in essence in the Old Testament already. We find it in the foreshadowings and prophecies of the Old Testament, which must be understood so as to appreciate the New. You should have a knowledge of both the Old and the New Testaments, but be particularly conversant with the New. The purpose of the Scriptures should be primarily for your own living of the Catholic Christian faith while at the same time making you proficient in sharing the faith with others. This is needed for an adequate defense and exposure of the fallacies of the fundamentalist's arguments.

Knowing the Bible is not merely having the ability to quote great portions of it from memory. Those who can quote memorized verses at the drop of hat, especially when they have introduced their own carefully chosen subject, may well demonstrate their gift of memory but in no way demonstrates the slightest Biblical scholarship. This is obvious to not only a Biblical scholar but to an ordinary Christian who is well acquainted with interpreting the Bible as a whole. By isolating texts, taking verses out of context and interpreting them in a way contrary to the intent of the original authors — indeed as God, the Primary Author, intended — it is easy to make the Bible contradict itself and prove almost anything one desires to prove. Even the devil will quote Scripture to his own advantage.

It is not possible that God, who is Truth Itself, could contradict Himself. But you can make it seem so if you isolate texts. The contradiction will be, however, not in God's Word but in one's interpretation or use of God's Word. This is precisely what fundamentalists do in attempting to make God's Word contradict the doctrines of Catholicism. To one unprepared, they can make themselves seem quite scholarly in doing so.

What fundamentalist evangelists present to their listeners as God's Word in attacking the Catholic Church are their own interpretations, which they use to speak for God, while their interpretations are very much at variance with the Christian experience of most of the world's Christians for two thousand years.

Have you ever seen optical illusions in the form of pictures or words? You may look at a picture of a word and not see at all what others see. Glance at the black and white formations below. Before you read on, decide what you see. What word do you see printed, if any?

The first time you saw those black and white formations, they probably made no sense. Or, you might have even said that you were seeing something written in Chinese, if you don't know the Chinese language. Some people have spent utterly hours before they figured out the word. Some, without help, have never figured it out.

Once your eyes focus in on the white portions, and not the black, and once your mind supplies for your eyes the missing lines at the bottom and top of each letter, the word "Jesus" is clearly seen. Once your eyes see the word, it is usually difficult to not see it henceforth.

This is what some do with the Word of God. They fail to see its full meaning. The infinite mind of the Supreme Being Who is God Himself is revealed in the words of the Bible. It cannot be read just like any other book. Some, however see another kind of Jesus. Some are limiting Jesus. Some read the Bible and do not come to faith in Jesus at all.

The Catholic Church insists that the Bible must be interpreted as a whole and with well-disposed hearts. Jesus Himself so insisted. In the fourth chapter of St. Mark's Gospel we are told that Jesus "began to teach them by the lakeside, but such a huge crowd gathered round Him that He got into a boat on the water and sat there . . . . He taught them many things in parables . . . " (4:1, 2). Then Jesus told the parable of the sower. Jesus told how people react differently to the Word of God. The seed stands for the Word of God; some falls on rocky ground, or among thorns, or onto rich soil. Jesus said to the Twelve:

> To you is granted the secret of the kingdom of God, but to those who are outside, everything comes in parables so that they may look and look, but never perceive; listen and listen, but never understand; to avoid changing their ways and being healed" (Mark 4:11, 12).

Read Luke 4 where the devil isolates and misinterprets texts while quoting Scripture to Jesus Christ. The devil attempted to use Scripture to prove a falsehood. The devil,

> led Jesus to Jerusalem and set him on the parapet of the Temple. "If you are the Son of God," he said to him, "throw yourself down from here, for Scripture says, 'He has given his angels orders about you, to guard you,' and again: 'They will carry you in their arms in case you trip over a stone.' But Jesus answered him, "Scripture says: 'Do not put the Lord your God to the test.' "

Jesus is telling us that one must never use Sacred Scripture to deceive. It amounts to attempting to make God lie, which could never be, for He is Truth Itself. Even if one does not intend to deceive, one must be careful that he is not using his own interpretation and presenting it as God's Word. The Bible was not written in modern English. To interpret it in a scholarly way one must have a knowledge of ancient and original languages in which it was written. One must know ancient history and the cultures of the time to interpret what the Sacred Author intended.

Biblical archeology, the science of Biblical origins based on the study of documents and monuments unearthed in Bible lands, permits scholars today to get keener and deeper insights into the meaning of the Sacred Writings than before. The Catholic Church, which is approximately two thousand years old, not only has passed the Sacred Writings down through the centuries but has had scholars and saints who have studied and meditated upon Scripture, and the fruit of their labors and prayers have been passed on.

We are dealing with the divinely inspired Word of God. As long as the world continues, it is always possible that there will be a deeper penetration into the revealed Word of God, the God

Who is infinite and has spoken in human fashion. Yet, the human medium of His expressions has the divine intelligence behind it. The co-operation of many scholars working together has been very beneficial. So it has been through the centuries. It is not the work of each man, each interpreter on his own, independently of others. There must be a sharing of insights. There must be the guidance of the Holy Spirit Who inspired the written Word of God and Who guides the Church yet today to keep it in the truth. This is what Jesus spoke of when He promised the Spirit of Truth (See chapters 16 and 17 of the Gospel of St. John).

That body of believers, put under the authority of the Apostles with Peter as head (Matt. 16:16-19), was to be kept in truth by the Spirit of Truth working in the one Church Jesus Christ established. Jesus promised to keep His Church in truth and to abide in His Church to the very end of the world. St. Matthew ends his Gospel with:

> Jesus came up and spoke to them. He said, "All authority in heaven and on earth has been given to Me. Go, therefore, make disciples of all nations; baptize them in the name of the Father and of the Son and of the Holy Spirit, and teach them to observe all the commands I gave you. And look, I am with you always, yes, to the end of time" (Matt. 28:18-20).

Jesus gave His very own authority to the Church with the Apostles in charge, and with Peter (and his successors) in particular. It was after Peter made his profession of faith, "You are the Christ, the Son of the living God," that Jesus replied,

> Simon son of Jonah, you are a blessed man! Because it was no human agency that revealed this to you but my Father in heaven. So I now say to you: You are Peter and on this rock I will build My Church. And the gates of the underworld can never overpower it. I will give you the keys of the kingdom of heaven; whatever you bind on earth will be bound in heaven; whatever you loose on earth will be loosed in heaven (Matt. 16:16-19).

Fundamentalists who claim that the Catholic Church had nothing to do with bringing about the New Testament of the Bible or passing the Sacred Writings down to the present, do violence to truth and to recorded history. The body of believers in Jesus Christ, with His authority and His powers, were first called Christians at Antioch in the year 44 A.D. Jesus had ascended into heaven, leaving His body of believers, the Church, behind and they were functioning before one line of the New Testament was written.

St. Matthew's Gospel was written in 42 A.D., according to some

estimates. But according to more recent scholarship, it was written after the destruction of Jerusalem in 70 A.D. None place it as having
been written when Jesus was still physically upon earth. Modern scholars consider the Gospel of St. Mark to have been written in Rome at
about 70 A.D. Early Christian traditions ascribe the companion volumes of St. Luke's Gospel and the Acts of the Apostles (the first history
of the Church) to approximately 75 A.D. They identify as the author,
Luke the physican, a friend of St. Paul, mentioned in Colossians 4:14,
Philemon 24, and 2 Timothy 4:11; St. John's Gospel may have been
written as late as 110 A.D. St. Paul, it is generally recognized, wrote
much of the New Testament. Most Biblical scholars do not place the
earliest works of the New Testament, e.g., Galatians, before 48-50 A.D.

The Roman Catholic Church is the only Christian community
which is verified as having been in the world for approximately two
thousand years since Jesus Christ was physically present and established His Church. This ancient Church is called "Roman" because
the successor of St. Peter, the Pope, resides in Vatican City, which is in
Rome. The stress of using the term, "Roman Church" or "Roman
Catholic Church," was found necessary after the Protestant Revolt.
The term is used to emphasize the distinctive quality of being not only
a Christian, because of being baptized, but of being a Catholic in communion with the Pope, of recognizing the Pope as the successor of St.
Peter to whom Jesus gave special authority in His Church before ascending into heaven and promising the Holy Spirit, the Spirit of Truth,
to keep His Church in true faith (see Matt. 16:16 quoted above).

Fundamentalists, especially of the southern variety, will often
deny that St. Peter was the first Pope. Some will ask, "If Peter was the
first Pope, who was the second?" One does not have to be a scholar of
history to answer that. It can be found in any public library where records of history are objectively recorded. The second Pope was Pope
Linus. He followed the end of Peter's reign in 67 A.D. Linus was Pope
until 76; Cletus until 88; Clement I to 97; Evaristus to 105; Alexander I
to 115; Sixtus I to 125; Telesphorus to 136; Hyginus to 140; Pius I to 155,
etc. What fundamentalists are really attacking is the papacy itself, denying by their question that Jesus Christ gave any special authority to
St. Peter.

It is also claimed that St. Peter never went to Rome. Secular historians who research with honest, objective minds would never buy that.
There is archeological evidence that Peter was in Rome. There have
been in modern times archeological excavations under St. Peter's Basilica in Rome and the conclusion was that the basilica where the Pope
today is frequently seen offering holy Mass and addressing thousands

of pilgrims was built over the tomb of the Apostle St. Peter. Constantine, the first Christian emperor, demolished sacred pagan burial grounds there in order to build St. Peter's. The tomb found there in modern times was something more sacred to the Christians, and archeologists are convinced by the evidence that it is the tomb of the Apostle Peter. A good book about this is *The Bones of St. Peter*, by John Walsh. This book tells the full story, complete with the archeological evidence. When one of the country's most popular fundamentalist television personalities declares there is no archeological evidence that Peter was in Rome, he simply is not telling the truth. He is threatened by the evidence which eminent scientists discovered when permitted by Pope Pius XII to make excavations under St. Peter's. Scripture itself verifies the special authority of St. Peter, even mentioning him more often than any other Apostle. It was Peter who presided over the special functions of the Apostles.

The Catholic Church existed years before the New Testament was written. History and Sacred Scripture itself verifies this. Only one Church can substantiate such a claim, the Church which has been in the world since the days of Jesus Christ and His Apostles. The book of Revelation (Apocalypse), has as its author John (1:1, 4, 9; 22:8), as the writer himself declares. Because of his faith in Christ, St. John had been exiled to the rocky island of Patmos. The date of composition is judged by scholars to be somewhat near the end of the reign of Domitian (81-96 A.D.), who was a fierce persecutor of the early Christians. This puts the date of the writing of the last of the Scriptures at about one hundred years after the birth of Jesus Christ and long after His Ascension into heaven and the descent of the Holy Spirit upon the Apostles.

Anti-Catholicism is nothing new to the American scene. Unfortunately, it has been a part of American history from the beginning of our country. America was found by people fleeing religious persecution, and yet complete freedom of worship was not granted to all from the beginning. The early colonies, with the exception of Maryland, were oriented against Roman Catholics. Catholic Irish immigrants were forced to leave Virginia in the 1620's. In Maine the first three Catholic Jesuit missionaries were hung, drawn, and quartered. Catholics were forbiddened by law to own a gun or horse valued at more than five pounds. A common sight in New York was the Union flag with the words "No Popery."

Nativism was a philosophy which declared "America for Americans." It flourished from 1834 to 1844. To be "Roman Catholic" was to be foreign. Mobs of people inflamed with this philosophy sometimes roamed the streets. In Philadelphia three churches, a semi-nary and a retreat house were burned within five months. The Ursu-line nuns in Boston became the victims of anti-Catholicism. On Au-gust 11, 1834, a mob broke into their religious school, destroyed every-thing, and finally burned it to the ground. From there they ransacked the contents of tombs and coffins in a nearby churchyard.

Sparry's *American Anti-papist* magazine was one of several which became the voice of the American Party. Efforts were made to form a Protestant common school system in its war against Romanism so as to protect Protestant interests. Malicious myths were perpetuated, which gradually won belief from even respectable citizens who be-came suspicious of the Catholic Church.

While the Civil War and Reconstruction focused America's atten-tion on other matters, the Ku Klux Klan continued as anti-Catholicism went more or less underground but nonetheless remained on the American scene, making itself more visible and bold in recent years. If crosses are not burned in front of Catholic Churches or accusations of guns being stored in basements of Catholic churches, the misrepresen-tations of Catholic teaching continues as every form of modern media is used. Even children's comic books have been distributed perpetuat-ing hatred once fostered by the "Know-Nothing" party of more than a hundred years ago. Posters have appeared in cities across the country accusing the Catholic Church of controlling the United Nations, the White House, Congress, federal, civic, and social governments, the IRS, the FBI, the Supreme Court, the judicial system, the armed forces, etc.

The influence of fundamentalists using the television industry ought not be underestimated. A recent nationwide survey revealed that television evangelists are watched in almost half of all households with television sets in the United States at least once a month. That is com-parable to the top-rated shows on prime time. The study revealed that over thirty-three million households, or 40% of all homes in the United States watch at least one of the ten best-known television preachers for at least six minutes once a month. Hardly any of the religious broad-casts rated were Catholic. (Of course, it is only fair to say that many of the broadcasts were sincere and not anti-Catholic.)

Some of the television evangelists, and all Protestant fundamen-talists, boast that as much as 30% of their financial support comes from Catholic viewers. Unfortunately, the average Catholic is not able to de-tect the subtleties of danger to his or her faith in the simplistic Biblical approaches, which are delivered full of zeal and are easy to grasp.

Thousands of Catholics belong to fundamentalist Bible study groups and flock to preaching-and-prayer services in convention centers and outdoor stadiums. Thousands of Catholics have thus been won away from the ancient Church of Christ into the Assembly of God, Baptist, and other Pentecostal churches.

Catholics who have fallen for Fundamentalism find themselves defenseless against attractive, simplistic interpretations of the Bible. They are totally unaware of the Catholic Biblical renewal launched by Pope Pius XII and the Scriptures as emphasized by the Second Vatican Council. Many Catholics remain unaware of Pope Pius XII's encyclical *Divino Afflante Spiritu* (1943), or the Pontifical Biblical Commission's *Instruction of the Historical Truth of the Gospels* (1964), or the Second Vatican Council's *Dogmatic Constitution on Divine Revelation* (1965). Some have left the riches and depth of Divine Revelation handed down for two thousand years for the fiery zeal of Fundamentalism, when they could have launched out into the deep waters of Catholicism. But as one popular fundamentalist preacher says, "Nothing in Catholicism remains simple." Unthinking people can be easily convinced, while the fundamentalist in simplistic presentations calls the two thousand-year-old Catholic Church "unthinking."

The fundamentalist frequently·contradicts the very Scriptures he quotes for his authority while distorting God's Word to suit his own interpretation. There is perhaps no manner in which the fundamentalist does this more consistently than in condemning Church authority and Sacred Tradition. This amounts to condemning God's Word itself, since it comes to us through the authority of the Church and Tradition, and ultimately from the one Source, God Himself. It is from God Himself that flows Sacred Tradition and Sacred Scripture. These two form the one sacred deposit of the Word of God.

The word "Tradition," as used by the Church, does not refer simply to devout practices which may change with the needs of the time. Such simple traditions, which vary from time to time in Church history, are speaking of customs or disciplines which may even vary from area to area within the universal Church. We must not confuse unchangeable doctrine with discipline. Jesus Himself gave His Church the authority to change its own human or Church-made laws. Jesus said to Peter,

> You are the "Rock," and on this rock I will build my Church, and the jaws of death shall not prevail against it. I will entrust to you the keys of the kingdom of heaven. Whatever you declare bound on earth shall be bound in heaven: whatever you declare loosed

on earth shall be loosed in heaven (Matt. 16:18-19).

Tradition literally means a "handing on," the passing down of God's revealed Word. In the first sense, Tradition means Divine Revelation, which extends from the dawn of human history to the end of the apostolic age, and passes on from one generation of believers to the next, and is preserved under divine guidance by the Church, by virtue of its establishment by Christ almost two thousand years ago. More technically, Tradition means that part of God's revealed Word which is not necessarily contained in Sacred Scripture. The fundamentalists have great problems with this just as they often confuse Tradition with traditions, and as they confuse doctrine with discipline.

The vision fundamentalists would give us of God's revealed Word is that of a luminous volume, the Bible, completed and delivered to man as the only source of all religious authority, and containing all religious truth. There is absolutely no foundation for such a view either in the Bible itself or in recorded history. The Bible just does not suddenly appear on the scene. Yes, the Bible *is* the Word of God, but it is written in the words of men, and as such its contents were gradually revealed. The Old Testament took more than a thousand years to complete. It was the authority of the early Church which determined for Christians which of the many writings, claimed by some to be Christian and inspired, were in fact inspired by God. In the early years of Christianity many such spurious writings were circulated.

God did not descend from heaven and deliver the Bible, either the Old or New Testament, as a finished work. There was no voice heard from heaven saying, "Take and read" as a mighty arm held down a great book from the clouds. It was, rather, within a faith-community that God's Word was gradually revealed. Even had there been a finished work of a Bible suddenly delivered to mankind there would still have been the problem of interpreting it. Whose interpretation would be the true one?

To say, "The Bible is our one certain authority; it alone contains religious truth," is to run into the same problem thousands of churches have today. As soon as one makes the Book itself the authority, rather than God (and at the same time excluding the means He gave us to keep faithful to the truth in interpreting His Divine Revelation), you have many who interpret revelation differently. It is little wonder that the *World Book of Religions* listed over eighteen thousand different Christian churches in 1980. If one were to look within those thousands of churches there would be found, since they have no central authority, countlessly different interpretations beyond the bond which somehow identifies them under the one general label of Christian.

We need the same authority God gave us to interpret the Bible correctly to determine what is called the *canonicity* of the Bible. Canonicity is the quality of a book, or part of a book of the Bible, as divinely inspired and therefore containing the Word of God. The important question is: How did the canon of the Bible come about? How do we know that all the parts of the Bible are divinely inspired?

There was a canon of the Hebrew Scriptures before the time of Christ but it was not until the first century of Christianity that there was a formal decision on the Jewish canon. Jewish religious authorities saw the need for a clearer definition of Judaism itself because of pressures from the Roman conquerors and internal pressure from various sects within Judaism, including the first Christians. The result was the Council of Jamnia, which formally defined the definitive sources of Jewish revelation.

The purpose and intention of the Jewish religion from its beginning was actually to bring Jesus-Messiah into the world for its salvation unto life everlasting. God revealed His will to that people through His prophets. God saved the Israelites from extinction through many horrible persecutions and wars.

The "Old Testament" of the Bible included in some way all the prophesies. The Old Covenant is the New Covenant in its infancy. In God's plan a mother and her child are inseparable. The original Jewish religion, known as the Old Covenant, is actually the *mother* of the New. The Old conceived and carried the infant from its conception until its appearance as the New Covenant, which is Christianity.

It is not accurate then to say that the Christian religion is a religion different from the Jewish religion. Christianity is a completion of the same religion. It is a full flowering of the bud. The Jewish religion without a Messiah never could and still cannot give everlasting life to anyone. Its purpose was to prepare this world for the Messiah of God who would by Himself alone be the "Lamb of Sacrifice" for His Jewish people and for all peoples, all nations until the end of time.

The Moses-Covenant never claimed the power to bring to its own Jews (or others) everlasting life. It rather claimed that the promised Messiah alone was to accomplish the Redemption of Israel and of all the peoples of the entire world.

There is but one God, who can give us only one religion. Truth is one. God is one. Christianity is the crown of Judaism, its fulfillment and glory. Judaism is crowned by its long-prophesied Messiah in Christ Jesus.

The author of this book once visited Jerusalem and stood at the retaining Western Wall of the ancient Jewish Temple. It is often called the "Wailing Wall" and is the holiest shrine of the Jewish world. It is revered as the last relic of the last Temple. It was built at about 20 B.C. When the great Temple was destroyed in 70 A.D., as Jesus predicted, it was because many did not accept Jesus as the Messiah, Lord, God and Savior. This western wall was spared by Titus so that its hugh blocks would show for future generations the greatness of the Roman soldiers who had been able to destroy the rest of the building. The custom of weeping over the ruins of the Holy Temple and praying at the wall has continued for centuries.

As I stood watching devout Jews praying at the Wailing Wall, some rhythmically moving their heads back and forth, my heart went out to the goodness of these people and their desire that they might realize that their longed-for Messiah had in fact come in Jesus Christ. As one Jewish man with strong features walked away from his prayers at the wall, I asked if I might be permitted to speak to him. "Yes," he said, "Why don't you Jews build yourself another Temple?" I asked. He looked at me with shock and disbelief that I had asked such a question. "You are a *Gentile.* You are a *Christian,* then?" He asked more in an accusing tone than as a question. I pleaded guilty to being a Christian. He explained that there is no Jew alive who would consider himself so purified as to be worthy to build for the Jews another temple after the destruction of their great Temple in 70 A.D. by Titus, who crushed the Jewish revolt and destroyed Jerusalem. The Jews could never hope for salvation either, without a Temple where they might fittingly worship and offer their sacrifices. They could therefore not be purified. The element of despair in their plight came through to me. "How will you ever get out of this dilemma, then?" I asked. "I don't know," said the man. "It will have to be a Messiah who will come to do it for us," he said in consternation.

How sad. If only they knew that the Body of Jesus was the Great Temple and that the Temple of His Body was offered on the altar of the Cross, once for all for the redemption of the entire world, and God no longer required the animal sacrifices in the Temple of Jerusalem, which exists no more. There was no need to remain in darkness when the Light came. Jesus said, "The truth will set you free" (John 8:32), and "I am the Way; I am the Truth and Life" (John 14:6).

The Jewish religion today is the same as it was in the hearts and minds of the Jews of Moses' lifetime. Added to this is its glorious fulfillment and completion through Jesus-Messiah. The religion of Adam and Eve could be called the Jewish religion if one considers

He has rather come to understand and love his people more than ever. He then desires for his fellow Jews with all his heart the saving faith which he has received in Jesus Christ. He is now a completed Jew as are in fact all Christians themselves in the spiritual realms, which are eternal.

What do we say of fundamentalists who water down the fullness of faith in Jesus Christ? We know that disunity among Christians, evident in its division into thousands of denominations, thousands of interpretations, is not the will of God. We know how strongly Jesus prayed for unity among His followers, His believers, the night before He died (John 17). We know from Scripture itself that the devil is the "father of lies" and the "spirit of disunity." Of Christians who ridicule the Catholic faith or refuse to accept the fullness of faith, can we not say that while they claim to truly accept Jesus Christ as their personal Savior, they have fallen victim to a half-truth about Christ? Disunity in faith is not from the Holy Spirit. If the evil one cannot succeed in keeping all from faith in Jesus Christ, accepting Him as Lord, God and Savior, is not the evil one's next best effort directed to presenting to them another kind of Christ so that at least they fail to recognize Christ Jesus in His fullness? And would not the evil one work as best he could to lead those within the fullness of true faith at least partially out to accept a lesser kind of Christ?

The author of this book remembers preparing a young couple for marriage, a marriage which in conscience I had to advise them I did not think could succeed. I remember another member of the Catholic girl's family coming to see me with tears because I "should at least give them a chance to prove themselves." Within two years their marriage failed. The young man preparing for the marriage was the son of a fundamentalist minister. He felt that his own faith was superior, and that the Eucharist was "merely symbolic, nothing more than a remembrance, like a father who the night before he died passed out candy mints to his children asking that they do the same thereafter and thus remember him." I asked, "You think that is a greater faith?" "Yes," was the answer. I replied, "That takes no faith. It takes real faith to believe that what looks like bread and wine after the consecration is in fact the Body, Blood, Soul and Divinity of Our Lord and Savior, Jesus Christ."

It is most important to determine how the Bible came about and where it came from. It must be understood and believed that God's Word came to us gradually over hundreds of years within a faith-community. We must appreciate the development, too, of the New Testament Scriptures in the early Church and realize the importance of oral tradition at that time. Jesus said, "Go, therefore, make disciples of all nations . . . " (John 28:19). The only tool they had ready to use was oral communication. Through preaching the Good News of Jesus Christ they began to spread the Gospel to the ends of the known world.

There was a scarcity of written materials in the first century and what existed was expensive and therefore not available to all. How many people could read? The answer is that memory was a highly developed human faculty at that time and is so today in the Near East. Even at the turn of the present century in the Americas, many who came from abroad with little or no formal literary training would listen to a sermon and later repeat the entire sermon almost word for word. The author has been to Europe frequently, spending each mid-summer on the mountaintop of Fatima and meeting original witnesses to the Fatima events of 1917 when supernatural happenings occurred that are scientifically unexplainable to the present day. These phenomena include the spinning of the sun, sent by God to prove that the Mother of Jesus had appeared with a message to draw mankind back to her Son, Jesus Christ. The memory of these mountain people is remarkable.

I remember interviewing Fr. John de Marchi, who wrote *Fatima from the Beginning.* Fr. de Marchi had served as acting pastor of the Fatima parish in the early years after the reported supernatural happenings of 1917. This is how he described the parents of the Fatima children and others at the time. "They were the type who could listen to a sermon and tell it all back to you later, word for word. In Italy or America with television and all the many distractions, that could never be." We make mention of this to gain some little appreciation of civilization at the time of the early Church and how they communicated.

The early Christians relied upon memory. The Good News was passed on by word of mouth from one person to another, from one generation to another. The early Apostles saw no need to hurry the Good News into written form. Christ's teachings were not immediately put into written form. Oral transmission was the more common, accessible and effective means of communication.

The Apostles themselves, at first thought that the Second Coming of Christ (the Parousia) would come in their own lifetime. There was no time for committing it to writing if the Parousia was to happen soon. As the Church developed and spread it became more clear that the Second Coming was not imminent and eventually it was found practical to help their teaching mission to put the Lord's teachings into written form. Even then there was no organized plan among the various sacred writers to sit down and write a book called the "Bible." The sacred authors were not necessarily aware of their writings being divinely inspired at the time they wrote. That declaration came later by the Church and their divinely inspired writings would have to be, as already indicated, separated from spurious writings. Some authority would be needed to tell believers in Christ which writings were truly written under the divine inspiration of the Holy Spirit.

Biblical inspiration is explained as follows: The writers of Sacred Scripture had a special influence of the Holy Spirit in virtue of which God Himself became the principal Author of the books written; the sacred writers were subordinate or secondary authors. In using human beings as His instruments in the composition, God did so in harmony with the person's nature and temperament but with no violence to the free, natural activity of the person's human faculties. The personality of the individual writer is still found in the style of the writing. According to the Church's teaching,

> by supernatural power, God so moved and impelled them to write, He was so present to them, that the things which He ordered and those only they first rightly understood, then willed faithfully to write down, and finally expressed in apt words and with infallible truth (Pope Leo XIII, *Providentissimus Deus,* Denzinger 3293.)

The inerrancy of the Bible has been the position of every papal encyclical on the Bible and also of the Second Vatican Council (1962-1965).

Regarding the Old Testament, from the fifth to the second century B.C., the time from Ezra and Nehemiah to the time of Jesus ben Sirach, the only document which refers to the collection of these sacred books is the Septuagint. The Septuagint was a Greek translation made from the divinely inspired Hebrew Scriptures. This translation was done by Jews residing at Alexandria in Egypt. The Septuagint contained all the books that are in the Catholic Bible and it was the Septuagint which Jesus Christ quoted when He referred to the Scriptures. Both direct and indirect references to the Greek Septuagint are frequent in the New Testament.

By the time our Lord was born, the original Hebrew writings had perished. Copyists are not guaranteed inerrancy in making their copies of the Scriptures in the New Testament, nor were they in the Old. About the second century after Christ, when Jewish Rabbis were determined to obtain a correct official Hebrew text, they used the Greek Septuagint translation to check discrepancies which they felt had crept into their texts from copyists. The fact that copyists are not guaranteed inerrancy points to the need for the living Church, guided by the Holy Spirit, which has received authority from Jesus Christ to teach. In accepting the authority of the Church in telling us what is the authentic canon of Scripture and how to interpret the Bible, we are accepting the authority of Jesus Christ who gave His Church the same authority He received from God the Father (Matt. 28:18-20).

The Catholic Church from its beginning, as founded by Jesus Christ, has accepted the Septuagint, the Greek version of the Old Testament (250-100 B.C.) which was read by the Jews in their synagogues of the Hellenistic and Roman world.

In 1947 there was found a collection of manuscripts and numerous fragments of ancient Scriptural texts at the site of the ancient Qumrum community, located close to the Dead Sea in Palestine.* The dry desert had kept its secret of these Scriptural writings, composed between 170 B.C. and 68 A.D., for two thousand years. This discovery was the find of the century, of great value to Biblical scholars. All seven parts of the Old Testament, omitted in some Protestant versions of the Bible, were found in remnants among the "Dead Sea Scrolls," the name by which they have become known.

Just as none of the texts of the Old Testament written under divine inspiration remain in their original writings, but only in copies, the same is true of the New Testament. This again points to the need of the living authority of Jesus Christ, which continues and is contained in the community of faith, Christ's Church. Christ's authority was not given to paper and ink, or to written scrolls. It was given to living human beings who were promised the Holy Spirit as special teachers in Christ's Church. God's Word is living, not dead.

The canon of the Bible as we have it today was accepted by the Council of Hippo (393 A.D.) and its decisions were reaffirmed by the two councils of Carthage in 397 and 419. The same canon has been reaffirmed repeatedly by Popes and councils throughout the centuries. The Council of Trent, on April 8, 1546, formally and dogmatically canonized these books consisting of 45 of the Old Testament and 27 of the New Testament. Unless there was an authority of the Church speaking in the name of Jesus Christ, we would have no way of knowing which writings were authentically inspired and which were spurious.

---

* For more details of the Dead Sea Scrolls and the Catholic position regarding Divine Revelation, see the author's book, *The Catholic Faith,* Our Sunday Visitor, Inc., Huntington, Indiana 46750.

The Scriptures of the New Testament were also ackn. common consensus until the sixteenth century. At that ti. Luther deleted some books from the Old Testament and also Already by the seventeenth century, Protestants began to retu. deletions to their canon. The canonization of the books of the Bi ie by the Council of Trent, mentioned above, was done in answer to the Protestant revisionists. What the Protestants did in changing the canon of the Bible was to attack the authority of the ancient Catholic Church and attempt to replace it with their own authority. The Bible's validity rests on the validity or authority of the Church, which is the authority of Jesus Christ clearly given it, as noted in the final paragraph of St. Matthew's Gospel.

It is more than simplistic to imagine that the Bible alone is the one authority of God in the world for guiding His people. It is to give authority to paper and ink. The Word of God is living, vibrant, and dynamic; our understanding of it in greater depth will go on as long as the world continues. The same Holy Spirit which illuminated the secondary authors of the Bible illuminates the Church today in interpreting the Bible. The Holy Spirit will never contradict Himself. But we need an authority — Christ's own authority given to His Church and kept in truth by the power of the Holy Spirit, to know which interpretations are in truth.

While all are free to read the Bible, and encouraged to do so, it must always be done as part of the faith-Community, the Church which Christ Jesus established and with the willingness to accept the official interpretations of the Church should our own private interpretation be at variance with it. The Church has not taken the Bible verse by verse and given us a final definitive interpretation of every sentence. The Church does not tie the living dynamic Word of God down, restricting it to a dead meaning incapable of growth in human understanding.

The living Tradition of the Church is that God lives and works in the Church through people, through the Mystical Body of Christ with head, soul, and members.

# Anti-Catholicism and the Scriptures — Is the Catholic Church Against the Bible?

*"You can't find in the Bible that you should pray to Mary the way Catholics do. You can't find in the Bible where it speaks about Transubstantiation the way Catholics speak about the Eucharist. Catholic worship of saints and images is condemned in God's own Word, the Bible. Having Mary dominate every aspect of Catholic religious life is the very opposite of Biblical Christianity. Catholic traditions do not match up with the Word of God. The Bible alone is the authority for our faith."*

The above paragraph contains just a few of the attacks made against the faith and practices of Catholicism by fundamentalists. Admittedly such attacks, which are made very strongly and with great enthusiasm, have disturbed not a few Catholics and have actually led some to abandon their Catholic faith. What kind of Christianity is it that its adherents are so insecure that it feels the need to attack the faith of other Christians? While the above accusations shall be answered in subsequent chapters I quote them here to demonstrate how some regard Catholic teachings and practices in relationship to the Bible. They actually believe that the Catholic Church is opposed to the Bible.

I turned on the television early one Sunday morning to hear a TV evangelist whose programs are rated highest in listener ratings. He was attacking any Church which has a liturgy and ritual. That attack, I thought, is aimed primarily at Catholics, but at some other Christians as well, including Lutherans and Anglicans. As the months went by, I realized I was listening to one whose attacks against the Catholic Church had become so direct and antagonistic at times that two television stations refused to accept his programs for airing in the future.

Yet, he continues on many stations throughout the United States.

Anti-Catholic organizations have been popping up in ever greater numbers in recent years. At times their boldness seems unlimited. They have even pasted their anti-Catholic posters throughout the South Dakota town where I have served as pastor. The same has occurred in countless cities and towns throughout the United States. Their accusations are so ridiculous that it is doubtful that more than a few could believe them unless they already are filled with hatred toward that Church which has existed upon this earth since the days of Jesus Christ and whose history confirms it as existing since the days of the Apostles. More dangerous are their subtle attacks.

I recognized the boldness in their approach when one of their representatives came to my rectory attempting to evangelize this Roman Catholic priest. He said, "We like to evangelize Catholics." The representative was a minister of one of the fundamentalist groups. He did not realize that he was insulting me. The approach is direct. The message is, "Catholics have nothing that is good or true." Now, evangelization means zealous proclamation of the Gospel in order to bring others to Christ. The man was saying to me, "You as a Catholic priest do not preach the Gospel. You do not preach Jesus Christ. Catholics do not believe in the Gospel," etc.

It was Pope Paul VI who wrote in *Evangelii Nuntiandi* (n. 18),

Evangelizing means to bring the Good News into all the strata of humanity, and through its influence transforming humanity from within and making it new. "Now I am making the whole of creation new" (Rev. 21:5). But there is no new humanity if there are not first of all new persons renewed by Baptism, and by lives lived according to the Gospel.

Gospel means the Good News of Jesus Christ, our Lord, God and Savior. To evangelize then, in general, means to preach the Good News as lived and taught by Jesus Christ. Specifically it means bringing the Revelation of Jesus Christ, God become Man, in order to save us, to persons and cultures to whom the Gospel has not yet been effectively proclaimed.

There is an organization known as Christians Evangelizing Catholics. The title tells of their concept of Catholicism. It works to show Catholics the "errors" of their ways. One of its pamphlets is titled, "Use Your Local Priest." Catholics who have been confused by high-pressure evangelists are asked to question their priest as to whether he knows he will go to heaven. Now a priest may well remember that

Sacred Scripture says "to work out your salvation in fear and trembling" (Phil. 2:12). Also, 1 Cor. 10:12 says, "Everyone, no matter how firmly he thinks he is standing, must be careful he does not fall." This verse goes on to say,

> None of the trials which have come upon you is more than a human being can stand. You can trust that God will not let you be put to the test beyond your strength, but with any trial will also provide a way out by enabling you to put up with it (1 Cor. 10:13).

But how can anyone declare himself saved in the sense that he is certain he will never neglect God's grace and die unrepentant? We live in trust of the promises of Christ and His beloved saving mercy, the salvation He won for us by His redeeming blood, as Scripture so clearly demonstrates and the Church teaches. At the same time, we must believe we will be saved by Jesus Christ if we remain faithful to his teachings and the Commandments of God. Would it not be presumptuous to declare oneself already saved in the sense of absolute certitude that one will go to heaven because one is certain he will never reject Jesus' saving graces? Should we not live in "fear and trembling" and also in the love of God to which Scripture, God's Word, calls us over and over again? If we remain true to the teachings of Jesus Christ we may believe confidently, that is in hope, that we shall indeed spend eternity with God in heaven. Christ has saved us but we are always free to reject His redemption.

Those who condemn the Catholic Church for declaring that certain souls of saintly people are now in heaven (canonization) will in the same breath declare themselves saved. Church canonization occurs only after careful investigation into the lives of saintly souls, when their virtuous lives are proven and usually miracles performed through their intercession. It has sometimes taken hundreds of years for the Church to declare by a process of canonization that extraordinarily saintly people are in heaven. Yet, some who will condemn their fellow Christians for believing that certain very holy people are now in heaven will declare themselves, while they still live upon earth, in human imperfection, to be certainly saved.

Bill Jackson is the leader of Christians Evangelizing Catholics, which puts out a newsletter and gives tips on how to show Catholics where they are "wrong." In one, titled "Use Your Local Priest," he said he once worked with a telephone ministry in San Francisco. His first call was to the local Catholic parish. "The layman that answered was quite put aback by my asking about the assurance of salvation, so he hurried to get the priest. Needless to say, the priest didn't know anything more about salvation than the layman had, but during our conversation," continued Jackson, "he specifically told me he did not have assurance of salvation." Accounts of the fundamentalist encounters with priests and other Catholics are generally related as much out of context as their verse-quoting of Sacred Scripture. Jackson continued his efforts in that parish and when speaking with a Catholic belonging to the parish, would say he had just talked with the person's priest. The priest said he was not sure of going to heaven, and wasn't that a disturbing thought? Surely a priest should be confident of his own salvation. How could one not sure about his own salvation direct another to salvation?

Jackson wrote: "I would then quote I John 5:13, and found this a very good way to initiate a Gospel presentation." Note this is what 1 John 1:13 says: "I have written this to you who believe in the name of the Son of God so that you may know that you have eternal life." This is interpreted by fundamentalists as certain salvation. If we read the words of Jesus Christ in the Gospels and in the other writings of the New Testament, we find there the Catholic teaching that grace in the soul which sanctifies, "sanctifying grace," as Catholics frequently call it, is a sharing in the life of God. Jesus speaks of our having "everlasting life." The Bible also speaks of some sins being unto death. Of temptation it says,

> Everyone is put to the test by being attracted and seduced by that person's own wrong desire. Then the desire conceives and gives birth to sin, and when sin reaches full growth, it gives birth to death (James 1:15).

The Apostle John writes in Sacred Scripture,

> If anyone sees his brother commit a sin that is not a deadly sin, he has only to pray, and God will give life to this brother provided that it is not a deadly sin. There is sin that leads to death and I am not saying you must pray about that. Every kind of wickedness is sin, but not all sin leads to death (1 John 5:16-17).

The death that God's Word speaks of is not the death of the soul. The soul is immortal. It cannot die. But a soul in grace, sharing in the life of God, can lose that sharing of God's life. It becomes dead to its sharing in God's life. There are sins which are of lesser seriousness. Catholics call them venial. God's Word says, as just quoted, "not all sin leads to death." God's Word also says "there is sin that leads to death." That is the meaning of mortal sin — it is deadly sin. Souls which share in God's life have *eternal life* within them. But being in the state of grace does not mean a person can never again sin. We do in fact have "eternal life" within us when we are in the state of grace. So long as we remain in that sharing in divine life, we shall be saved. We have no absolute guarantee that we will never sin against faith and reject the divine and eternal life within us. The Apostle therefore tells us to "work out your salvation in fear and trembling."

By isolating texts, one can prove almost anything from the Bible. Therefore, the Bible must be interpreted as a whole. The preaching of the Gospel — evangelizing — means preaching the Good News. It is not evangelizing to condemn other Christians and say they are going to hell. There are non-Catholic preachers who are positive, who do not tear down, who do not feel that their own salvation depends on opposing everything Catholic. They are actually uplifting. They teach in honesty as they know it and believe it. They are brothers in Christ who do not look upon everything Catholic as diabolic. We embrace them as our brothers and sisters in Christ.

Unfortunately, anti-Catholic literature is about as truthful as *Pravda* newspaper was seen to many. *Pravda* is the official newspaper of the Communist Party, now translated into English. As the official organ of the Communist Party, *Pravda* stuck to the party line and extolled the Soviet work ethic. To understand *Pravda* well, one had to understand the jargon. Russian readers, it is reported (especially before glasnost) were adept at reading between the lines. *Pravda*, which means "truth" in Russian, was not as interested in getting the latest news out as it was in getting the latest party line out. They were driven not by the scoop, but by party ideology.

Another Russian newspaper, *Izvestia,* is the official newspaper of the Soviet government. *Izvestia* means "news." There was a saying among Russians that there is no truth in *Pravda* and no news in *Izvestia.*

I have before me as I write this chapter a series on Catholicism written by Jimmy Swaggart which appeared in his magazine, *The Evangelist*, from 1985 to 1986. Jimmy Swaggart has obviously studied teachings of the Catholic Church, but not with an open mind. His insecurity finds him repeatedly attacking things Catholic. Half-truths can be very dangerous. His use of language and his personal interpretations of the Bible are repeatedly passed on as the Word of God.

At the time of the writing of this book, it has been noticed that there has been a mellowing in the approach of Brother Swaggart since he has been subjected to public attacks against him, both from his own denomination and the media. Jimmy is now reportedly separated from his denomination with which he ran into a crisis after a scandal in which he was involved. Jimmy's words against Catholicism, however, are not exclusively his. He is merely repeating in his own words other attacks against Catholicism. According to the Catholic expert on Fundamentalism, Karl Keating, a common source book, *Roman Catholicism*, is used. This book would be more appropriately called, *Anti-Roman Catholicism*.

I wrote to Brother Jimmy Swaggart the following:

Jimmy, I am not interested whether the attacks made against you more than a year ago were true. What is important is that *you did publicly say that you had sinned.* I saw you do so live .... Isn't now the time to publicly do the same in regard to your past attacks against the Catholic Church? Not just a general vague apology but one that is explicit. Do we not have to make reparation for the harm we have done others?

Jimmy, you are more Catholic than you know. Your basic teachings are in harmony with Catholicism, real authentic Catholicism — except when you are anti-Catholic. *Yes, I've noticed a profound change in you since the public attacks and accusations have been made against you. It would seem to me that God permitted this great suffering for your purification.* Jimmy, of late you no longer seem to be that abrasive, cockey, proud, holier-than-thou ... that loomed so large on the screen in the past. Doubtlessly there is pride left in you as there is in me, but you do indeed preach with more compassion.

My memory tells me, Jimmy, that you have called to Catholics to "come on out." You seem to state now that we should not have denominations among Christians. I believe that Catholicism is not a denomination. So I believe I have a certain calling to call out to you, "Brother Swaggart, come on over." If you did so, you would not give up your basic faith. All of your talents could be used for the fullness of faith, as you have so much already that is good, beautiful and true. You could go down as one of the giants of Christianity, but what is needed is humility, more humility, honesty, and openness to the Holy Spirit .... .

Brother, your past hatred of the Church has been against what you wrongly believed to have been Catholicism.

I would be happy to share with you my book, *Protestant Fundamentalism and the Born-Again Catholic.*

I pray the Rosary for you daily. I offer, daily, my Divine Office, which consists mainly of Bible readings, for you and Frances. In fact, I've written your names at the beginning on the inside cover. I've told my parishioners from the pulpit that we ought not to rejoice over the attacks upon you. I prayed for you before my congregation last Sunday.

It is hoped that no Catholic will be shocked to learn that I pray daily for the conversion of Brother Jimmy Swaggart to come to the fullness of Catholic faith. At times, when I am making a thanksgiving after having received our divine and loving Lord and Savior Jesus Christ in Holy Communion, and have his Real Presence within me, I think of Jimmy. I pray for him. I've told him that when he was attacking the Catholic Church he was not preaching the Gospel. Jimmy Swaggart has begun to respond to my letters. He has been showing more and more understanding. He now calls me "Father," and admits that Catholics can be saved and that among Catholics are found the born-again. However, at the time of this second edition, he has made no direct apology for his remarks. Any apology for public damage should be made publicly. The apology of St. Paul was divinely inspired and recorded in Sacred Scripture.

The fundamentalist hatred of Catholicism is seen in the false statements of *The Evangelist*, as shown below:

> . . . *The Catholic church had absolutely nothing to do with the formulation of the Scriptures. Neither did they have anything to do with preserving them except for their own benefit, because it certainly was not for the people. And even today the Catholic church does not want the people to read the Bible* . . . .
>
> *The fact is, the Catholic church doesn't like the Bible because the Bible contradicts the teachings of the Catholic church. The teachings of the Bible set men free; the teachings of the Catholic church put men in bondage. The teachings of the Catholic church can never be reconciled with the Word of God because they are 180 degrees opposite the Word of God. Any man who puts his faith in the traditions of the Catholic church to save himself will be eternally lost because those traditions do not match up to the Word of God* . . . .
>
> (The Evangelist, January 1986)

> *The Roman Catholic position is that God the Father and His Son, Jesus Christ, are, through normal human efforts, unreachable. By extension, they then propose that since Christ's mother is available, that petitions delivered by her will not be ignored.*
>
> (The Evangelist, December 1985)

> . . . *All of my statements either come from documented Catholic teaching, the Bible, or from former Catholic priests. And*

*you must understand, for anyone to testify against himself in a court of law presents within itself the most damaging of testimony. So when a former Catholic priest points out error, that is the most credible testimony against the doctrine of the Catholic Church that could be tendered from anyone. No, I have never misinterpreted or misrepresented anything.*

(The Evangelist, January 1985)

*. . . Yes, Catholics do worship Mary. To be tragically concise, most Catholics don't understand the worship of God the Father or of His Son, Jesus Christ. Their real focus and conception of worship is to Mary. And of course their perception of worshipping God is the worship of God through Mary. Everything must go through Mary to God — and everything must come from God through Mary.*

*The Roman cult of Mary erects a barrier between the individual and the Trinity. It confuses the Catholic believer's perception of the work and functions of the individual members of the Godhead. It robs Christ of His unique creatorship . . . .*

(The Evangelist, December 1985)

The above is typical of the misrepresentations, and twisting of truths that occur among anti-Catholics. In effect, such anti-Catholic persons say, "Never mind what Catholics or their Church say about Mary when they claim they don't worship Mary. I'll tell you what they believe and what their Church teaches."

The above statements about Mary and her being "a barrier between the individual and the Trinity . . . " struck this writer, who recently published a book, *Immaculate Heart of Mary — True Devotion.* The books states on its cover:

> The purpose of this book is to present the Immaculate Heart of Mary in the Trinitarian and Christological light that illumines the authentic Christian life. Many have mistakenly thought that God has given Mary only a minor role in the economy of salvation because there seem to be few Biblical references to Mary. This fallacy is a tragic one. If the importance of Mary depends on how many verses in Scripture explicitly deal with her, what are we to say of the central events of the life of Jesus Christ?

We are living in times when what has been secret to many is being discovered about Mary in the very pages of the inspired Word of God, the Sacred Scriptures. Mary is emerging as the great Woman of the Bible . . . as a teacher of true faith. The Mother of God is now seen more clearly as the spouse of the Holy Spirit and close collaborator of the Holy Spirit in making Jesus, the risen

Lord and Savior, present in us and among us. True devotion to Mary brings Jesus Christ, in fact, the entire Blessed Trinity, into our lives. (*Immaculate Heart of Mary — True Devotion*. Our Sunday Visitor Publishing Division, Huntington, Ind. 46750).

Perhaps a more general view of the problem at hand would shed light on the subject. The late internationally-known preacher and author, Archbishop Fulton J. Sheen, had a prime-time television program, "Life is Worth Living." He wrote:

There are not over a hundred people in the United States who hate the Catholic Church. There are millions, however, who hate what they wrongly believe to be the Catholic Church — which is, of course, quite a different thing. These millions can hardly be blamed for hating Catholics because Catholics "adore statues"; because they "put the Blessed Mother on the same level with God"; because they say "indulgence is a permission to commit sin"; because the Pope "is a Fascist"; because the "Church is the defender of Capitalism." If the Church taught or believed any one of these things it should be hated, but the fact is that the Church does not believe nor teach any one of them. It follows then that the hatred of the millions is directed against error and not against truth. As a matter of fact, if we Catholics believed all of the untruths and lies which were said against the Church, we probably would hate the Church a thousand times more than they do.

If I were not a Catholic, and were looking for the true Church in the world today, I would look for the one Church which did not get along well with the world; in other words, I would look for the Church which the world hates. My reason for doing this would be, that if Chirist is in any one of the churches of the world today, He must still be hated as He was when He was on earth in the flesh. If you would find Christ today, then find the Church that does not get along with the world. Look for the Church that is hated by the world, as Christ was hated by the world. Look for the Church which is accused of being behind the times, as Our Lord was accused of being ignorant and never having learned. Look for the Church which men sneer at as socially inferior, as they sneered at Our Lord because He came from Nazareth. Look for the Church which is accused of having a devil, as Our Lord was accused of being possessed by Beelzebub, the Prince of the devils. Look for the Church which, in seasons of bigotry, men say must be destroyed in the name of God as men crucified Christ and thought they had done a service to God. Look for the Church which the world rejects because it claims it is infallible, as Pilate rejected Christ because He called Himself the Truth. Look for the Church which is rejected by the world as Our Lord was rejected by men. Look for the Church which amid the confusion of conflicting opinions, its members love as they love Christ, and respect its Voice as the very voice of its Founder, and the suspicion will grow, that if the Church is unpopular with the spirit of the world, then it is unworldly, and if it is unworldly, it is other-worldly. Since it is other-worldly it is infinitely loved and infinitely hated as was Christ Himself. But only that which is Divine can be infinitely hated and infinitely loved. Therefore the Church is Divine.

If then, the hatred of the Church is founded on erroneous beliefs, it follows that the basic need of the day is instruction. Love depends on knowledge, for we cannot aspire nor desire the unknown. Our great country is filled with what might be called marginal Christians, i.e., those who live on the fringe of religion and who are descendants of Christian living parents, but who now are Christians only in name. They retain a few of its ideals out of indolence and force of habit; they know the glorious history of Christianity only through certain emasculated forms of it, which have married the spirit of the age and are now dying with it. Of Catholicism and its Sacraments, its pardon, its grace, its certitude and its peace, they know nothing except a few inherited prejudicies. And yet they are good people who want to do the right thing, but who have no definite philosophy concerning it. They educate their children without religion, and yet they resent the compromising morals of their children. They would be angry if you told them they were not Christian, and yet they do not believe that Christ is God. They resent being called pagans and yet they never take a practical cognizance of the existence of God. There is only one thing of which they are certain and that is that things are not right as they are. It is just that single certitude which makes them what might be called the great "potentials," for they are ready to be pulled in either of two directions. Within a short time they must take sides; they must either gather with Christ or they must scatter; they must either be with Him or against Him; they must either be on the cross as other Christs, or under it as other executioners. Which way will these *marginal Christians* tend? The answer depends on those who have the faith. Like the multitudes who followed our Lord into the desert, they are as sheep without a shepherd. They are waiting to be shepherded either with the sheep or goats. Only this much is certain. Being human and having hearts, they want more than class struggle and economics; they want Life, they want Truth, and they want Love. In a word, they want Christ.

... The Catholic Church is the only Church existing today which goes back to the time of Christ. History is so very clear on this point, it is curious how many minds miss its obviousness ... . We ask you to go not only to the written records but to the living Church which begins with Christ Himself. That Church or that Mystical Person which has been living all these centuries is the basis of our faith ... .

The late Archbishop Sheen, known the world over and who, shortly before his death, was embraced by Pope John Paul II as the Pope whispered in his ear, "You have written well of Christ," had a deep love for the Church. For this great man of God, Jesus and His Church were one, "the Body of Christ." It is such that the Scriptures teach. It was this great priest who inspired the writer of this book as a boy and I feel hurt when the Church is attacked. To attack the Church is to attack Jesus Christ.

Hatred can blind the intellect to light, and weaken the will. Hatred hinders embracing the fullness of faith and one another in Christ. The Gospel is the preaching of the Good News, not condemning others to hell. It is easy for men to hate in order to make countless attacks against those whose petition threatens their own. It can be difficult to counter such accusations, not because they cannot be clarified as to their falsehoods but it can take much time and space to answer accusations and misrepresentations. It is impossible to dialogue with anyone who hates, who will not listen, and is intent only on proving others wrong.

I have been a Roman Catholic priest for over thirty years. I am acquainted with many Catholic priests and have frequently traveled in Europe. Never in my life have I ever heard a sermon in the Roman Catholic Church attacking other Christians and never have I given a sermon that would discredit other Christians. I have received many into the Catholic Church as adults. When anyone who already believes in Jesus Christ as Lord, God and Savior comes to me for instructions in the Catholic faith, in one of my first classes I explain that I will not ask those who have been members of various Christian churches to deny the faith they have been taught. I tell them that if ever they come to the point where they desire to embrace Catholicism they will not be asked to deny things of faith they have believed since childhood. They will keep the Christian faith they had and simply add to it. It will be like a beautiful bud they have long had, now blossoming out more fully. The Catholic Church is grateful for truths other Christians share with us in common.

Catholics must not hate those who are anti-Catholic. Other Christians who have their faith attacked ought not to hate the attackers. For that matter, no man, regardless of his faith, Christian or otherwise, should ever hate. Jesus said,

> Blessed are you when people abuse you and persecute you and speak all kinds of calumny against you falsely on my account. Rejoice and be glad, for your reward will be great in heaven; this is how they persecuted the prophets before you (Matt. 5:11-12).

Fundamentalists say, "the Catholic Church doesn't like the Bible and even today the Catholic Church does not want its people to read the Bible." On the contrary, the official position of the Catholic Church in regard to the Bible can be found in the document issued by the latest ecumenical council of the Catholic Church, Vatican Council II. The council's sixteen documents are the fruit of the deliberations of the world's Roman Catholic bishops and the Holy Father, the Pope. What an ecumenical council has promulgated is henceforth the official position of the Catholic Church. The Ecumenical Council of Vatican II (1962-1965) issued the *Dogmatic Constitution on Divine Revelation* (*Dei Verbum*). After its short preface in which it reaffirmed what the Church had taught on the Word of God in the Councils of Trent and of the First Vatican Council, it continues as follows, with the selected passages below being only a small part of the total document.

> In His goodness and wisdom, God chose to reveal Himself and to make known to us the hidden purpose of His will (cf. Eph. 1:9) by which through Christ, the Word made flesh, man has access to the Father in the Holy Spirit and comes to share in the divine nature (cf. Eph. 2:18; 2 Peter 1:4). Through this revelation, therefore, the invisible God (cf. Col. 1:15; 1 Tim. 1:17) out of the abundance of His love speaks to men as friends (cf. Ex. 33:11; John 15:14-15) and lives among them (cf. Bar. 3:38), so that He may invite and take them into fellowship with Himself. This plan or revelation is realized by deeds and words having an inner unity: the deeds wrought by God in the history of salvation manifest and confirm the teaching and realities signified by the words, while the words proclaim the deeds and clarify the mystery contained in them. By this revelation, the deepest truth about God and the salvation of man is made clear to us in Christ, who is the Mediator and at the same time the fullness of all Revelation (n. 2).

> ... And so the apostolic preaching, which is expressed in a special way in the inspired books, was to be preserved by a

continuous succession of preachers until the end of time. There-fore, the Apostles, handing on what they themselves had received, warn the faithful to hold fast to the traditions which they have learned either by word of mouth or by letter (cf. 2 Thes. 2:15), and to fight in defense of the faith handed on once and for all (cf. Jude 3). Now what was handed on by the Apostles includes everything which contributes to the holiness of life, and the increase in faith of the People of God; and so the Church, in her teaching, life, and worship, perpetuates and hands on to all generations all that she herself is, all that she believes.

This tradition which comes from the Apostles develops in the Church with the help of the Holy Spirit. For there is growth in the understanding of the realities and the words which have been handed down. This happens through the contemplation and study made by believers, who treasure these things in their hearts (cf. Luke 2:19, 51), through the intimate understanding of spiritual things they experience, and through the preaching of those who have received through episcopal succession the sure gift of truth. For as the centuries succeed one another, the Church constantly moves forward toward the fullness of divine truth until the words of God reach their complete fulfillment in her ... (n. 8).

Sacred Tradition and Sacred Scripture form one sacred deposit of the Word of God, which is committed to the Church. Holding fast to this deposit, the entire holy people united with their shepherds remain always steadfast in the teaching of the Apostles, in the common life, in the breaking of the bread, and in prayers (cf. Acts 2:42; Greek text), so that in holding to, practicing and professing the heritage of the faith, there results on the part of the bishops and faithful a remarkable common effort.

But the task of authentically interpreting the word of God, whether written or handed on, has been entrusted exclusively to the living teaching office of the Church, whose authority is exer-cised in the name of Jesus Christ. This teaching office is not above the word of God, but serves it, teaching only what has been handed on, listening to it devoutly, guarding it scrupulously, and explaining it faithfully by divine commission and with the help of the Holy Spirit; it draws from this one deposit of faith everything which it presents for belief as divinely revealed.

It is clear, therefore, that Sacred Tradition, Sacred Scripture, and the teaching authority of the Church, in accord with God's most wise design, are so linked and joined together that one can-not stand without the others, and that all together and each in the action of the one Holy Spirit contribute effectively to the salvation of souls (n.10).

. . . since everything asserted by the inspired authors or sacred writers must be held to be asserted by the Holy Spirit, it follows that the books of Scripture must be acknowledged as teaching solidly, faithfully, and without error that truth which God wanted put into the Sacred Writings for the sake of salvation. Therefore "all Scripture is inspired by God and useful for teaching, for reproving, for correcting, for instruction in justice; that the man of God may be perfect, equipped for every good work" (2 Tim. 3:16-17, Greek text) (n. 11).

However, since God speaks in Sacred Scripture through men in human fashion, the interpreter of Sacred Scripture. in order to see clearly what God wanted to communicate to us, should carefully investigate what meaning the Sacred Writers really intended, and what God wanted to manifest by means of their words (n. 12).

. . . The word of God, which is the power of God for the salvation of all who believe (cf. Rom. 1:16), is set forth and shows its power in a most excellent way in the writing of the New Testament. For when the fullness of time arrived (cf. Gal. 4:4), the Word was made flesh and dwelt among us in the fullness of grace and truth (cf. John 1:14) (n. 17) . . . .

It is common knowledge that among all the Scriptures, even those of the New Testament, the Gospels have a special preeminence, and rightly so, for they are the principal witness of the life and teaching of the incarnate Word, our Savior.

The Church has always and everywhere held and continues to hold that the four Gospels are of apostolic origin. For what the Apostles preached in fulfillment of the commission of Christ, afterwards they themselves and other apostolic men, under the inspiration of the divine Spirit, handed on to us in writing: the foundation of faith, namely, the fourfold Gospel, according to Matthew, Mark, Luke, and John (n. 18).

. . . The Church has always venerated the divine Scriptures just as she venerates the body of the Lord, since from the table of both the Word of God and of the Body of Christ she unceasingly receives and offers to the faithful the bread of life, especially in the Sacred Liturgy. She has always regarded the Scriptures together with Sacred Tradition as the supreme rule of faith, and will ever do so. For, inspired by God and committed once and for all to writing, they impart the Word of God Himself without change, and make the voice of the Holy Spirit resound in the words of the prophets and Apostles. Therefore, like the Christian religion itself all the preaching of the Church must be nourished and ruled by Sacred Scripture ... (n. 21).

... Easy access to Sacred Scripture should be provided for all the Christian faithful. That is why the Church from the very beginning accepted as her own that very ancient Greek translation of the Old Testament which is named after seventy men; and she has always given a place of honor to other translations, Eastern and Latin, especially the one known as the Vulgate. But since the word of God should be available at all times, the Church with maternal concern sees to it that suitable and correct translations are made into different languages, especially from the original texts of the Sacred Books. And if, given the opportunity and the approval of Church authority, these translations are produced in cooperation with the separated brethren as well, all Christians will be able to use them ... (n. 22).

... This sacred synod earnestly and specifically urges all the Christian faithful, too, especially religious, to learn by frequent reading of the divine Scriptures the "excelling knowledge of Jesus Christ" (Phil. 3:8). "For ignorance of the Scriptures is ignorance of Christ." Therefore, they should gladly put themselves in touch with the sacred text itself, whether it be through the Liturgy, rich in the divine word, or through devotional reading, or through instructions suitable for the purpose and other aids which, in our time, are commendably available everywhere, thanks to the approval and active support of the shepherds of the Church. And let them remember that prayer should accompany the reading of Sacred Scripture, so that God and man may talk together; for "we speak to Him when we pray; we hear Him when we read the divine sayings" (n. 25).

... Each and every one of the things set forth in this Constitution has won the consent of the Fathers of this most sacred Council. We too, by the apostolic authority conferred on us by Christ, join with the Venerable Fathers in approving, decreeing, and establishing these things in the Holy Spirit, and we direct that what has thus been enacted in synod be published to God's glory (n. 26).

The above is the official teaching of the Catholic Church forevermore; it reaffirms previous Church teaching, and hardly suggests that the Catholic Church is not in favor of the Bible. In fact, a person who could not accept the Bible as the inspired Word of God could not be accepted into communion with the Roman Catholic Church. Contrary to what anti-Catholic individuals spread about the

Catholic Church, it has never forbidden the reading of Sacred Scripture.

What the Church has been cautious of is the opinion that each individual could pick up the Bible and be assured of guidance by the Holy Spirit to interpret it always according to truth. If each individual was guided by the Holy Spirit — "the Spirit of Truth," then we would not have thousands of Christians churches in the world today claiming their different interpretations of the Word of God as the correct one. The 1980 *World Book of Religions* listed over eighteen thousand different Christian denominations. It is this abuse of the Word of God, bringing it down to man's level and fallen nature and distorting the Word of God, which the Church does not approve.

If one studies carefully the words of Vatican Council II above, it is seen that whereas each individual is encouraged to read the Bible prayerfully, each one of us must be aware that our individual interpretation is not necessarily the infallible one. If all were interpreting Sacred Scripture according to Truth, according to the Holy Spirit, all Christians should be one in their interpretations. It is important that we look to the Church Jesus founded, and to which He promised the Holy Spirit to keep it in the truth (Matt. 16:13-20; John 14:16-21).

The teachings of the ancient Catholic Church are essentially contained in the Bible and preserved and taught today. The Bible is a Church-book, written by churchmen under the inspiration of the Holy Spirit, for the Church's use. The same Holy Spirit who inspired the writings guides the Church in them. The Holy Spirit is the primary Author of Sacred Scripture.

When I was in the seminary, after many years of study of philosophy and theology, and after studying in depth what I had been taught as a child in the simple catechism, it occurred to me as I got a more Scriptural background of our holy Catholic faith that all the basics of the Catholic catechism were to be found in the Bible. Admittedly in my years as a boy, I studied the catechism without Bible in hand. One does not have to go directly to the Bible to discover what God teaches. He founded a Church, not a book, to do His teachings. The Bible is the Church's book, written by churchmen under the inspiration of the Holy Spirit for the Church's use. This distinction has caused some people outside the Catholic Church to claim that the Church teaches that it is not good to read the Bible. As stated earlier, half-truths are very dangerous and lead to falsehoods when taken out of the context of historical circumstances.

The Pharisees read the Scriptures and managed to use and abuse the Word of God, quoting from the Bible as an argument against Christ, just as men today quote Scripture in arguing against the Catholic Church. This universal Church has been upon this earth for almost two thousand years, since the days the Son of God became Man. Jesus lived, taught, died, rose, and ascended into heaven leaving behind His Church with the command,

> Go, therefore, make disciples of all nations; baptize them in the name of the Father and of the Son and of the Holy Spirit, and teach them to observe all the commands I gave you. And look, I am with you always; yes, to the end of time (Matt. 28:19-20).

In this time of modern communication there are still many who accept the falsehood that Catholics are not permitted to own and read the Bible and that the teachings of the Bible are hidden from Catholics. On the contrary, the doctrines of the Bible are constantly taught to members of the Catholic Church. There are three readings of the Bible at every Sunday Mass, and at least two at every weekday Mass. Catholics are encouraged to have a Bible in their home and to read it.

It is untrue to say that Catholics are only now discovering or rediscovering the Bible. The Bible has been carefully preserved, treasured, translated and retranslated by the Church since the days of Christ and His Apostles. Before the days of the printing press it was a fortunate community which could own hand-inscribed scrolls of all the Scriptural texts. When the printing press was invented by the German Catholic Gutenberg in 1445, the first book printed was the Bible. This was before the existence of Protestantism and the many different Christian denominations of today.

Scripture itself testifies that interpreting God's Word brings no guarantee of divine guidance for each individual. Jesus founded a Church, and promised it the Holy Spirit to keep it in the truth (Read 2 Peter, chapters 1-3).

Some attack the Church for its respect for tradition. "The Bible alone" is their theory. The two thousand years that the Church has had to meditate and come to a deeper and better understanding of God's Word means little to them.

Holy Scripture itself denies that it is the only rule of faith. The Apostle St. John ends his beautiful Gospel written under divine inspiration with these words,

> This disciple is the one who vouches for these things and has written them down, and we know that his testimony is true. There was much else that Jesus did; if it were written down in detail, I do

not suppose the world itself would hold all the books that would be written" (John 21: 24-25).

St. Paul pays great respect to tradition in his Scriptural writings:

> Through our Gospel He called you to this so that you should claim as your own the glory of our Lord Jesus Christ. Stand firm, then, brothers, and keep the traditions that we taught you, whether by word of mouth or by letter (2 Thes. 1:14-15).

If Sacred Scripture only is our authority, independent of a divinely founded and guided Church, then each one is his own authority in interpreting the Bible and there is no one faith, one Baptism, and we could have as many churches or opinions as we have people reading the Bible.

> I, the prisoner in the Lord, urge you therefore to lead a life worthy of the vocation to which you were called. With all humility and gentleness, and with patience, support each other in love. Take every care to preserve the unity of the Spirit by the peace that binds you together. There is one Body, one Spirit, just as one hope is the goal of your calling by God. There is one Lord, one faith, one Baptism, and one God and Father of all, over all, through all and within all (Eph. 4:1-7).

If one isolates texts, and does not interpret the Bible as a whole, one can prove almost anything he desires and attempt to put the authority of God's Word behind one's private interpretations. For example, some quote Matthew 15 and claim that the words of Christ Himself condemn tradition:

> Then the Pharisees and scribes from Jerusalem came to Jesus and said, "Why do your disciples break away from the tradition of the elders? They eat without washing their hands." He answered, "And why do you break away from the commandments of God for the sake of your tradition?" (Matt. 15:1-4).

Some quote this part of the Bible simply because it contains the word tradition without regard to its sense, that Jesus referred to *their* tradition, condemning their erroneous and merely human tradition, which was apart from divine authority.

Anti-Catholics have claimed that the Catholic Church had absolutely nothing to do with the composition of the New Testament. The Church teaches that while the Holy Spirit is the primary Author of the Bible, God used early churchmen as His secondary authors. The New Testament was written by early members of the one Church of Christ and His Church existed before a line of the New Testament was written. The thousands of denominations calling themselves Christian today came on the scene hundreds of years later, each quoting and interpreting Scripture differently, not as "one faith." Some have been started only in recent years. The Gospels are writings of early Church members and there was only one Church that came from the hands and heart of Jesus Christ. History testifies that only the Roman Catholic Church goes back to the days of Jesus and His original Apostles.

Jesus Christ established His Church as the rule of faith, promising it the Holy Spirit to keep it in truth, and giving to the Apostles, with Peter as the chief Apostle, the authority to teach in His Name. Historically and Scripturally, even logically, the Catholic Church is the only Church that can be demonstrated to have been founded by Jesus Christ upon His Apostles, Peter in particular, and to have been preserved in an unbroken line for the past two thousand years.

While the above is true, the Catholic Church in no way condemns other Christians. The following quotes from the Ecumenical Council of Vatican II, in the *Decree on Ecumenism,* reveals in brief the Church's charitable attitude toward other Christians:

> Promoting the restoration of unity among all Christians is one of the chief concerns of the Second Sacred Ecumenical Synod of the Vatican. The Church, established by Christ the Lord, is indeed, one and unique. Yet many Christian communions present themselves to men as the true heritage of Jesus Christ. To be sure, all proclaim themselves to be disciples of the Lord, but their convictions clash and their paths diverge, as though Christ Himself were divided (cf. 1 Cor. 1:13). Without doubt, this discord openly contradicts the will of Christ, provides a stumbling block to the world, and inflicts damage on the most holy cause of proclaiming the Good News to every creature. [Introduction]

> What has revealed the love of God among us is that the only-begotten Son of God has been sent by the Father into the world, so that, being made man, the Son might by His redemption of the entire human race give new life to it and unify it (cf. 1 John 4:9; Col. 1:18-20; John 11:52). Before offering Himself up as a spotless victim upon the altar of the Cross, He prayed to His Father for those who believe: "That all may be one even as Thou, Father, are in Me, and I in Thee; that they also may be one in Us, that the world may believe that thou hast sent Me (John 17:21). .... [n. 2]

> From her very beginnings there arose in this one and only Church of God certain rifts (cf. 1 Cor. 11:18-19, Gal 1:6-9; 1 John 2:18-19), which the Apostle strongly censures as damnable (cf. 1 Cor. 1:11ff.; 11:22). But in subsequent centuries more widespread

disagreements appeared and quite large Communities became separated from full communion with the Catholic Church — developments for which, at times, men of both sides were to blame. However, one cannot impute the sin of separation to those who at present are born into these Communities and are instilled therein with Christ's faith. The Catholic Church accepts them with respect and affection as brothers. For men who believe in Christ and have been properly baptized are brought into a certain, though imperfect, communion with the Catholic Church. Undoubtedly, the differences that exist in varying degrees between them and the Catholic Church — whether in doctrine and sometimes in discipline, or concerning the structure of the Church — do indeed create many and sometimes serious obstacles to full ecclesiastical communion. These the ecumenical movement is striving to overcome. Nevertheless, all those justified by faith through Baptism are incorporated into Chirst. They therefore have a right to be honored by the title of Christian, and are properly regarded as brothers in the Lord by the sons of the Catholic Church (n. 3).

Moreover some, even very many, of the most significant elements or endowments which together go to build up and give life to the Church herself can exist outside the visible boundaries of the Catholic Church: the written Word of God; the life of grace; faith, hope, and charity, along with other interior gifts of the Holy Spirit and visible elements. All of these, which come from Christ and lead back to Him, belong by right to the one Church of Christ.

The brethren divided from us also carry out many of the sacred actions of the Christian religion. Undoubtedly, in ways that vary according to the conditions of each Church or Community, these actions can truly engender a life of grace, and can be rightly described as capable of providing access to the community of salvation.

It follows that these separated Churches and Communities, though we believe they suffer from defects already mentioned, have by no means been deprived of significance and importance in the mystery of salvation. For the Spirit of Christ has not refrained from using them as means of salvation which derive their efficacy from the very fullness of grace and truth entrusted to the Catholic Church.

Nevertheless, our separated brethren, whether considered as

individuals or as Communities and Churches, are not blessed with that unity which Jesus Christ wished to bestow on all those whom He has regenerated and vivified into one body and new-ness of life — that unity which the Holy Scriptures and the revered tradition of the Church proclaim. For it is through Christ's Catholic Church alone, which is the all-embracing means of salvation, that the fullness of the means of salvation can be obtained. It was to the apostolic college alone, of which Peter is the head, that we believe our Lord entrusted all the blessings of the New Covenant, in order to establish on earth the one body of Christ into which all those should be fully incorporated who already belong in any way to God's People. During its pilgrimage on earth, the People, though still in its members liable to sin, is growing in Christ and is being gently guided by God, according to His hidden designs, until it happily arrives at the fullness of eternal glory in the heavenly Jerusalem. [n. 2-3].

The quotations above reflect the official position of the Roman Catholic Church in its position regarding other Christians. Notice, the Catholic Church states that other Christians can receive grace; they can be saved. How unlike the extremism of anti-Catholics who hate Catholicism and state that Catholics are going to hell. They will quote Revelations 17 and conclude that the Catholic Church is "the whore of Babylon." They pass out their tracts distorting Sacred Scripture. In their attacks against Catholicism, they go door to door, onto the streets, and at times even into Catholic churches, placing their biased litera-ture in hymnals, etc., or onto windshields of cars while Catholics are participating in Mass.

Biblical tracts attacking Catholicism were handed out in a New-man Center near a former parish of mine. One young man receiving the anti-Catholic tracts came from a home where the mother had joined the Catholic Church only to please her husband. This woman had been brought up with anti-Catholic bias against Catholic doc-trines such as Purgatory and the veneration due the Mother of God. After many years her emotions could not forget the bias in which she was formed. In reality, no one should in conscience go through a cere-mony of receptence into the Catholic Church without accepting all of its dogmas of faith. A priest in conscience could not knowingly receive anyone into full union who rejects dogmas of faith. Somehow this woman got by in the husband's hurry during World War II to have her join the Church, and in the rush of things they prepared for marriage at a young age. Thirty years later the woman's dilemma remained the same, for she refused to open her mind. A ceremony of reception does not make one a Catholic unless the faith be first in the heart.

The above state of affairs could not but help influence the children. A child experiences, from pre-school years, a parent's sincerity if there is happiness, conviction, and commitment to it. What happens to such children then when they know a parent is not happy with the faith and is presented literature attacking the Catholic Church? In the case sited above, the young man not only left the Catholic Church after studying the hate literature which distorted the Catholic position, but proceeded to so influence other members of his family. His younger brother came to me, a young man who had been in my parish for more than twelve years and had heard hundreds of times, in the Scriptures and in sermons that Jesus Christ was our Lord, God and Savior. Below, in summary is what the college youth holding a Bible stated:

"I do not know if you are saved. I know I am saved. I never once heard in the Catholic Church that Jesus Christ is my Savior. You shouldn't be worshipping statues of Mary. You shouldn't be teaching children to worship statues. I was never told in the Catholic Church who Jesus Christ is."

That young man had completely blanked out of his mind what I and other members of the parish had taught him for over twelve years. He had been so worked over by extremists, by fundamentalists who study and quote the Bible with a view to condemning Catholicism, that he appeared sincere. He believed what he was saying. I found notes of innumberable sermons I had given, in the context of Mass where three Scriptural readings occur, and at which that young man had been present. He had heard me hundreds of times emphatically declare that Jesus Christ is our Lord, God and Savior, that Jesus Christ had shed His precious blood for our salvation, etc. He had been exposed to these truths thousands of times in the Catholic Church. He sat before me glassy-eyed, his father at his side, claiming never to have heard in Catholicism, "Jesus is our Savior."

After the heart-breaking encounter with this young man, in the same parish in which he grew up but, from which he had just separated himself, I went into the first and second grade CCD religion classes. I started by asking, "Who is Jesus Christ?" The first answer I received from a second grader was: "Jesus Christ is our Savior." The young man's little brother was a first grader and volunteered, "Jesus Christ is our God." That amounts to, "Jesus Christ is Lord, God and Savior." I could only wonder what message the beautiful Stations of the Cross in the church with Scriptural meditation I led each Lent and the beautiful large Cross with the Body of Christ hanging upon it over the altar had given to the young man who had separated himself. These instruments of devotion to convey the message of salvation now were condemned by him. Now he was acting as though he had discovered the Bible for the first time. In each of our CCD classrooms were copies of the Bible for teachers and students to use and in which that young man had participated for twelve years. So strongly had fundamentalists worked on that youth that he had blanked out of his mind his Catholic education.

The series of anti-Catholic tracts I have before me as I write this chapter present themselves as highly documented. But if they were evidence in a trial, they would quickly be thrown out in any court. Their bibliography does not include a single authentic source from official Church pronouncements, such as the councils of the Church, unless it be to make glaring and incomplete statements out of context. Such is done in the case of the Inquisition, "bad Popes," etc. Not one word of favor toward Catholicism can be found. Unfortunately some individuals are so psychologically put together that they cannot well endure such direct attacks. Not knowing well how to interpret the Bible with proper guidance and the scholarship needed, these people can easily be led astray.

A beautiful ecumenical spirit was fostered among Catholics at the time of the Second Vatican Council (1962-1965) which had as a chief purpose the promotion of unity among all Christians. Catholics were encouraged to take a first step toward other Christians. Catholics were told to emphasize, together with other Christians, not our differences but to recognize where we already had unity.

In a small parish in South Dakota in 1964, on the first Sunday of Advent, I with my parish and every minister of the town and our parishioners met together for an ecumenical Advent service in the local public school auditorium. More people participated than the total population of the town.

Vatican II's *Decree on Ecumenism* (*Unitatis Redintergratio*) had been promulgated only days before, on Nov. 21, 1964. My bishop had given permission from Rome for my parish to participate. The event was highlighted in secular and religious papers across the United States as a first in the country. Much good will resulted. We had all met, read the Sacred Scriptures together, said prayers in common which were agreeable to all. We sang hymns, each according to our faith, and finally in common, "O Come, O Come Emmanuel."

For some years a beautiful Christian spirit of unity grew among Catholics and fellow Christians. We were encouraged to bury past grievances. The days of the Counter-Reformation were over. Seldom, if ever, were young Catholics taught courses in apologetics, the science which give "a reason for the faith that is in us."

Now in the spirit of ecumenism, the Christian unity movement, it hardly seemed fitting with the passing of the Counter-Reformation period to spend our time justifying our Catholic positions. We would bring up a whole new generation of Catholics filled with positive attitudes toward fellow Christians. That noble aspiration and ideal exists to the writing of this book for the most part. It was that good will which anti-Catholics and fundamentalists have taken advantage of in recent years. With the new openness to fellow-Christians, even some older Catholics have been lead astray. Older Catholics who had led religiously-sheltered lives never read a leaflet unless it was under Catholic auspices, never listened to a radio or watched a religious TV program unless it was Catholic, had a new spirit of openness toward other Christians fostered by the spirit of ecumenism. But they were not always immune to the zeal of fundamentalists who were convinced they needed to save the souls of Catholics enslaved in "superstition."

Many young people have been led astray with the fire of evangelists, toting and quoting the Bible, shouting, "I'm saved. Do you know for certain that you are saved?" Added to the problem for youth has been the failures too often of not having been taught the basics of Catholicism. Too often, the Modernists who gained control in catechetical fields, in a false sense of ecumenism, have failed to teach our youth the basics of Catholicism, solid Church history or any apologetics. Many religion textbooks resembled mere sociological and psychological approaches. There were efforts to present the faith with the least common denominator so that many growing young Catholics had no sense of the fullness of faith found in their Church which has been around for two thousand years. These youth were hardly taught how to protect themselves from attacks on their faith. In some cases, as the late Cardinal Wright said, "They are not losing their faith. They never had it."

For over a quarter of a century, in the post-Vatican II era, we have failed to teach young Catholics apologetics. The truths of the faith are often above — but not contrary — to the use of right reason. We cannot understand how an eternal God could make all things out of nothing, but it is the only reasonable conclusion for the existence of the universe. Scripture tells us to have a reason for the faith that is in us. Catholics from their youth on should be taught how to explain their faith and to defend it from those who attack our faith with over-simplifications. If our young people are not taught some of the techniques of those who attack Catholicism in the name of Christianity, they are unsuspecting victims and easy prey to feverish hunters.

Once faith in God is accepted and faith in God's Son become Man in Jesus Christ and that Jesus as Lord, God and Savior founded a Church, as mentioned in Matthew 16, and as testified by early history, then the Scriptures can be used to verify the logical conclusions of Catholicism. Then one can have a reason for the faith that is in him. This takes study. It takes time. It requires prayer. The reward is a discovery of a deeper faith, a personal relationship with our Lord Jesus Christ. One can then see the perfect soundness of the holy Catholic doctrines. We shall demonstrate this in various doctrines discussed in this book as shall be seen especially in the case of the doctrines of the Church concerning the Holy Eucharist to be dealt with in the very next chapter. One who can study the Catholic faith with an open mind will discover that the Catholic Church is indeed a Bible-based Church and one's growth in knowledge and love of Jesus Christ need never end but go on expanding more and more.

People opposed to the Church or who have doubts about its authority are highly suspicious. They think Catholics are trying to hide something, the way Mormons hide their real doctrines from the initiates. This suspicion leads to mistrust, and sometimes with a hatred that is handed down from one generation to another. Thus, even quoting conciliar documents may not be convincing. Then too, because of some misunderstanding, some imprudence or even uncharitableness on the part of a Church member, even a priest or a religious, prejudice can have built up in one's mind so that emotions blank out making judgments objectively. It takes humility to come back when one has been hurt.

Mr. Karl Keating, an attorney in San Diego, who heads a Catholic organization concerned with the attacks of the fundamentalists, advised the author of this book as follows: "If it came to a choice between relying on the authority of a conciliar document or the persuasiveness of Father Robert Fox's own words, I think most readers, at least those suspicious of Catholicism, would pay more attention to the latter, on the theory that a priest should really know what Rome teaches and should be able to put things in perspective."

Obviously, those who refuse to recognize that any authority was given by Jesus Christ to a Church two thousand years old, and who will not recognize that the Catholic Church today is the same as that Church which has been in the world for all those years, are going to find it difficult to accept as authentic any of its official pronouncements. In doing so, however, they go contrary to the positions of most educated men, even the secular media, which in general is not favorable to the Catholic Church. For example, when Pope John Paul II went to the Jewish Synagogue in Rome on April 13, 1986, the evening news reported, "It was the first time in two thousand years that a Roman Pontiff visited a Jewish synagogue."

Such comments, made frequently by the secular media, are explicit and implicit recognition that the Catholic Church has a history extending back to Jesus Christ and His original twelve Apostles. Even then, however, the news media erred a bit regarding that incident. Acts 3:1 states: "Now Peter and John were going up into the Temple at the ninth hour of prayer." (There was no sudden break with the past — the disciples had their own Sacrifice, the Eucharist, in their houses where they also took their evening meal beforehand, as our Lord did at the institution of the Eucharist.)

Karl Keating, the expert on Fundamentalism, also advised the author that the fundamentalist will ask, " 'What's this? A Catholic priest who evidently knows the Bible?' The fundamentalist *will* be surprised, because he's been taught priests studiously keep their distance from the sacred text."

Pope John Paul II has warned about "narrow Fundamentalism." On April 7, 1986 the Pope said,

> attention must be given to the literary forms of the various Biblical books in order to determine the intention of the sacred writers .... And it is most helpful, at times crucial, to be aware of the personal situation of the Biblical writer, to the circumstances of culture, time, language and so forth which influenced the way the message was presented.

Pope John Paul voiced his concern for Fundamentalism — the strictly literal and narrow interpretation of the Scriptures — in an address to the World Catholic Federation for the Biblical Apostolate. In his address, the Pope said that those who teach Scriptures must approach the Bible from the context of the "the living tradition of the Church."

While the fundamentalist may mistrust papal or conciliar pronouncements, if he reads them he will doubtlessly be surprised over the high regard the Church has for the inerrancy of the Bible. He will discover that the Church holds to the absence of error in the Bible as it is believed by the Church to be the revealed Word of God.

It was precisely because many challenged the truth of events and sayings recorded in the Gospels that the Vatican issued guidelines for

Biblical interpretation. The instruction, "On the Historical Truth of the Gospels," was issued on April 21, 1964 with the approval of Pope Paul VI.*

A summary of the instruction follows:

1. Catholic Biblical exegetes, working in accord with the rules of rational and Catholic hermeneutics, must make skillful use of the new aids to exegesis, especially those provided by the historical method, in its widest sense, including textual and literary criticism, and linguistic studies to help them understand more fully the character of the Gospel testimony of the religious life of the first churches, and of the significance and force of the apostolic tradition. But they must also be careful not to be misled by advocates of the method of form-history (*Formgeschichte*) who, led by rationalistic prejudices, deny any supernatural order, including the possibility of miracles or of divine revelations; or by those who *a priori* deny the historical value of the documents of revelation; or who underestimate the authority of the Apostles as witnesses of Christ and overestimate the creative capacity of the early Christian Community itself. "All these aberrations are not only opposed to Catholic doctrine, but are also devoid of any scientific foundation, and are foreign to the general principles of the historical method."

2. The exegete must note the stages by which the teaching and life of Jesus have come down to us. Jesus chose certain disciples who were with him from the beginning, who were qualified to become witnesses. In His teaching, Jesus used methods of reasoning and exposition accommodated to the mentality of His hearers, so that His teaching would be impressed on their minds and easily remembered. The apostles realized that His miracles were performed to induce belief in him as the Christ, and to accept by faith the doctrine of salvation. From being witnesses of His Resurrection, their faith in Jesus and their memory or what he had done and taught was further strengthened. To pass on the teaching of Jesus the Apostles used various forms of speech, according to the mentality of their hearers. Each followed a method suited to his immediate

---

* This authorized translation appeared in the *Canon Law Digest,* volume 6, pp. 789-97, which was taken from *The Catholic Biblical Quarterly,* volume 26, pp. 305-12.

audience, selecting certain things out of the many which had been handed on, at times synthesizing them. They recounted events as they recalled them, without trying to place them in a precise chronological order.

Exegetes are free to try to determine more precisely what each writer intended to teach or exemplify, while always ready to accept the Church's teaching authority.

3. *Teachers in seminaries* and similar institutions should make theological doctrine the main subject of their exposition, so that Sacred Scripture "may become for the future priests of the Church a pure and never-failing source of spiritual life for themselves and of nourishment and vigor for the office of sacred preaching which they are to undertake" (Pius XII, *Divino Afflante Spiritu*). When they apply modern methods, especially literary criticism, they should do so to produce a deeper insight into the sense intended by God speaking to them through the sacred writer and go on to show how such findings contribute to a better understanding of revealed doctrine or towards the refutation of misleading views.

4. *Preachers* must be especially prudent, sticking to certain doctrine and avoiding futile novelties and uncertain matters. In narrating Biblical events, they should not introduce imaginary additions at variance with the truth. The same holds especially for *writers* on the popular level, so that they never depart in the slightest from the common doctrine and tradition of the Church. They can rely on real advances in Biblical knowledge, but stay clear of rash fancies of innovators.

Fundamentalists who have had drummed into them the idea that the Catholic Church is against the Bible, even fears the Bible, are often greatly threatened when confronted with facts that the Catholic Church dearly loves the Bible and looks to it as a chief tool in its divine mission of teaching in the Name of Jesus Christ. After all, many a fundamentalist thinks the Bible is not a Catholic book. The public is even treated to movies and television programs that have fictitious characters which make statements in this manner, "How do you expect me to know anything about the Bible. I'm a Catholic .... Catholics don't read the Bible."

In the Dakotas where this book is written, in one of our larger cities, the daily newspaper carried quotations from a talk the Pope had delivered in which the Pope was quoted as proclaiming that the Catholic Church was a Bible-based Church. Fundamentalists reading the news report were horrified and hastened to write letters to the editor offering their proof that the Catholic Church has always been against the Bible and that the Pope was obviously lying to trick people into the Church or keep people there. This is not to suggest that the writers to the editor in that fashion were insincere. They were doubtlessly most sincere. Hundreds of thousands of fundamentalists really do believe that the Catholic Church is against the Bible and that the faith of Catholics is opposed to the Bible. To the credit of the editor, the newspaper afterwards published a letter from a Catholic who for some years had become convinced by fundamentalistic interpretations of the Bible but had found his way back into Catholicism. The former Catholic re-discovered that the Catholic faith of his childhood was indeed the faith given us by Jesus Christ and is consistent with the Bible. The Pope was not preaching that the Church flowed from the Bible but that the Church proclaims the Bible as the inerrant Word of God.

Fundamentalists, even in this modern day, persist in their idea that the Catholic Church has kept the Bible chained so that the average Christian could not read it. Every heresy has some truth and while their image of the Bible chained to a desk has substantially been correct in history, their interpretation of it is not. Just as they misinterpret the "chaining of the Bible" by taking it out of the context of historical circumstances, so they misinterpret the Bible itself in many instances by ignoring the language, the culture, the historical circumstances, and the intentions of the authors.

In cases where the Bible was chained in churches — before the invention of the printing press — each Bible had to be laboriously hand-inscribed, and it was a fortunate community which could have an entire Bible. The chaining was done precisely to make the Bible available to all. Since it was so valuable, the Bible could easily have been stolen if it had not been protected from theft in some way, such as are large phone books in our major cities.

It is often claimed that various Popes, e.g., Pope Pius VII, Pius VIII, Leo XII and Pius IX denounced Bible societies and warned Catholics about them. What these Popes did was to warn against the circulation of inaccurate translations, and against the principle that all can interpret the Bible to their own private judgment, however little qualified they may be. The Popes have warned that with private interpretation and without proper translations and scholarship there would be many different conclusions. This would contradict the ideal given by St. Paul:

Brothers, I urge you, in the name of our Lord Jesus Christ, not to have factions among yourselves but all to be in agreement in what you profess; so that you are perfectly united in your beliefs and judgments (1 Cor. 1:10).

Pope Pius VII quoted St. Augustine's words, "Heresies would not have arisen unless men had read good Scripture badly, and rashly asserted their own mistakes to be the truth." The result of replacing the authority Christ gave His Church with private interpretation of the Bible has been innumerable Protestant divisions, even many radical differences within the same sects. Cults have arisen, which have rashly interpreted the Bible. Hundreds, even thousands of such divisions have brought disrespect to Christianity and to the Bible so that many are drifting from faith in the Bible altogether. What the Catholic Church has done in reality is defend the Bible against the very ones who accused her of hostility towards it.

Just as God's Word is living so the living voice of an authentic interpreter is needed. In the course of this book, as the nature of the Church as Christ's Body with the Holy Spirit becomes more evident, we see that the Holy Spirit that is the primary Author of the Bible is also the Soul of the Church, which is the official interpreter of the Bible. The same Holy Spirit which inspired the human writers to write only what was divinely true — although in human form and according to the human personality and culture of each writer — is the Holy Spirit which guides the universal Church in interpreting the Bible.

Is the average citizen capable of interpreting the laws of their country correctly? We have lawyers who spend many years in difficult studies and even then lawyers with extended education will wrangle long over the interpretation of individual laws and often disagree with each other. This is something natural. God's Revelation is of the supernatural order of truth and has the infinite mind of God behind it.

An individual priest, as an individual minister, as any individual Christian, can be mistaken in the interpretation of Sacred Scripture. Even individual bishops can mistakenly interpret the Bible. The authoritative voice of Jesus Christ speaking for His Church is found only when the bishops speak collectively and in union with the Pope. This is called the college of the bishops. The bishop alone without the successor of St. Peter would not suffice. The teaching Church is not an individual priest or bishop. The teaching Church involves the Magisterium of the Church. The Magisterium is the Church's teaching authority, vested in bishops, as successors of the Apostles, under the Pope as the successor of St. Peter. The Biblical as well as historical evidence that Jesus set up His teaching Church in this manner shall be dealt with in the contents of this book.

One can easily see the importance of an authoritative interpreter of God's Word when the four simple words of Jesus Christ, "This is my body," have been interpreted in many conflicting and different ways. The truth does not lie in one's individual interpretation but in what the God-Man actually meant in giving us the Holy Eucharist.

Some have asked that if God is truly the Author of the Bible why could He not make it so simply clear that no one could doubt its meaning? The very question escapes the realization that God is the Supreme Being, infinite in nature, Infinite Truth. The limitation is not on God's part. It is on man's part. Man, in addition, is a fallen creature with weakened will and darkened intellect.

Catholics are accused of putting more emphasis on the Church and Christian Tradition than they do on the Bible. The truth is that authentic Catholics put reliance on both. Both Scripture and Tradition come from the one Source, which is God. We are not talking about mere human traditions, but Divine Tradition. It is not possible for Divine Tradition to be opposed to Sacred Scripture, since both come from God, who is Truth. It is not possible for Catholic dogma to be opposed to either Sacred Scripture or Divine Tradition because dogma is a divinely guided interpretation of God's Revelation.

The hundreds of different non-Catholic Christian churches do not claim infallibility for themselves. They do not claim to be guided by the Holy Spirit Who is Truth. Therefore they admit that their interpretations of God's Word, the Bible, are not necessarily correct.

While the Catholic Church encourages Bible reading for its individual members, the Church insists that it should be read humbly and from the perspective of faith and within the context of the Church's living Divine Tradition, guided by the Holy Spirit. In other words, if one's personal interpretation is at variance with an official interpretation of the Church, one should humbly admit that the authority of Christ in His Church, guided by the Holy Spirit, is the interpretation to follow. Private interpretation can lead to erroneous conclusions, which are testified by the lack of unity among Christians. In the Acts of the Apostles, as Philip comes upon the Ethiopian eunuch, Philip asks him if he understands the Scriptures he is reading. Without hesitation, the man answers, "How can I, unless someone explains it to me?" (Acts 8:27-31).

A Catholic is as free to read the Bible as any Christian. One should make use of good Bible commentaries and guides put out by Biblical scholars who have dedicated much of their lives to the study of the Scriptures, as well as Biblical history, cultures, languages, etc.

Martin Luther, who at first encouraged private scriptural interpretation, later revoked that teaching when he saw the great harm resulting from unqualified people interpreting Scripture who were working with the assumption that their interpretation was of equal value to that of scholars.

In interpreting the Bible, the Catholic Church makes use of the work of scholars. It is not only bishops in union with the Pope who contribute to the accumulated wealth of wisdom of the centuries in better understanding Divine Revelation. But since scholars, like lawyers, may disagree, the authority of Christ in the official teaching Church (Magisterium) is needed. There must be preserved the unity in faith called for by Christ.

The Catholic Church does not suppress personal reflection in the reading of the Bible. It encourages it. We should pray to the Holy Spirit even as individuals when we read the Scriptures. Each one ought not to consider himself on a level with the Church, or being divinely guided so as to always interpret infallibly.

Usually the Church will use its infallible authority to interpret a part of the Bible only when a serious need for that arrives. The Church's authority of interpreting the Bible does not include such technicalities like secondary authorships of parts of the Bible or the exact date each part was written.

A person who is suspicious of the Catholic Church may form the idea that the Catholic Church is sitting there like a tyrant telling us the exact meaning of each verse. Nothing could be further from the truth. The Church exercises great restraint in making authoritative interpretations of individual verses. While such proclamations are important, fewer than a dozen such instances can be pointed out in the two thousand-year history of the Catholic Church. Most of these were at the Ecumenical Council of Trent following the Protestant Revolt, when a serious need was obvious, since Christians were dividing into warring and contradicting factions.

When the Church has given definitive interpretations of parts of Scripture it has been when there has been a real historical need in the lives of Christians. There has not been such a need for most of the verses in Scripture. The Church, in acting authoritatively, has first consulted the best of Biblical scholars of the day and called upon the divine guidance that Jesus has promised His Church (John 14:26; John 16;13, etc.).

The Blessed Sacrament in public procession

# CHAPTER 6

# The Eucharist
# — Reality or Symbolism?

Attacks against Catholic doctrines on the Eucharistic Body and Blood of Jesus Christ and the Mass's perpetuation of Christ's Sacrifice of the Cross are centuries old. Below we quote modern-day misrepresentations containing half-truths aimed at disturbing Catholics and keeping others from investigating the two thousand-year-old Church. The quotes are from the publication of a popular TV evangelist:

> *The Roman Catholic church teaches that the Holy Mass is an expiatory (sin removing) sacrifice, in which the Son of God is actually sacrificed anew on the cross . . . . This esoteric sacrifice was to be a recreation of His suffering and death on Calvary, perpetually repeated within His church until He should come again. Therefore, He is today the truly present body, blood, soul, and divinity (although, admittedly, disguised as wine and bread) on all Catholic altars and in all Catholic tabernacles, and will so remain until such time as He may choose to come again.*

> *The Catholic doctrine of Transubstantiation is, without question, one of the most absurd doctrines ever imposed on a trusting public. As we've already discussed, this doctrine states that the priest is endowed with the power to transform bread and wine into the literal body and blood of Christ . . . .*

> *Roman Catholic errors are inevitably human innovations that were inserted into the church during the early centuries . . . . From the third century, Old Testament ideas of priesthood were used by some to interpret the eucharist as the "Christian sacrifice." At first the sacrifice was thought to consist of praises, but gradually it came to be held that an offering*

*was made to God to gain the forgiveness of sins. By the Middle Ages this had been developed to make the eucharist a re-offering of Christ's sacrifice on the cross . . . .*

*This doctrine of Transubstantiation, which simply means that the bread and wine change to His body and blood, was first formulated by Paschasius Radbertus, Abbot of Corbey, at the beginning of the ninth century . . . .*

*In all honesty, we must repudiate this dogma on two counts: It is opposed to Scripture.*

*It is contradicted by the evidence of the senses. When one handles the wine or the wafer, their textures remains the same. When one tastes them, they are as before. And when one smells them, there is no transformation in odor. They are still bread and juice, with all the original qualities. They are physically unchanged and will ever remain unchanged. They are merely, as blessed and holy as they might be, a memorial to our Savior's sacrifice as a sin offering in our stead. Therefore, we reject this erroneous doctrine because of its basically superstitious nature and the idolatrous connotations connected with it . . . .*

*The Catholic doctrine of Transubstantiation forces one to humiliate Christ, even beyond the supreme humiliation He suffered on the cross at Calvary . . . . Yet the very concept of bread and wine, which He Himself created — being mysteriously transformed into His living body and blood — forces Him into further humiliation, which is unacceptable and unthinkable . . . .*

*Further, Paul does not say, "ye shall repeat the sacrifice of Christ until He comes." He says, "ye do shew the Lord's death . . . ."*

*It seems obvious that, if the expiatory death of Jesus was a perfect work, we have no need for additional sacrifices . . . .*

*If the celebration of the Mass were a true sacrifice, then it would be wicked and cruel on the part of the priests to repeat it so frequently . . . . No true sacrifice exists without pain and suffering . . . .*

*The New Testament clearly shows that the Lord's Supper was only a peripheral element in the overall majesty of the Gospel message. It was obviously not considered an essential part of salvation . . . .*

The above quotations are all from *The Evangelist* (October 1985), written by Jimmy Swaggart; it was his fourth in a special series on

Catholicism. The article which seriously misrepresents Catholic teaching was titled, "The Mass — The Holy Eucharist."

Some of the things in the article from which I quoted are so ridiculous and degrading to the Holy Eucharist and the Catholic Church it would not be in good Christian taste to quote them. Apparently people who want to believe such things easily do. In the article it is emphasized over and over again that the Mass is a sacrifice, "wherein the Lord's death is repeated over and over again." The truth is that the Catholic Church *does* teach that the Mass is a Sacrifice but it is *not*, according to Catholic doctrine, a "repeated" Sacrifice. It is the *one and same* Sacrifice that Christ Jesus offered physically once and for all on Calvary. The Catholic Church does not teach that Jesus again undergoes pain and physical death. The writer knows this but he uses words according to his own definitions when he concludes, "No true sacrifice exists without pain and suffering."

In Catholic doctrine the Mass does not *repeat* the Sacrifice of Jesus on the Cross, as the writer keeps saying. The Mass is not a new or different or additional Sacrifice. It is not Jesus Christ dying physically over and over again. It is not the place of those outside the Church to attempt to explain what the Church teaches, especially when their purpose is to ridicule and condemn its teachings. If one wants to know what the Catholic Church teaches, the Church's own explanations are quite adequate. I shall offer the reader some help in this direction. When the Catholic Church teaches that the Mass is an "unbloody" sacrifice it is teaching that the Sacrifice of the Cross is not repeated physically, that there is not a painful physical death of Christ again. In a sacramental way, in a different manner of offering, Jesus Christ in His Church can perpetuate His Sacrifice, which is infinitely pleasing to God the Father, without repeating it. This is of course, a mystery of faith. The incarnation, God become man, is also a mystery.

This is how the Catechism of the Council of Trent summarized the Church's teaching on the Holy Eucharist as Sacrifice:

> We therefore confess that the Sacrifice of the Mass is and ought to be considered one and the same Sacrifice as that of the Cross, for the victim is one and the same, namely, Christ our Lord, who offered Himself, once only, a bloodly Sacrifice on the altar of the Cross. The bloody and unbloody victim are not two, but one victim only, whose Sacrifice is daily renewed in the Eucharist, in obedience to the command of our Lord: *Do this for a commemoration of Me.*

The priest is also one and the same, Christ the Lord: for the ministers who offer Sacrifice, consecrate the holy mysteries, not in their own person, but in that of Christ, as the words of consecration itself show, for the priest does not say: *This is the Body of Christ,* but, *This is My Body;* and thus, acting in the Person of Christ the Lord, He changes the substance of the bread and wine into the true substance of His body and blood.

This being the case, it must be taught without any hesitation that, as the holy Council [of Trent] has also explained, the sacred and holy Sacrifice of the Mass is not a Sacrifice of praise and thanksgiving only, or a mere commemoration of the Sacrifice performed on the Cross, but also truly a propitiatory Sacrifice, by which God is appeased and rendered propitious to us. If, therefore, with a pure heart, a lively faith, and affected with an inward sorrow for our transgressions, we immolate and offer this most holy victim, we shall, without doubt, obtain mercy from the Lord, and grace in time of need . . . .

This universal catechism quoted above was presented as a handbook to help teachers, preachers, etc. present the authentic Catholic faith.

The Catholic Church teaches that whereas the Mass is an unbloody Sacrifice of the Cross perpetuated, there is also thereby made present the real, living Jesus Christ, the same resurrected Christ who ascended into heaven and now sits at the right hand of God the Father. It is not a dead Christ we behold in the Holy Eucharist. It is the risen, glorified Christ. Under the veils of bread and wine His glory is hidden to us as His glory was hidden to men while He walked upon the earth teaching, and while He was redeeming mankind.

Jesus Christ spoke of the climax of His redeeming life as "His hour." God the Father received infinite glory, infinite adoration from Jesus Christ, true God and true man when He was offering His life in Sacrifice upon the Cross in reparation for our sins, for the salvation of the world. God the Father accepted Christ's Sacrifice for all men. God the Father did not look down upon Christ for this humiliating act but rather raised Him up again and looks upon all mankind as saved as a consequence, if only each one of us in faith and love turn to Jesus Christ and His redeeming act of the Cross. This is what Catholics do when they participate in the Mass, which does not repeat but perpetuates into our lives the infinite act of glory. This is not double talk but the precise expression of our faith. The Eucharist *perpetuates* the Sacrifice of the Cross. If the sacrifice were "repeated" as those who oppose the Catholic dogma of faith claim, each time a priest offered the Mass it would be different, or an additional sacrifice. By now there would have been offered millions of sacrifices since Jesus first instituted His Church. Such a position is clearly and completely opposite of the teachings of the Roman Catholic Church. These anti-Catholics present as Catholic doctrine what the Church does not teach. Then they use Scripture to "prove" the Church wrong. The Second Vatican Council stated:

> At the Last Supper, on the night when He was betrayed, our Savior instituted the Eucharistic Sacrifice of His Body and Blood. He did this in order to perpetuate the Sacrifice of the Cross throughout the centuries until He should come again, and so to entrust to His beloved spouse, the Church, a memorial of His death and resurrection: a sacrament of love, a sign of unity, a bond of charity, a paschal banquet in which Christ is consumed, the mind is filled with grace, and a pledge of future glory is given to us. (*Constitution on the Sacred Liturgy*, n. 47).

It is a mystery of faith, and we ought not place any limitation on what God can do in His Son made man in Jesus Christ. It took faith for those who lived two thousand years ago when Jesus Christ was physcially present upon earth with His Body and Soul united to His Divinity, to accept that this was truly the Son of God the Father and therefore God become man. Jesus was sentenced to death for claiming to be just that. Those who came into contact with Jesus Christ did not sense His glory. They were asked to believe, and He gave testimony by the works He performed, the ultimate work being His Resurrection from the dead. His Resurrection was the supreme sign to us that God the Father was well pleased with Jesus' Sacrifice and we are indeed redeemed, saved.

Fundamentalists, who generally hold that the words of Sacred Scripture are to be taken literally, make a glaring exception. Jesus tells us He is changing bread and wine into His Body and Blood and gave the Apostles the same power (Matt. 26:26-28; Mark 14:22-24; Luke 22:19-20; 1 Cor. 11:23ff). Furthermore, it is seen in John 6 that Jesus labors to demonstrate that He is *not* speaking figuratively and means exactly what He says. Yet, it is precisely here where opponents of the Church will attempt to explain away Catholic doctrine, the words and teaching of Christ Himself, by having our Lord's most solemn words reduced to meaning little or nothing but symbolism. Those who hold to literal interpretations suddenly switch and see these things figuratively.

The Catholic Church teaches that there is the Real Presence of

Jesus Christ in the Holy Eucharist. Under the appearances of bread and wine there is the real living Body, Blood, Soul and Divinity of our Lord and Savior Jesus Christ. It is the most intimate union with God made in, with and through Jesus Christ that is possible upon this earth. There is no personal relationship with Jesus Christ that can exceed this coming of the Lord in His Body, Blood, Soul and Divinity into our very person than when we receive Him in Holy Communion.

It is indeed sad and tragic that fundamentalists who keep calling for the assurance of salvation and for a personal relationship with Jesus Christ will deny the greatest means the God-Man gave us to have a personal relationship with Him — a necessary means for our salvation. "In all truth I tell you, if you do not eat the flesh of the Son of man and drink his blood, you have no life in you" (John 6:53). What could be more personal in a relationship than for Jesus to come into our very being with the entire substance of His Sacred Body, His precious Blood, and His Soul with His plenitude of divine life (Col. 1:19; Col. 2:9; Eph. 3,19). Let us read on to discover how Jesus labored to instruct us that He would indeed give us His Body and Blood to eat and drink unto salvation.

First, I quote the popular TV evangelist already mentioned in his fundamentalist attacks against Catholic doctrine:

> *On the same basis we should accept without thinking that Jesus gives us literal living waters which will produce eternal life (John 4:14), or that Jesus is truly a door (John 10:7-9), that He is a lamb (John 1:29), or that He is a growing vine (John 15:5). If the Catholic hierarchy is to be consistent, they should foster adoration of doors, vines, and lambs. Certainly, these figures of speech are descriptive and colorful, but they are transparently figurative, just as are the terms "my body" and "my blood."*

The lack of thinking of which fundamentalists accuse the hierarchy and those who accept the Catholic faith is not on the part of the leadership and membership of the Catholic Church. It has a two thousand year old line of ancestors, including numerous scholars, who have believed in exactly the same manner. While there are literally thousands of spiritual writers from the first centuries to the present whose writings are preserved and who speak of the Real Presence of the Lord's Body and Blood in Holy Communion, we can find the most valuable accounts in Sacred Scripture itself, e.g., St. Paul.

"Is not the cup of blessing we bless a sharing in the Blood of Christ? And is not the bread we break a sharing in the Body of Christ?" (1 Cor. 10:16-17). Our divine Lord was certainly telling us that He was not giving us an ordinary bread like the manna sent as food to the Israelites in the desert (Exodus 16:4-36). The multiplication of loaves of bread and fish were multiplied to feed thousands, and the bread of which He spoke undergoes a marvelous change in becoming His Body and Blood:

> I am the bread of life. Your forefathers ate manna in the desert, and they died. This is the bread that comes down from heaven; anyone who eats this bread will never die. I am the living bread come down from heaven. Anyone who eats this bread will live for ever . . . (John 6:48ff).

The Gospels of Sts. Matthew, Mark and Luke are known as the synoptic Gospels because these three evangelists follow the same general plan and reflect great similarity in their telling of the life and teachings of Jesus Christ. The fourth Gospel was written by the Apostle John. Now John's Gospel was written later and so he does not repeat what Matthew, Mark and Luke have written — with one exception: he too writes of the Holy Eucharist, and of that most extensively. He obviously had knowledge of the synoptic Gospels. And since he was writing late in the first century there was more time to reflect deeply on the teachings of Jesus Christ. This John does and he does so profoundly, laboring extensively regarding the Holy Eucharist, which immediately became central in Christian worship.

Among the first Christians, before the century ended, there were doubtlessly some who asked whether Jesus' teaching that He was to give us His Body and Blood was a real divine life-giving of His actual substantial Body and Blood. St. John gives us more details about the Holy Eucharist than do the other three evangelists who wrote earlier. This most extensive explanation on the part of Jesus, as we shall see, removes the possibilities of mere figurative meanings.

It is also to be noted that John was the Apostle especially close to Jesus. He is the Apostle who writes so profoundly on the love of God. St. John does not use his own name in writing of himself but speaks simply of "the disciple whom Jesus loved." He acknowledges his special closeness to Jesus. John sat closest to Jesus at the Last Supper. John was allowed to accompany Jesus to Jairus' home when the latter's daughter was brought back to life. John was present at the Transfiguration (Matt. 17:1-2). John was one of the three who went with Jesus to Gethsemane (Mark 14:33). John was the Apostle who hurried with Peter to the tomb on Easter Sunday morning and was the first Apostle to proclaim faith in the Risen Christ (John 20:1-10). John is in the upper room after the Ascension (Acts 1:13) and accompanies Peter on special occasions as he had done with Jesus. (Acts 3:1-10, 8:14-17). As Jesus was dying on the Cross, John was the only Apostle present at the foot of Calvary's Cross of Redemption on which our Savior hung. John heard Him say, "Behold your Mother" after which he took Mary into his own home (John 19:27).

It is this John, commonly thought to be the youngest of the Apostles, "the disciple whom Jesus loved," who does not repeat the other events mentioned by Saints Matthew, Mark and Luke, but does record Jesus' teachings extensively about the Holy Eucharist. It is through the Holy Eucharist that we can especially come close to Jesus in a personal relationship, become one with Him, and this great Apostle of love to whom Jesus commissioned His own Mother from the Cross, did not miss the opportunity in writing His Gospel to quote extensively on the Sacrament of Unity, the Sacrament of Love, the Body and Blood of Jesus Christ received in Holy Communion.

The only union with God in, with and through the Mediator, Jesus Christ that can be greater than our union with the Blessed Trinity through Jesus Christ in Holy Communion, will be our union with God in heaven when we will behold Him "face to face." A person with authentic Catholic faith does indeed have a personal relationship with Jesus Christ in the Holy Eucharist.

It is impossible to imagine a closer personal relationship with God in His Son, our Lord and Savior Jesus Christ than His coming into our very being in Holy Communion and becoming one with Him. We become one in Christ. Among the many things the Apostle John relates, he tells of the time when Jesus' hour had come, when the time for the Passover of the Lamb of God arrived and Jesus had His last meal with His disciples. Jesus then spoke of His love for the Father, the Father's love of Him and their love for the one who keeps Jesus' word. (See John chapter 13). "We shall come to him and make a home in him" (John 14:23). Remember, these words are being spoken at the Last Supper when Jesus institutes the Blessed Sacrament — that is — the Holy Eucharist, and makes it possible for us to receive Him in Holy Communion. The keeping of Jesus' word included "Do this . . . " as the other three Gospel writers carefully record.

As we read on in the chapters of St. John, as he records the words of Jesus at the Last Supper — the first Mass — Jesus says,

> May they all be one, just as You Father, are in Me and I am in You, so that they also may be one in Us . . . . Father, I want those

You have given Me to be with me where I am, so that they may always see My glory which You have given Me because You loved Me before the foundation of the world (John 17:21, 24).

Now Jesus had previously said in John 6, that unless we eat His Flesh and drink His Blood (verse 53) we can have no life in us. "Anyone who does eat My Flesh and drink My Blood has eternal life, and I shall raise that person up on the last day" (John 6:54). It is through receiving Jesus in Holy Communion that we shall come to the glory that is the Son's from the beginning, which is what Jesus continues to pray for at the Last Supper, as seen in chapter 17 of St. John.

If we were to accept the fundamentalists' interpretation of God's Word making Jesus' solemn words on the Holy Eucharist only figurative, what is to stop one from interpreting Jesus' promise to rise from the dead figuratively? Many modernists who water down the faith are doing precisely that. Under that interpretation our own future resurrection at the end of the world would be doomed as well. But Jesus promised our own future bodily resurrection as His pledge when we eat His Body and drink His precious Blood. Repeatedly, Jesus speaks of our future resurrection in connection with the reception of His Body and Blood. During His discourse on His intention to institute the Holy Eucharist (John 6), the only thing that Jesus repeats more often than the future bodily resurrection is the constant repetition, more emphatically stated each time, that He will give His Flesh and His Blood for us to receive so that we may have eternal life. This is the grace necessary to enter heaven. "Anyone who does eat My Flesh and drinks My Blood has eternal life, and I shall raise that person up on the last day" (John 6:54).

The Catholic Church has always taught that the reception of Our Lord's Body and Blood in faith and love in Holy Communion is necessary for salvation. That means salvation of the whole man, body and soul. The Church has always taught this because Jesus taught it from the beginning. The life that the Father communicates to the Son passes to the faithful through the Eucharist. "As the living Father sent Me and I draw life from the Father, so whoever eats Me will also draw life from Me" (John 6:57).

Some fundamentalists think Catholics have a faith-problem and a thinking problem, as already noted. A closer analysis will clearly show the problem is on the part of the fundamentalists. "How can this man give us his flesh to eat?" they asked Him (v. 52). Jesus reemphasizes:

"In all truth I tell you, if you do not eat the Flesh of the Son of Man and drink His Blood, you have no life in you ... ." After hearing it, many of His followers said, "this is intolerable language. How could anyone accept it?" (vv. 53-60).

Those crowds of Jews knew the language of Jesus. They knew how He meant "My flesh . . . My blood" and they knew that they must not use merely human judgment in interpreting His words "the flesh." They were well acquainted with Jewish expressions and understood Jesus correctly, but many put no faith in what He taught. That is why John concluded the account with:

> "But there are some of you who do not believe." For Jesus knew from the outset who did not believe and who was to betray Him. He went on, "This is why I told you that no one could come to Me except by the gift of the Father." At this, many of His disciples went away and accompanied him no more" (vv. 64-66).

It is not human judgment or human intellectual understanding but dispositions for the gift of faith from the Father that were required.

> Then Jesus said to the Twelve, "What about you, do you want to go away, too?" Simon Peter answered, "Lord, to whom shall we go? You have the message of eternal life, and we believe; we have come to know that you are the Holy One of God." Jesus replied to them, "Did I not choose the Twelve of you? Yet one of you is a devil." He meant Judas, son of Simon Iscariot, since this was the man, one of the Twelve, who was to betray Him (vv. 67-71).

Thus ends the famous chapter 6 of St. John's Gospel. It ends with the moment of truth for the Twelve. It is the moment for faith. They too may go away, Jesus tells them, with that crowd of thousands, but He is not taking back His words. Judas, it seems obvious, even though one of the Twelve, did not believe. Let us answer with Simon Peter who said in effect for the eleven of them: "We believe. We don't understand how you can give us your Flesh to eat and your Blood to drink. But you are, we know, the Holy One of God. If you say you will do it, we believe it. We have no one else to turn to. In you we put our faith — you, the Son of the living God."

When God's Word, the Scriptures, speak in allegories and symbols it makes itself quite obvious that it is doing so. We have the Apostle John, writing under the inspiration of the Holy Spirit, to thank for demonstrating from Jesus' own teachings that what St. Matthew, Mark and Luke so carefully record, "This is My Body . . . This is My Blood," is to be taken literally.

Jesus not only labored at great length to make sure people did not take His words figuratively but He stood there and watched the entire crowd of thousands depart and follow Him no longer rather than take back His words or explain them away figuratively. Jesus meant exactly what He was saying when He said that He would give us His sacred Flesh to eat and His precious Blood to drink.

There is no example in the Bible where Jesus labors more diligently, and repeats Himself more emphatically to explain that He means to be taken literally. It is just as obvious that when Jesus uses words like "door, gate, vine, lamb, living waters," etc., He is speaking figuratively. In doing so He is explaining that His role is that of the one essential Mediator, and it is within the mystery of His Church, which will be His body, where He will have a real union with us.

Yes, Jesus is the "gate" if we understand His words, "No one can come to the Father except through Me" (John 14:6). Jesus is the gate, the Mediator between mankind and the Father. Yes, Jesus is the "Vine" and we "are the branches" (John 15:5) if we understand that He intends to have a real union with us through the Holy Eucharist, as Jesus spoke those words at the Last Supper when He gave us the Holy Eucharist. Yes, Jesus is a lamb, if we understand that He is the sacrificed Lamb "Who takes away the sins of the world," (John 1:29) the fulfillment of what the sacrificial lamb of the Old Testament represented, and that which Jesus became in the New Testament actualized in Holy Week.

After the paschal sacrificial meal of the Last Supper at which they ate the paschal lamb, He offered Himself as the true "Lamb of God that takes away the sins of the world." Jesus became the reality of what the lamb had only signified. The true Lamb of God laid down His life for us on the Cross. Yes, Jesus is "living water" if we understand that we must be born again in Him through the waters of Baptism so as to share in the life of God, which is grace, and which is necessary for entrance into heaven. "In all truth I tell you, no one can enter the kingdom of God without being born through water and the Spirit" (John 3:3).

In the ancient catacombs, in the underground burial places just outside of Rome where the early Christians worshipped during the persecutions of the early Church, there are found, even today, on the walls, symbolic references to the Holy Eucharist. These inscriptions tell of the faith of the first Christians.

The catacombs of the first centuries contain images of the Last Supper, and the Sacraments, indicating the high regard that the early Christian community had for the Holy Eucharist. Images of the Holy Eucharist are frequent in the catacombs. I have repeatedly visited these catacombs of the early Christians and offered Mass in one of the catacombs, in one of the larger rooms where early Christians once offered the same Eucharist. For the most part, the catacombs are narrow passageways with places for burials in the walls of both sides. Of the thousands of frescoes, drawings, and inscriptions found in the catacombs dating from the first centuries of Christianity, the most frequent representations refer to miracles that relate to the Holy Eucharist. It is difficult to understand how those who attack the Catholic doctrine of the Last Supper — the Eucharist — will consider the Last Supper and Christ's institution of the Holy Eucharist as only an insignificant part of the life and teachings of our Lord, and to be taken only figuratively. The early Christians obviously did not think so.

The miracle most frequently depicted in the catacombs is that of the multiplication of the loaves of bread and the fish, which scholars agree refers to the Holy Eucharist. Through these miracles, Jesus was preparing the minds of the people, the Apostles in particular, to accept in faith that if He could feed thousands with a few loaves of bread and fish, He could likewise feed millions through the ages with Eucharistic bread which would be Himself. If the Holy Eucharist is unimportant and only figurative, why did the early Christians risk their lives under pagan persecutions to celebrate it?

The catacomb images of the multiplication of the loaves and fishes is followed second in frequency by representations of the "breaking of the bread." A fresco from about the year 190 in the catacombs of St. Callixtus depicts a *joyful* gathering at a banquet of seven persons with nothing but bread — twelve enormous baskets of bread for seven persons. This recalls the Biblical account: "They filled twelve baskets with the fragments." Frequently, the Mass has been, through the centuries, called a "Eucharist banquet." Seven is a Biblical number meaning completeness, perfection. The Holy Eucharist was instituted for all.

Jesus worked miracles to bring people to faith. He cited the work of His miracles as a reason why they should believe. The wedding feast of Cana, where Jesus worked His first public miracle (John 2) at the request of His Blessed Mother, indicated more than God's recognition of the holiness of Matrimony. If Jesus could change water into the best of wines, His Apostles (and others) ought to be able to believe He could change wine into His own precious Blood. "This first of his signs Jesus worked at Cana of Galilee; and He manifested His glory, and His disciples believed in Him" (John 2:11-12).

In the catacombs of Sts. Peter and Marcellinus there is found the image of a very early "breaking of bread." What is especially noticed about it is that before the gathering of people for the Eucharistic banquet, there is depicted an altar with three legs in front of the banquet table. An altar with three legs was traditionally used for bloody sacrifices of the Old Testament, before it was replaced by the Eucharistic liturgy. The message from the early Christians is that their faith was that the Holy Eucharist was both Sacrament and the Sacrifice of the New Covenant.

When those opposed to the Catholic faith state that there is nothing in the Bible to state that the Holy Eucharist is a Sacrifice, we must point to the concept of Sacrifice running through the whole length of the Bible from the beginning of the Old Testament to the conclusion of the New Testament.

The sacrifices of the Old Covenant, especially the sacrificial paschal lamb, leads up to the offering of the true Lamb of God who takes away the sins of the world, Jesus Christ. And when Jesus institutes the sacrificial meal at the Last Supper He commands that the Apostles do the same.

> Then He took bread, and when He had given thanks, He broke it
> and gave it to them, saying, " ... This is My Body given for you;
> do this in remembrance of Me." He did the same with the cup after supper, and said, "This cup is the New Covenant of My Blood
> poured out for you" (Luke 22:19-20).

As a sacrifice of the lamb was commanded under the Old Covenant (Testament), so Jesus commands ("do this ... ") as a sacrifice of Body and Blood in the New Covenant.

The very definition of "priest" is one who offers sacrifice. There were priests in the Old Covenant. Jesus Christ is presented as the high priest of the New Covenant. All Christians who have seen some connection between the Holy Eucharist and sacrifice call their ministers "priests," as do the vast majority of the world's Christians today, including the millions of Orthodox whose faith and practices are very close to Catholicism. Anglicans (Episcopalians) also refer to their ministers as priests.

In the first book of the Bible, Genesis (14:18-20) the priest Melchizedek, a king of Salem, is mentioned. When Abraham returned from battle after rescuing Lot, Melchizedek greeted him and gave him a blessing in honor of his victory, offering bread and wine. It is interesting that with all the bloody sacrifices offered in the Old Testament, this unique event, very early in Biblical history, of the offering of bread and wine is mentioned. The priesthood according to the Order of Melchizedek, which is forever, becomes associated in the

Bible with the priesthood of Jesus Christ, which carries through the New Testament.

Jesus Christ the High Priest offers Himself in the form of bread and wine at the Last Supper which begins as the Old Covenant sacrificial meal of worship and ends with a New Covenant offering of the Body and Blood of the true Lamb of God with the command to continue the same action with the Apostles thereafter. Jesus, in replacing the Old Covenant with the New, is commanding that His action and His offering be perpetuated throughout the centuries.

In a Psalm devoted to the dual role of priest and king, David exclaimed, "Yahweh has sworn an oath which He never will retract, 'You are a priest of the order of Melchizedek and forever' " (Ps. 110:4). Only two references to this priesthood in the Old Testament occur. Yet, in the New Testament, in the Epistle to the Hebrews, there is an association of Christ's priesthood with Melchizedek's by quoting in three successive chapters the invocation from Psalm 110: "You are a priest of the order of Melchizedek and forever." This is also a Biblical basis for the Catholic doctrine that once a man is ordained a priest of Jesus Christ, like Christ's priesthood, it is forever.

Chapter 10 of Hebrews tells us of the first act of the soul, the intellect and will, of Jesus Christ upon coming into the world:

Bull's blood and goat's blood are useless for taking away sins, and this is what He said, on coming into the world: "You who wanted no sacrifice or oblation, prepared a body for me. You took no pleasure in holocausts or sacrifices for sin; then I said, just as I was commanded in the scroll of the book, "God, here I am! I am coming to obey your will."

Notice that He says first: "You did not want what the Law lays down as the things to be offered, that is: the sacrifices, the oblations, the holocausts and the sacrifices for sin, and you took no pleasure in them"; and then He says: "Here I am! I am coming to obey your will." He is abolishing the first sort to replace it with the second. And this "will" was for us to be made holy by the offering of His body made once and for all by Jesus Christ" (Heb. 10:4-10).

The first act of the soul of Jesus refers to the centuries of sacrifices God had offered in the Old Covenant which would be replaced by the single perfect Sacrifice of Jesus' own death on the Cross. God could not die as God. The God-Man would die in His human nature. And He would do so freely.

The Father loves me, because I lay down my life in order to take it up again. No one takes it from me: I lay it down of my own free will, and as I have power to lay it down, so I have power to take it up again, and this is the command I have received from my Father (John 10:17-20).

Those with any acquaintance with the Old Covenant will remember the repeated and frequent sacrifices offered to God. None of these sacrifices of themselves sufficed to take away sin. They were all symbolic of the perfect Sacrifice of the Cross to come. Who has not been impressed with Abraham being commanded by God to offer his only son Isaac, when he was still a boy, as a burnt offering? Abraham, the man of faith and obedience in the Old Testament, without hesitation, but with great pain of heart, sets out with Isaac to the designated spot. He built an altar, and prepared to kill his son as an offering to Yahweh-God. An angel intervened. Isaac was spared, and Yahweh praised Abraham and had an animal offered instead. Isaac, an only son, even carried the wood for the sacrifice up the mountain as Christ the only-begotten Son of the Father would one day carry the wood of the Cross up Mt. Calvary.

Those acquainted with the Old Testament — the time before the coming of our Lord and Savior Jesus Christ, the time of preparation for His coming and perfect Sacrifice which would redeem mankind — know the importance of the paschal lamb being sacrificed and the deliverance of God's people, the Jews, from the bondage of Egypt. This deliverance commanded the sacrifice of an unblemished lamb or kid, bones unbroken, whose blood was to be sprinkled on the doorpost of every Hebrew house on the night before their passage. The angel of death, passing over Egypt, would kill the firstborn of every home where there was not found the blood of the lamb. The deliverance of the Jews from Egypt was a foreshadowing of the Christian Pasch when, through the Sacrifice of Jesus Christ, the true Lamb of God and the application of the merits of His Blood, the human race would be freed from the bondage of the devil and of sin.

Good Friday in the early Church was called the Pasch (Passover) of the Crucifixion. Easter Sunday was called the Pasch of the Resurrection, and the Sundays from Easter to Whit-Sunday were always referred to as "after the Pasch." Easter is the Christian Passover. The lamb was eaten at the Passover Feast of the Jews. According to Mosaic law, the lambs were first to be sacrificed on the afternoon of the fourteenth of Nisan and then taken to the homes, where the people ate the lamb during the night (Exodus 12). Christ, the Messiah, "was sacrificed for us" (1 Cor. 5:7), "and thus became for those who believe in Him the Paschal Lamb who takes away the sins of the world" (John 1:29). "Paschal Mystery" is a general term used to describe the redemptive work of Jesus Christ, especially the events of the Last Supper and the Passion, until they reach their climax on Easter Sunday. The first Christians immediately recognized the celebration of the Eucharist as the fulfillment of the paschal lamb offered at the high point of their worship. They called themselves "Sons of the Resurrection" and gathered each Sunday to offer the Eucharist. Rather than Saturday, they met on Sunday, the day Jesus passed over from death to life.

Under the Old Law, which described the kind of sacrifices to be offered, there were two kinds required: bloody and unbloody. There were four kinds of bloody sacrifices: 1) The whole burnt offering or holocaust. The victim, often an animal, was entirely consumed by fire, and this was done twice daily as a perpetual sacrifice; 2) Sin offering, which was to expiate misdeeds committed through ignorance or inadvertence; the victim was determined by the gravity of the offense; 3) Guilt offering, required for sins demanding restitution; 4) Peace offerings, offered in thanksgiving or to fulfill a vow or which were simply voluntary (in this kind of sacrifice, part of what was offered was returned to the offerer to be eaten in a sacrificial meal).

Unbloody sacrifices, which were really oblations, were offerings of articles of solid or liquid food along with incense. These food offerings were made at every holocaust and peace offering but never at sacrifices for sin or guilt, except at the cleansing of a leper.

The concept of sacrifice in worship, we see from the study of the Bible, is a part of Divine Revelation extending from the earliest days of recorded Divine Revelation until the coming of Jesus Christ. The Apostle Paul in his Biblical writings identifies Jesus Christ as the Sacrificial Victim (1 Cor. 5:7; Eph. 5:2). This sacrificial victimhood is confirmed by the epistles (1 Pet. 1:19; 1 John 2:2). There is assumed the eternal nature of Christ's Sacrifice (Rev. 13:8). The entire letter to the Hebrews is dedicated to the high priesthood of Christ, who by His perfect obedience has "offered one single Sacrifice for sins, and then taken His place forever at the right hand of God" (Heb. 10:12).

As the time for the coming of Christ approached, the prophet Malachi (Mal. 1:10-11) spoke for God to the Jewish priest and looked ahead to a time when a Sacrifice would be perpetually offered:

> I am not pleased with you, says Yahweh Sabaoth; from your hands I find no offering acceptable. But from farthest east to farthest west my name is honored among the nations, and everywhere a sacrifice of incense is offered to my Name, and a pure

offering too, since my Name is honored among the nations, says Yahweh Sabaoth.

That prophecy is being fulfilled at every moment today in the Roman Catholic Church. At every moment, day and night, somewhere throughout the world, the Sacrifice of the Mass is being offered, perpetuating the Sacrifice of the Cross. When Jesus rose from the dead and ascended into heaven He retained the wound marks in His hands, feet and side, only now they are glorified. He is ever before our heavenly Father making intercession for us, as Sacred Scripture testifies. There is never a moment but which Jesus is offering the Sacrifice of Himself for us. It is not repeated; it is not renewed in the sense of being offered again. It is *continuous* in the soul of Jesus. It is perpetuated.

Furthermore, the priest at the altar of the Catholic Church is acting *in persona Christi* — in the very person, the very priesthood of Jesus Christ. We tune in to that perpetual Sacrifice. Jesus has never changed His mind. He has never withdrawn His sacrificial offering. In space and time, we tune in to His perpetual Sacrifice that was physically, in a bloodly manner, offered once for all. Jesus is always at the right hand of God the Father with His glorified wound marks in His risen-ascended body. Having offered the Gift of Self in Sacrifice once, Jesus never withdraws the Gift. What He offered once and for always, we too join in.

The *Didache* (Teaching of the twelve Apostles), is a treatise written before 100 A.D. It was discovered in 1833 by Bryennios, the Greek Orthodox Metropolitan of Nicomedia. The *Didache* is divided into three parts: 1) The Two Ways: the Way of Life, and the Way of Death; 2) a liturgical manual treating Baptism, fasting, Confession and Holy Communion; 3) a treatise on the ministry. Doctrinal teaching is presupposed. The Way of Life is the love of God and of neighbor; the Way of Death is a list of vices to be avoided. There is a brief instruction on Baptism, references to Apostles, bishops, and deacons, and an exhortation to watch and be prepared for the coming of Christ. The oldest tradition as found in the *Didache* has referred to the prophecy of Malachi in speaking of the Holy Eucharist, namely as a Sacrifice.

The very words that Jesus Christ used in instituting the Holy Eucharist reveal its sacrificial character. "This is My Body which shall be given up for you." "This is My Blood, which shall be shed for you." These are Biblical sacrificial expressions, "to give up the body" and "to shed blood." Furthermore, Christ makes clear that His Blood is the Blood of the Covenant. The Old Covenant of God with Israel concluded by the proffering of the bloody sacrifice (Exod. 24:8); "This ... is the blood of the covenant which Yahweh has made with you ... ". The blood of the covenant is synonymous with the blood of sacrifice.

The original Greek words used in Luke, Matthew, and Mark indicate the *present tense* of the offering of Christ's blood in sacrifice. Biblical scholars assert this is true especially in Luke 22:20, where the pouring out of the chalice is asserted. Reference is thereby made to the Eucharistic practice. There is also the mandate: "Do this as a memorial of Me" (Luke 22:19; see 1 Cor. 11:24). The context is that the Eucharistic Sacrifice is to be a permanent institution of the New Testament. The message, then, of the Holy Eucharist as Sacrifice is in the Sacred Scriptures from beginning to end — first foreshadowed, then fulfilled.

The Apostle Paul, after relating the manner in which our Lord instituted the Holy Eucharist at the Last Supper, added, "Until the Lord comes, therefore, every time you eat this bread and drink this cup, you are proclaiming his death" (1 Cor. 11:26).

Revelation 5:6 presents to us the Messiah as Lamb, standing as if slain. Sometimes Christian symbols of Christ as the Lamb of God slain are seen with blood flowing from the side of the lamb, while the lamb stands alive. Christ, although sacrificed for us, lives still. Jesus offers us the same Sacrifice today.*

As we begin to see the role of sacrifice in the Bible, and while we interpret Scripture as a whole, let us return to the Gospel of the Apostle St. John, in chapter 6, as he quotes at length our Savior Jesus Christ repeating Himself more and more emphatically,

> I am the bread of life .... Your fathers ate manna in the desert and they are dead; but this is the bread which comes down from heaven, so that a person may eat it and not die. I am the living bread which has come down from heaven. Anyone who eats this bread will live forever; and the bread that I shall give is my Flesh, for the life of the world.

Readers of this book are encouraged to read for themselves the entire sixth chapter of John. Notice that twice the Apostle John interrupts the account to say that the Jews were complaining because He said, "I

---

* For additional treatment by the author on the Holy Eucharist as Sacrifice and Sacrament, see his book, *The Catholic Faith,* Our Sunday Visitor, Inc. Huntington, Ind. 46750.

am the bread that has come down from heaven" (v. 41). As Jesus makes Himself more emphatic, the Apostle interrupts the account again to say,

> Then the Jews started arguing among themselves, "How can this man give us his flesh to eat?" Jesus replied to them: "In all truth I tell you, if you do not eat the Flesh of the Son of man and drink His Blood, you have no life in you. Anyone who does eat My Flesh and drink My Blood has eternal life, and I shall raise that person up on the last day. For My Flesh is real food and My Blood real drink. Whoever eats My Flesh and drinks My Blood lives in me and I live in that person. As the living Father sent Me and I draw life from the Father, so whoever eats Me will also draw life from Me. This is the bread which has come down from heaven: it is not like the bread our ancestors ate: they are dead, but anyone who eats this bread will live for ever" (vv. 52-58).

Those who had been following and listening to Jesus up to now seem to think He is speaking of cannibalism. Instead of retracting His words, Jesus leads them deeper into the mystery and comes on all the stronger. He shows them that He will actually give them His Flesh to eat and His Blood to drink. "Jesus was aware that his followers were complaining about it and said, "Does this disturb you? What if you should see the Son of Man ascend to where He was before?" (vv. 61-62). Jesus knows their complaints, which were caused by His words, but He neither revokes nor dilutes anything of what He has said. The elliptic question, "What if you should see the Son of Man ascend to where He was before?" (v. 62) is to rectify a cannibalistic interpretation. The Ascension should eliminate their chief difficulty about eating the Flesh of One who in celestial glory takes His place where He was from all eternity.

Verse 63 of John 6 is used as a key reference by those who would discount the Catholic teaching for two thousand years that Holy Communion is in reality the reception of the Lord's Body, Blood, Soul and Divinity: "It is the spirit that gives life, the flesh has nothing to offer. The words I have spoken to you are spirit and they are life."

Here is how fundamentalists and anti-Catholics explain the above: "See, our Lord says, 'the flesh has nothing to offer.' Does this not say that it was not His Flesh He would give? Jesus is therefore speaking figuratively." However, such an explanation is unrealistic in the light of almost an entire chapter that has preceded it in which Jesus emphasized that He is the living bread come down from heaven and that He would give us His Flesh to eat and His Blood to drink, repeating this truth all the more emphatically, to counter the growing amount of complaints and murmurs which broke out in the crowd. Why the continued murmuring, if all is only symbolic? Why did Jesus lose the crowd if His words were only figurative?

As already mentioned, instead of retracting, Jesus leads deeper into the mystery of the Son of Man's Ascension. What Jesus goes on to say can hardly be said to be removing the scandal from His immediate hearers. The remedy for the deserters on the part of Jesus was not to take back His words but to invite them to a deeper faith. The Ascension, making a heavenly reality of Jesus' Real Presence, is essential for the Christian understanding of the Holy Eucharist, which contains the three great mysteries of the Son of Man: Incarnation, Redemption, and the Ascension. It is the Word made flesh, Who died on the Cross for our salvation, who rose from the dead, Who ascended into heaven and sits in glory at the right hand of the Father Who comes to us in the Holy Eucharist. Those who will not believe Jesus' words that He is the living bread come down from heaven are being asked by Jesus, "what will they think if they see Him ascending into heaven?"

Now the term, "the flesh," which Jesus uses in verse 63, is not the same as "my Flesh" used in verse 53 and the following verses. "The flesh" is Biblical for human judgment without faith (See John 4:48 and Rom. 8:4). Again, it must be remembered that the Church does not isolate Biblical texts but interprets the Word of God as a whole, and according to the intention of the authors. Isolating texts and interpreting them in a fundamentalistic way, as if the Word of God was written in late twentieth century English, leads to very dangerous and false conclusions. A knowledge of ancient languages, customs, religious practices of the time, etc., are essential for interpreting Scripture and any one individual unguided is incapable of infallibly interpreting the Scriptures. Even each Pope, visible head of the Church as chief vicar of Christ on earth, respects the defined teachings of all his 264 papal predecessors, beginning with St. Peter.

The mystery of the heavenly bread accepted in divine faith is only open to the life-giving Spirit (Gen. 2:7; Ezek. 37; John 3:6; 4:24). Jesus tells us that we cannot believe without the gift of the Holy Spirit. "Nobody is able to say, 'Jesus is Lord' except in the Holy Spirit" (1Cor. 12:3). Without divine help no one can believe Jesus is Lord and nobody can have faith that Jesus can give us Himself under the forms of bread and wine. "In all truth I tell you, no one can enter the kingdom of God without being born through water and the Spirit;

what is born of human nature is human; what is born of the Spirit is spirit. Do not be surprised when I say: You must be born from above. The wind blows where it pleases; you can hear its sound, but you cannot tell where it comes from or where it is going. So it is with everyone who is born of the Spirit" (John 3:5-8).

When it is said that there cannot be the Real Presence of the Lord's Body, Blood, Soul and Divinity in the consecrated species of bread and wine, because our bodily senses do not experience any properties other than bread and wine, the entire mystery of faith is forgotten. It is a reduction of the mysteries of Christ entirely to human judgment without faith. This is exactly what is meant in Biblical language by "the flesh" as used by Jesus in John 6:63.

The Catholic Church is accused of making everything complicated and leaving nothing simple. Over-simplification is the error of the fundamentalist who so simplifies the Word of God, which has infinite wisdom behind it, that at times the divine mysteries of eternal life remain hidden and not perceived under the guidance of the Holy Spirit. The Bible is God's inspired Word. The Catholic Church has been studying and meditating the Word of God for two thousand years. Its understanding, its penetration of the divine mysteries goes on and on, just as Christ worked to lead His followers to a deeper penetration of the faith and the mysteries which He was revealing.

The expression, "development of doctrine," is used in Catholic theology. Theology is faith seeking greater understanding. Development of doctrine is growth in the Church's understanding of the truths of Divine Revelation. It is a gradual unfolding of the meaning of what God has revealed. It is always presumed that the substantial truth of a revealed mystery remains unchanged. What changes is the subjective grasp of the revealed truth, but never in contradiction to the defined doctrines of preceding centuries.

The source of this progressive understanding is the prayerful reflection of the faithful, especially recognized in the Church's saints and mystics, the study and research by scholars and theologians, the practical experience of living the faith among the faithful, and the collective wisdom and teaching of the Church's hierarchy under the guidance of the Bishop of Rome, the Holy Father, the Pope. Even with the valuable input by the various members of the Church, it is not authentic doctrine until recognized by proper Church authority, namely the Magisterium (the world's bishops together with the Pope). In all this it is the Holy Spirit which guides it towards deeper understanding.

Without the above position, each generation would have to start anew in comprehending God's Word, with no recognition of the Church as the living divine organism, "the body of Christ" which St. Paul repeatedly calls the Church. The (Mystical) Body of Christ, the Church, is made of its *members,* which are all the baptized faithful. The *Soul* of this Mystical Body is the Holy Spirit. The *Head* is Jesus Christ Himself. Jesus is the eternal invisible Head while the Pope on earth is His chief visible representative (Matt. 16:13-19). The Word of God is living and dynamic. It is not confined to dead pages in a book. "The Word of God is something alive and active; it cuts more incisively than any two-edged sword" (Hebrews 4:12).

Unfortunately for many fundamentalists, "early Church" means only what is written in the pages of the Bible and then only their interpretation of those words is the correct one. In fact, all of the original texts of the Bible long ago turned to dust. None are known to exist in the original writing. It was the ancient Catholic Church of which history testifies is identical with the Catholic Church of today in an unbroken line, which has passed the Scriptures down to us.

The last book of the Bible, Revelation, sees the Church as the new people of God. The Church is presented in this book as an uninterrupted continuation of the people of the Old Testament. It is a "kingdom of priests" (1:6; 5:10), constituted so by the blood of the Lamb. The dead, especially the martyrs, are united to their suffering brethren on earth (6:9-11; 19:2).

The relation of the Church to Christ is expressed through the Biblical marriage image, (19:7; 21:2, 9.). Jesus Christ is ever active in His Church, (1:13-16) and ever directing it. Christ's union with the Church will reach its consummation in the joy of the Parousia (the second coming of Christ to the earth. (See 1 Cor. 15:23; 1 Thes. 4:15-17; Matt. 24:3-14; II Peter 1:16).

For those who can accept no teaching of this living Body of Christ, which is the Church, guided by the Holy Spirit, as Christ Jesus promised it would be through the "Spirit of truth" (John 14:17; John 15:26; John 16:13), Eucharistic miracles will be slighted and explained away. The truth is that Eucharistic miracles have existed in the Church for centuries and every scientific investigation fails to explain them naturally. I present several examples to help appreciate Christ's continued power today and through the centuries.

I have held in my hands each year since 1974, even repeatedly each year, the bleeding host of Santarém, in Portugal. In the tabernacle of the Church of the Holy Miracle is to be found a consecrated Host that *bled* early in the thirteenth century when a lady took the host from her mouth with the intention of taking it to an evil woman who was known to be a sorceress. After the lady wrapped the Sacred Host in her veil, great drops of precious Blood fell from the veil. The parish priest was informed. Eventually the bleeding Host was put into the tabernacle, and a crystal pyx was miraculously formed around the Host, containing the Body and Blood of Christ. For more than six hundred years that same bleeding Host has been preserved and venerated.

In 1984 a medical doctor stood immediately beside me when I opened the tabernacle to venerate the miraculous Host at Santarém. At close range I permitted the doctor to study the Blood of the Host. He declared that it was certainly blood.

There are many documentations of many Eucharistic miracles that are continuous but I shall summarize only one more of the most famous here, the Eucharistic miracle of Lanciano, in Italy.

For twelve centuries the city of Lanciano has been the scene of a Eucharistic miracle that even the latest scientific investigations support as unexplainable by the laws of nature. Historical and scientific data are in agreement as a testimony for those who wonder about the authentic reality of this miracle.

According to the Catholic faith, under the "species" of bread and wine, the Sacrament of the Altar, the Holy Eucharist, are the Body, Blood, Soul and Divinity of our Lord and Savior, Jesus Christ. The bread and wine are no longer present in *substance* after the words of consecration of the priest. Only the *appearances*, what appears to the senses, remain. The substance has been changed. (Even according to philosophy no one has ever *seen* a substance. We see and experience *accidents*, i.e., the size, weight, color, resistance, taste, and odor of something. By the power of God, upon consecration, the substance in which the accidents of bread and wine adhere *is* the Body of Christ. A correct term to describe what takes place at the consecration of the Mass is "transubstantiation," although the Church does not speak of the "doctrine of transubstantiation" as some people outside the Church do. The faith of the Church is simply that it is the real, living, substantial Body, Blood, Soul and Divinity of Jesus Christ.

The Lanciano miracle appears to reaffirm what is already a part of the Catholic faith, while it is not the source of our faith. The Church teaches that miracles can and do happen. But the Church does not require belief in any particular miracle that has reportedly happened since the days of the Bible as an absolute subject of faith. While Catholics must believe the miracles of Jesus Christ recorded in the Bible, it is only some miracles since then, after careful investigation, that are declared worthy of belief. An example of one such miracle which may be accepted is the Eucharistic miracle of Lanciano. Below in summary is its history of over twelve hundred years.

In ancient days Lanciano was called Ansiano and was famous for its fairs. About the year 750, in the Monastery of St. Legontian, lived the monks of St. Basil. Today it is known as the Monastery of St. Francis. In this monastery, about the middle of the eighth century, lived a monk, educated in the sciences of his time but not strong in the faith. He had serious doubts about whether the Body and Blood of Jesus really exist in the appearance of the consecrated bread and wine.

The same monk, in prayer, begged God to resolve the doubt in his heart. According to documents of that time, one morning when he was offering the Sacrifice of the Mass, after pronouncing the words of consecration, the priest-monk was again overcome by his doubts. Then he *saw* the bread change into Flesh and the wine into Blood.

According to the documents handed down through the centuries, the monk became confused and frightened at the stupendous miracle of the Eucharist. He stood looking at the miracle as if in divine ecstasy. Finally, filled with joy and shedding tears, he spoke to the congregation:

> O fortunate witnesses, to whom the Blessed God, to confound my unbelief, has wished to reveal Himself in this Most Blessed Sacrament and to render Himself visible to our eyes. Come, brethren, and marvel at our God, so close to us. Behold the Flesh and the Blood of our Most Beloved Christ.

The people rushed to the altar and beheld the miracle, and reports of the miracle spread throughout the city. The miracle had a profound effect on the city, on old and young alike. Some invoked the divine mercy of God while others beat their breasts in sorrow, accusing themselves of sins. Still others praised God in thanksgiving, that He had willed to have their mortal senses behold His immortal and incomprehensible majesty.

Authorities in the city had an exquisite tabernacle made of ivory to contain the priceless relic. Later they made a magnificent silver vase in the form of a chalice, and finally a crystal *de Rocca*, in which it was preserved.

Flesh appeared around the Host. Through the centuries the Host pulverized and disappeared while the Flesh remains today intact after twelve hundred years. Scientists have identified it as flesh of the heart muscle. On the outside rim it is thick, but almost paper thin on the inside, where it was in contact with the Host. Scientists have been unable to find any trace of chemical preservatives, as in mummies.

There are five parts to the Blood in the Eucharistic miracle of Lanciano. Each part, though different in size, nonetheless weighs as much as the sum of the weight of all the parts. Also, two parts weigh as much as three, and the smallest as much as the largest. The Blood has divided and dried into five pellets. Its entire weight is 15.85 grams or .56 ounce.

Accounts of the preservation of this Eucharist continue through the centuries. At present, the holy relics are contained in this manner. The Flesh is in a round, gold-plated silver lunette between two crystals. This lunette is in an ostensorium, or monstrance, of silver, into which the holy relic was placed on April 16, 1713. The Blood is contained in a chalice of crystal with a cover of crystal and is part of the base of the ostensorium, which contains the Flesh.

With the approval of Church authorities, on rare occasions the holy relics have been investigated. Monsignor Rodrigues made an authentication on February 17, 1574, in the presence of people who testified to the preternatural weight of the congealed Blood, viz, the total weight of the five pellets is equal to the weight of each pellet. This is attested on a marble tablet in the church. A second authentication was made in 1637, when the holy relics were transformed to the Valsecca Chapel. A third authentication was made on October 23, 1770, when it was desired that the reliquary be refurbished and the Host of Flesh was removed for a short time.

In 1886 the seals and silk cords were broken which sealed the chalice of Blood at its authentication in 1770. The archbishop of Lanciano, Monsignor Petrarca, and a commission of canons and ecclesiastics joined in breaking the seals and cords of the chalice, but the seal of the Host was not touched. It was certified that fragments of the species of bread were still clearly visible in the Flesh.

Two hundred more years elapsed since the authentication of 1770, when, on July 1, 1972, before well-known witnesses, the holy relics were enclosed in a new lunette, sealed, and placed in a renovated ostensorium. This was after a careful scientific investigation, according to advanced scientific procedures, conducted from November 18, 1971, to March 4, 1972, by Professor Odoardo Linoli, an expert in histology and human anatomy. A summary of the results of modern scientific investigations lists the following points:

1. The Blood of the Eucharistic Miracle is real blood and the Flesh is real flesh.

2. The Flesh consists of the muscular tissue of the heart.
3. The Blood and the Flesh belong to the human species.
4. The Blood type is identical in the Blood and in the Flesh and this indicates that the donor is a single person, whilst there remains the possiblity of their origin from two different persons who, however, have the same blood type.
5. In the Blood there were found normally fractioned proteins in the proportions that are found in the sero-protein scope of normal fresh blood.
6. In the Blood there were also discovered the minerals, chlorides, phosphorus, magnesium, potassium, and sodium in a reduced quantity, whereas calcium was found in an increased quantity.

The Catholic Church, which numbers more members than the thousands of other Christians denominations combined, would not be so foolish as to approve of a miracle as worthy of belief if every opportunity to give a natural explanation had not been explored. Even then, the Church merely says "worthy of belief" and that we may have human faith in such. We must have divine faith in the Biblical miracles of Christ, and the teachings of Jesus Christ. There have been unbalanced people who have claimed miracles. The Church is most cautious as will be explained in a later chapter. The Eucharistic miracle of Lanciano, however, for twelve hundred years has consistently met the tests of the time and continues to be naturally unexplainable.

The Church insists that the Sacrifice of the Last Supper, the Sacrifice of the Cross, and the Sacrifice of the Mass today, are *not* three different sacrifices. It is one and the same Sacrifice of Jesus Christ; only the manner of offering it is different. God is not bound by time or space. We should put no limitations on the power of God. The power of God does not depend upon our human understanding. We put divine faith in what God has revealed. To ridicule the doctrine of the Holy Eucharist as Sacrament and Sacrifice because our human senses and mind cannot grasp it is to ridicule God and bring Him down to our level, even in His divine Persons. When we accept in faith the mysteries of Christianity, we put our faith not in our human understanding, but in the power and Persons of God, and in His authority as He has revealed.

The conditions of a sacrifice are verified at the Last Supper. The Paschal Lamb is first offered as had been done for centuries in memory of the Night of the Passover, the Hebrews' deliverance from slavery in Egypt, when they smeared the blood of the sacrificial lamb upon the doorposts. They did not break a bone of the lamb. They ate its flesh, with unleavened bread, etc. In the account on the institution of the Holy Eucharist St. Mark begins,

On the first day of Unleavened Bread, when the Passover lamb was sacrificed, His diciples said to Him, "Where do you want us to go and make the preparations for You to eat the Passover?" So He sent two of his disciples, saying to them, "Go into the city and you will meet a man carrying a pitcher of water. Follow him, and say to the owner of the house which he enters, 'The Master says: "Where is the room for me to eat the Passover with my disciples?" ' He will show you a large upper room furnished with couches, all prepared. Make the preparations for us there." The disciples set out and went to the city and found everything as He had told them and prepared the Passover.

When evening came he arrived with the Twelve . . . .

And as they were eating He took the bread, and when He had said the blessing He broke it and gave it to them, "Take it," He said, "This is My Body." Then He took a cup, and when He had given thanks He handed it to them, and all drank from it, and He said to them, "This is My Blood, the Blood of the covenant, poured out for many . . . (Mark 14:12ff).

For a true sacrifice a priest is needed. The Priest of the Sacrifice of the Last Supper is the High Priest, Jesus Christ Himself. An altar and a victim are also needed, as well as a covenant. Jesus Christ is both Priest and Victim in the Sacrifice of the Last Supper, on the Cross and in the Mass today. At the Last Supper and at Mass it is Christ Himself under the appearances of bread and wine. They are separately consecrated to represent the separation of Body and Blood on Calvary which brought about the Sacrifice of His death. The offering is the same in the Mass, but without the physical pain.

At the Last Supper Jesus offered Himself under the forms (species) of bread and wine as He would offer Himself in physical, bloody forms the next day. In reality, according to the Biblical reckoning of a day, Holy Thursday evening was already Good Friday because their day began in the evening. Recall how Jesus had to be buried before evening when the Sabbath began. It is the modern mentality that counts a new day as beginning at midnight. According to Biblical times, Jesus offered the Sacrifice of the Last Supper and the Sacrifice of the Cross, (two manners of offering the same Sacrifice) on the same day, *Good Friday*.

The Sacrifice of the Last Supper looked ahead to what Jesus

would offer in a physical, bloody manner in a matter of hours. The Sacrifice of the Mass today looks back, so to speak, to make the past present as far as we are concerned. With God there is no time. God the Father sees one and the same Sacrifice being offered whether at the Last Supper, the Cross or the altar of today.

St. Paul, the Apostle to the Gentiles, clearly sees the celebration of the Eucharist as a covenant-Sacrifice.

> "This is My Body, which is for you; do this in remembrance of Me." And in the same way, with the cup after supper, saying, "This cup is the New Covenant in My Blood. Whenever you drink it, do this as a memorial of Me." Whenever you eat this bread, then, and drink this cup, you are proclaiming the Lord's death until He comes. Therefore anyone who eats the bread or drinks the cup of the Lord unworthily is answerable for the Body and Blood of the Lord ... (1 Cor. 11:23-27).

Attempts by some outside the Church to say that only in later centuries did the Church teach the dogma that the Mass is a sacrifice is without foundation. The Church has constantly reaffirmed its teachings in this regard through the centuries. If the belief in the Eucharist as sacrifice comes only centuries after Jesus founded the Catholic Church, how do we explain the historical record, such as references in Catacombs, and that St. Irenaeus in the year 180 wrote that Christ commanded His disciples to offer sacrifice to God, not because God needed it but that they might become more pleasing to God? St. Irenaeus then shows that the continued offering of the Eucharistic Sacrifice is the fulfillment of the prophecy of Malachi which predicted that the Jewish people would cease to offer to God, and that a new and pure sacrifice would be offered to Him in every place by the Gentiles (*Adv. Haer.* IV., 17, 5.).

Those attacking the position of the Catholic Church today regarding Holy Communion under only one form seem not aware that millions of Catholics do receive under both forms — the consecrated Bread and consecrated Wine — both of which, they believe to be truly the Body and Blood of our Lord and Savior, Jesus Christ. Yet, it is not necessary to receive under both forms to receive the entire Christ Jesus. In fact, Jesus is whole and entire in every particle of consecrated Bread and in every drop of consecrated Wine. The consecration of both bread and wine are essential, however, whenever Mass is celebrated because the Eucharist is Sacrifice as well as Sacrament. Both must be consecrated in order to keep the Eucharist complete as Sacrifice, as explained earlier. There must always be a twofold consecration to represent the separation of the Lord's Body and Blood, his sacrificial death.

Christ can no longer die a physical death. There will never be a physical separation of His Body and Blood again. He exists in the His same ascended glorified Body. To receive the Body is to receive the Blood. Jesus Christ is wholly under the appearances of bread or wine which have been consecrated by an ordained priest.

Note St. Paul's words "or" and "and" in the verse below. Some non-Catholic translations incorrectly have changed the "or" to "and" so that the word "and" occurs in both cases. The correct version is, "Therefore anyone who eats the bread *or* drinks the cup of the Lord unworthily is answerable for the Body and Blood of the Lord" (1Cor. 11:27). The Apostle says that whether we eat or drink unworthily we are guilty of both.

While fundamentalists and/or anti-Catholic individuals claim that the Eucharist is not really the Lord's Body and Blood, but only symbolically so, and that there is no Sacrifice of the Cross perpetuated, we must agree that in their case this is true. They have lost the powers of Christ's priesthood and therefore cannot celebrate a valid Eucharist. For those separated from the Apostolic Chain, in breaking away from the ancient Catholic Church, the powers of sharing in Christ's priesthood has been lost. Jesus gave to the first Apostles (bishops) the fullness of His priesthood to be passed on to succeeding generations. The Apostolic Chain for Christians who cannot trace their specially ordained bishops and priests back for two thousand years in an unbroken line has been broken. Therefore, their ministers do not have the power of Jesus Christ.

At the time of the Protestant Revolt at the beginning of the sixteenth century, there was a denial on the part of the reformers of the Sacrament of Holy Orders, of a special priesthood with special powers to consecrate the elements of bread and wine, to be able to forgive sins in Jesus' name, etc. They did not have validly ordained bishops who broke with them to ordain their ministers. In fact, the early reforms did not see the need, and denied any special powers of special successors of the Apostles. The attacks on Catholic doctrines regarding the Eucharist amounts to an attempted justification for their loss of Christ's special priestly powers.

In rejecting a specially ordained priesthood, those who separated from the ancient Catholic Church separated themselves from the reality of the Eucharist as Sacrifice and Sacrament. For them, it is in-deed mere symbolism. There is lacking the reality of the living Christ in their eucharist. There is not perpetuated in their ceremonies, even when attempted, the eucharistic-Sacrifice of the Cross, nor is there accomplished the Real Presence of the Lord's Body and Blood.

There is much evidence in the New Testament that Jesus Christ established a priestly office. In St. Luke 6:13, we read "He called together His followers, and chose twelve." In John 20:20, Jesus said, "As the Father sent Me, so am I sending you." In verse 22, Jesus gives them the power to forgive sins in His name: "Receive the Holy Spirit. If you forgive anyone's sins, they are forgiven; if you retain anyone's sins, they are retained." In Mark 16:16, Jesus said to the Eleven, "Go into the whole world and preach the Gospel to every creature. He who believes and is baptized shall be saved . . . . In Matthew, Jesus said, "Go, therefore, make disciples of all nations; baptize them in the name of the Father and of the Son and of the Holy Spirit, and teach them to observe all the commands I gave you. And look, I am with you always; yes, to the end of time." We have recounted several times in this chapter Jesus' words giving the Apostles, the first bishops and priests of the Church, the power to consecrate bread and wine into Himself. The book of Hebrews speaks eloquently of the priesthood of Jesus Christ. Jesus ordained a special priesthood to teach, to sanctify and to govern for the good of souls and the glory of God.

Bishops have the *fullness* of the priesthood of Christ. That means they have the power to ordain other bishops and priests. Were I to leave the Catholic Church and start another denomination, which others have done many times, I as a Catholic priest would have the powers of Christ's priesthood to consecrate bread and wine, etc., as long as I lived. Being an author of many books, having a leading role in apostolates that are known even internationally, I doubtlessly could influence quite a following. But I would not have the power to ordain others. I could not pass on the priestly powers of Jesus Christ I received from the bishop who ordained me, who in turn was consecrated a bishop by another bishop, and so on for two thousand years in an unbroken line to Jesus Christ Himself. I could not pass on the powers of Christ's special priesthood by the imposition of hands, because I am not a bishop with the fullness of Christ's priestly powers. At the same time, if I left the Catholic Church, I believe I would be sinning in celebrating the Eucharist unworthily. I would be going against the will of God, in breaking from the unity of His Church for which Jesus prayed so strongly at the Last Supper. Read John chapter 17 for Jesus' priestly prayer for unity.

It is true that every baptized Christian has a priestly dignity, but the priesthood of the faithful differs not only in degree but also in essence. St. Paul says that Christ gave various gifts. "And to some, his 'gift' was that they should be Apostles; to some prophets; to some evangelists; to some, pastors and teachers; to knit God's holy people together for the work of service to build up the Body of Christ, until we all reach unity in faith and knowledge of the Son of God and form the perfect Man fully mature with the fullness of Christ Himself." (Eph. 4:11-13). Ordination by the imposition of hands is often mentioned and Timothy was instructed not to neglect the grace of God given by imposition of hands. "You have in you a spiritual gift which was given to you when the prophets spoke and the body of elders laid their hands on you; do not neglect it" (1 Tim. 4:14).

If the Mass is what Catholics claim it to be — according to the mistaken beliefs of those who deny Catholic doctrines regarding Sacrament and Sacrifice — then it is humiliating to Christ to offer Mass repeatedly; they are causing Christ to suffer yet more. For the educated Catholic who understands his or her faith appreciatively, that accusation is ridiculous. It is the *glorious* Sacrifice of the Mass that is celebrated. Christ is not slain again, as clearly pointed out in Catholic teaching. God the Father, and in fact the entire Blessed Trinity, is given infinite adoration every time the Mass is celebrated as it tunes in to Christ ever living to make intercession for us. Jesus is always presenting His Body with the glorified wound marks to the heavenly Father as testimony that He has redeemed all his brothers and sisters upon earth in a New Covenant-Sacrifice. Each time we offer the Holy Mass we enter into the reality of that New Covenant which Christ Jesus struck on Mt. Calvary. This is infinite adoration, not because we of ourselves could do anything of infinite value but because the essential Priest of the Mass is the High Priest Jesus Christ. The Priest and Victim of the Sacrifice of the Mass today is the same Priest and Victim of the Sacrifice of the Cross. They are one and the same, only the manner of offering is different.

Those who protest and complain about Catholic teachings regarding the Real Presence of the Body and Blood of Jesus Christ under the appearance of bread and wine, and the perpetuation of Jesus' Sacrifice, make it clear that our teachings are hard sayings and intolerable language. That accusation is nothing new. The same was given to Jesus Christ directly in his eloquent and lengthy discourse on the Holy Eucharist in John 6. "After hearing it, many of his followers said, 'This is intolerable language. How could anyone accept it?' " (vv. 59, 60).

The sixth chapter of John closes by telling us, "After this many of his disciples went away and accompanied Him no more" (v. 66). Jesus was the perfect Teacher. If they had misunderstood Him, and He was only to be taken symbolically, would He have kept repeating that He was really going to give mankind His sacred Body to eat and His precious Blood to drink? As people departed, would He not have called them back? "Oh! you have misunderstood Me. I am not really going to give you Myself to eat and drink. I am only using figurative expressions." When fundamentalists quote verse 63 to claim that Jesus meant His words only figuratively, then, why does the very next verse tell us that Jesus said, "But there are some of you who do not believe"? This is followed by telling us that many departed from Jesus thereafter.

The final verses of St. John's beautiful chapter presents Jesus saying to the Twelve, "What about you, do you want to go away too?" (v. 67) In other words, it was as if He had said, "you have witnessed the thousands departing. I mean what I say when I say I am going to give you My Flesh to eat and My Blood to drink. This is your moment of truth, your moment of faith. If you do not want to believe as that crowd did not, then you too are free to depart. But I mean what I have said." "Simon Peter answered, 'Lord, to whom shall we go? You have the message of eternal life, and we believe; we have come to know that you are the Holy One of God' " (vv. 68-69). Peter in effect says, "I don't understand it Lord. But I believe it. You are the Son of the Living God and if You say it is true I believe it."

The very last lines concludes, "Jesus replied to them, 'Did I not choose the Twelve of you? Yet one of you is a devil.' He meant Judas son of Simon Iscariot, since this was the man, one of the Twelve, who was to betray Him" (vv. 70-71).

Why did Jesus call Judas to become one of the Twelve when He knew ultimately he would betray the Lord? Scripture says of the one who would betray Him, "Alas for that man by whom the Son of Man is betrayed! Better for that man if he had never been born" (Mark 14:21).

Judas was not the last of Apostles who would betray the Lord. There have been some bishops and priests, successors of the original Apostles through the centuries who have also betrayed the Lord. Some have left the Church with hatred in their hearts. Worldliness, sensuality, failure to live up to the high standards of any Christian life, let alone the added responsibility of the priesthood, have led some, like Judas given to clutching purse strings, to betray Jesus, His priesthood, His Church. It is sad to see anti-Catholics quote former priests attacking the Church with falsehoods and bitterness, as if they could find no higher authority as proof against the Catholic Church. Such proof against the two thousand-year-old Church is no more valid than it would be to use Judas as proof against Jesus Christ as the Son of the Living God who came to earth to redeem us.

There will always be some who will set up for themselves another kind of Christ. The Jesus Christ of the Gospels is a Christ who invites us to take up our cross and follow him daily if we would be His true disciples (Matt. 10:38; 16:24; Mark 8:34; Luke 9:23; 14:27).

To present the word "transubstantiation" as a doctrine first formulated in the Middle Ages is a misrepresentation of Catholic teachings. The faith behind the term was believed in the Church from the time of Jesus Christ and His Apostles. Theology is faith seeking understanding of what has been revealed. The word "transubstantiation" itself is not the faith, but the use of human language to explain the faith. Humanly speaking, we can never understand the power of God to change bread and wine into the Body and Blood of Jesus Christ while still having the appearances and the taste of bread and wine. Not to accept that God could do it would be to sin against faith. In explaining the faith of the Church in the Holy Eucharist the word "transubstantiation" is used.

The Eastern Fathers of the Catholic Church before the sixth century favored the expression *meta-ousiosis,* meaning "change of being." The Latin tradition, the Church in the West, eventually coined the word *transubstantiation*, meaning "change of substance." The Council of Trent used the words, "wonderful and singular conversion of the whole substance of the bread into the Body, and the whole substance of the wine into the Blood" of Christ, and added, "which conversion the Catholic Church calls transubstantiation."

The fundamentalist interpretation of the Body and Blood of Jesus Christ having only a figurative meaning is not only incorrect but a rather new interpretation. The early Church interpreted the words of Jesus literally. There is no record from the time of Christ and the early centuries that even implies that Christians who accepted Jesus as Lord and Savior doubted the constant interpretation of the Catholic Church from the first. There has never been found any document in which the literal interpretation is opposed and only the metaphorical accepted by any body of Christians, that is, until modern times, especially after the Protestant Revolt.

In picking up the Scriptures and giving them a simplistic interpretation without regard to the intent of the writers or the mode in which they wrote, one runs into all kinds of difficulties and contradictions which escape those who read the Bible as if it were writtten yesterday. The expression "to eat the flesh and drink the blood" when used figuratively among the Jews of old as among the Arabs of today, meant to inflict upon a person some serious injury, especially by calumny or by false accusation. The fundamentalists don't seem to realize that in their figurative explanation they have our Divine Lord promising everlasting life to the culprit for slandering and hating him, which would reduce Jesus' words to nonsense.

The only New Testament record of the followers of Jesus forsaking Him for purely doctrinal reasons is in John 6 when Jesus refused to take back His words that He will give us His Flesh to eat and His Blood to drink. Jesus said twelve times that He was the bread come down from heaven. Four times He said they would have "to eat my Flesh and drink my Blood."

The popular TV fundamentalist whose anti-Catholic writings we studied bragged how he confused "a lovely young lady," a Catholic who believed that Jesus was present with His Body and Blood in Holy Communion, by quoting for her verse 63 of John 6. The fundamentalist preacher again distorted the words of Jesus and made the words mean something other than Biblical scholars would accept. The "flesh" of John 6:63, as explained earlier in this chapter, does not refer to Christ's own flesh, but to mankind's inclination to think on the natural, rather than a spiritual, supernatural level. The word "spirit" used in that verse does not mean "What I have just said is symbolic." The word "spirit" is never used that way in the Bible. Jesus is calling us to faith in what He is teaching, even though the human mind cannot grasp the marvel. The fundamentalists are guilty of the very things Jesus cautions against when they ridicule Catholic doctrine on the Holy Eucharist in their words, "the senses of the body tell us it is only bread and wine."

A record of a homily written by Origen in 244 A.D. expresses faith in the Real Presence of Jesus Christ in the Holy Eucharist. "I wish to admonish you with examples from your religion. You are accustomed to take part in the divine mysteries, so you know how, when you have received the Body of the Lord, you reverently exercise every care lest a particle of it fall and lest anything of the consecrated gift perish . . . ."

Athanasius, the bishop of Alexandria, wrote the following to some newly baptized Christians in 373 A.D.,

> So long as the prayers of supplication and entreaties have not been made, there is only bread and wine. But after the great and wonderful prayers have been completed, then the bread becomes

the Body and the wine the Blood, of our Lord Jesus Christ.

Still on record is a catechetical lecture given by Cyril of Jerusalem in the middle of the fourth century.

Do not, therefore, regard the bread and wine as simply that; for they are, according to the Master's declaration, the Body and Blood of Christ. Even though the senses suggest to you the other, let faith make you firm. Do not judge in this matter by taste, but be fully assured by faith, not doubting that you have been deemed worthy of the Body and Blood of Christ.

The writings of Ignatius of Antioch are precious since he had been a disciple of the Apostle John, whom we have quoted so much in this chapter, and who wrote other parts of the New Testament. Copies of an epistle which St. Ignatius wrote in about 110 A.D. to the Smyrneans are in existence today. Referring to "those who hold heterodox opinions," he said that,

They abstain from the Eucharist and from prayer, because they do not confess that the Eucharist is the Flesh of our Savior Jesus Christ, Flesh which suffered for our sins and which the Father, in his goodness, raised up again.

Forty years, later, St. Justin Martyr wrote,

Not as common bread nor common drink do we receive these; but since Jesus Christ our Savior was made incarnate by the Word of God and had both Flesh and Blood for our salvation, so too, as we have been taught, the food which has been made into the Eucharist by the Eucharistic prayer set down by him, and by the change of which our blood and flesh is nourished, is both the Flesh and the Blood of that incarnated Jesus.

When critics among the fundamentalists claim that there is nothing in the Bible which suggests the Catholic celebration of the Mass they are demonstrating not only prejudice but a failure to interpret the Bible, as a whole, with a basic message running from beginning to end. Jesus was a Jew and observed the prescriptions of the religion of the Jews. Jesus chose a meal, a very special meal in Jewish worship, to institute the Holy Eucharist. The Jews considered a meal as a ritual action. The Passover meal which Jesus chose was the high point of Jewish annual observance, filled with religious meaning which called forth the memory of Jewish history in relationship to God. As always, in interpreting Sacred Scripture we must enter into the historical, cultural and religious observances in use when it was written. We will discover that for a Jew to remember someone or an event was to represent the benefits of that person, of that event, of that relationship.

One must recall all of Jewish history to appreciate what Jesus is doing, what He is instituting at the Last Supper.

Especially important in understanding this is Exodus 12. It is important to interpret the New Testament (Covenant) in terms of the Old Testament (Covenant) to gain a full appreciation and meaning of this. The Passover Meal was indeed the sacrificial meal and high point of Jewish annual worship. It is about to pass away and its meanings be fulfilled in actuality. In order to seal a Semitic covenant, a real victim was required (Genesis 15:7-8; Exodus 24:5ff). Jesus is about to seal the New Covenant with Himself as Victim and in His own Blood.

The Holy Eucharist which Jesus institutes at the Last Supper for sealing the New Covenant looks toward Calvary and its Sacrifice which will save all men until the end of the world (Hebrews 9). The Apostles, with their Jewish minds, were aware of the sacrificial meaning of Jesus' words in the process of giving them the Eucharist with the command to do in like manner when He spoke of His Body "to be given for you" (Luke 22:19) and "the New Covenant in my Blood, which will be shed for you" (Luke 22:20). The nature of the Eucharist is much more than a meal. It is a meal having its greatest meaning from the sacrifice, the Body being "given up" and Blood "poured out" or shed.

If the effecting of the Holy Eucharist was intended by our Lord to be simply a memorial meal with the weakened sense of "memory" in modern terms and with no great implications in Christian faith and practice, not only is such an interpretation contrary to the Scriptures in its basic message running throughout the Bible but an interpretation clearly not understood even by those who persecuted the early Christians. The first-century Roman historian Tacitus wrote of the Christan religion that the death of Christ at the hands of Pontius Pilate "checked the abominable superstition for the while." But then he notes that belief in Christ broke out in Rome itself. Associated with Tacitus' concern was the celebration of the Eucharist.

Writers in the second century, Tertullian and Minucius Felix, corroborate with earlier accusations against Christians concerning charges of cannibalism and infanticide, which resulted from pagan misunderstanding of the nature of the Eucharist according to the Christian faith that it is the perpetuation of the Sacrifice of Jesus and the eating of His Body and Blood. Their accusations of cannibalism were identical with those who walked away from Jesus (John chapter 6) and followed Him no longer.

If the reception of the Eucharist is no more than a holy memory with bread and wine, why is it that St. Paul, when he had established a

Christian community in Corinth, did he become so concerned about the reverence with which the Eucharist must be celebrated and received? (1 Cor. 10:14-22; 11:17-34). " . . . Anyone who eats the bread or drinks the cup of the Lord unworthily is answerable for the Body and Blood of the Lord." Other translations from the original languages have it: "guilty of the Body and the Blood of the Lord"; "sins against the Body and the Blood of the Lord."

Each time the Holy Eucharist is celebrated, the reality of the merits of Jesus' redeeming death for our salvation are re-presented; the very Person of Jesus Christ is made present to us; there is an actual vital relationship with Calvary's Cross and all its benefits offered to us here and now. This is the real sense of the Jewish meaning of memory. A personal relationship with Jesus Christ is established for those who enter into the Mass — the Holy Eucharist — with faith and love. No one of any century need be denied the reality of the Cross and its effects.

While some fundamentalists are willing to grant that a general outline of the Mass has a Scriptural foundation, yet, they are bothered by vestments, incense, candles and all the other external things they connect with Catholic devotions and worship. They forget that all these Catholic liturgical practices have roots in the liturgy (worship) which was offered in the Great Temple at Jerusalem. We know from Sacred Scripture that Jesus, as a devout Jew Himself, participated regularly and devoutly in the Liturgy of the Temple. Even the sanctuary lamp that burns night and day beside the Catholic tabernacle today in honor of the Real Presence of Jesus Christ in the Most Blessed Sacrament contained therein takes its origin from the Temple. The Jewish Temple had such a lamp burning in honor of the presence of God where the Ark of the Covenant was contained. At times God manifested His presence. The Temple had its altar of sacrifice, its tabernacle, and its burning fire or lamp.

We should expect to find remains of the Jewish religion in the Christian religion which fulfilled everything to which the Old Covenant looked forward. In His Sermon on the Mount, Jesus our Lord and Savior said, "Do not imagine that I have come to abolish the Law or the Prophets. I have come not to abolish but to complete them" (Matt. 5:7).

The commandments of God are still in force. The New Covenant did not do away with the Old Covenant but perfected it in every way. From the liturgy of worship in the Temple and its sacrifices to the Sacrifice of Christ in the New Covenant, the New Sacrifice completes what the old merely symbolized.

Pope John Paul II recognized this on April 13, 1986 when he visited the main Jewish Synagogue in Rome and embraced Elio Toaff, Rome's chief rabbi. Pope John Paul spoke against the hatred and persecution of the Jews throughout the centuries of which even Christians have been guilty.

"You are our dearly beloved brothers and, in a certain way, it could be said that you are our elder brothers," Pope John Paul said to a resounding applause from the crowd of about one thousand people. They entered the synagogue to the accompaniment of a choir singing a psalm. The white gown and stole worn by Toaff were not strange to devout Catholics. Nor were the Scriptural readings in Hebrew which were translated into Italian. Each Catholic Mass has readings from the Psalms, and every Sunday, in addition to New Testament readings, there is an Old Testament reading.

The chief attack of fundamentalists on the Catholic religion is on the Holy Eucharist. Those who take issue with the mystery of the Catholic faith are unwittingly casting themselves into the role of those souls who in Jesus' time refused to believe. With Peter, however, sincere Catholics say to Jesus regarding the Real Presence in the Holy Eucharist, "Lord . . . You have the message of eternal life."

May the readers of this book profess their faith in this way, and not depart from it. May it inspire any who have departed from the Church to come back home.

**END OF CHAPTER**

# CHAPTER 7

# Saints, Images and Miracles

The fundamentalist mentioned in the previous chapter attempts to describe the Catholic faith regarding saints and images in the following words:

> *The worship of saints and images is an integral part of the Roman Catholic religion. Let's examine it as the Roman Catholic church teaches and proclaims it — and then let's look at it in the light of the Word of God.*
>
> *The saints are mediators between the faithful and God.*
>
> *... We should address prayers to the saints and kneel before them to obtain their favor.*
>
> *... The saints are pleased to see their images venerated and adorned with costly treasures — and they (the saints) will recompense the faithful who are generous in their worship.*
>
> *... The images of the blessed virgin and the Lord Jesus Christ may be venerated under different names. This can give rise to competition between different images of the same person.*
>
> *... According to the Catholic position, "saints" are individuals of the New Testament (or later martyrs or notable persons of "The Church") who have died and subsequently been declared to be saints by the pope. ... In this enlightened age it is difficult to realize that the majority of Catholics are unaware of the direct contradiction between a belief in an omnipotent God and the worship of saints as advocates and intercessors. ... In a conversation between an evangelical and several Roman Catholics, the following question was proposed: "Everyone*

*accepts that the saints are finite beings — not only on earth but in heaven as well. So how can finite beings hear the prayers of men who are on the earth? If one would stop to think about this, it would seem impossible for a finite being to hear the prayers of not just two or three people, but those of multiplied thousands who are all praying at the same time.*

*The only way they could hear so many thousands of prayers, and discern the heart attitudes of all of these people, would be if they were both omniscient and omnipresent. In other words, each saint would have to be God in order to accomplish this."*

*When this question was put to the Roman Catholic represent- atives, they didn't know how to reply. Finally, after a whispered conference, one of them offered this: "There is no difficulty. Even if the saints can't hear our prayers, God can and He could reveal them to the saints."*

*Did you anticipate the resulting question in this dialogue? This would then mean that we would be approaching the saints through God — instead of God through the saints.*

*The idea becomes more absurd the further we pursue it.*

*The very thought of individuals speaking to frail and finite humans — and expecting them to carry their ideas to God — is ludicrous. The Word of God states clearly that we can go direct- ly to the Father at any time, in the name of the Lord Jesus Christ (John 16:23).*

*The Catholic system of patron saints is nothing more, nor less, than a continuation of ancient heathen beliefs in gods de- voted to days, occupations, and the various needs of human life. Since the worship of saints is really a perpetuation of these false gods, Romanism is patently guilty of worshiping "other gods" — a practice that is repeatedly condemned in Scripture.*

*To make the apostasy less obvious, the leaders of the Roman Catholic church substituted Christian-sounding names that were similar to the original pagan names.*

*It wasn't until the fifth century that pictures of Mary, Christ, and the saints were made and used as objects of worship.*

*Scripture specifically condemns idol worship in countless places, as there is not a hint or a suggestion in the Word of God that the Early Church deviated from these age-old injunctions.*

There is no indication in the Word of God that a person becomes a saint after he dies. *In fact, it is not the pope who makes someone a saint, it is God. In Scripture, saints are always living people — never the dead.*

*For example, when Paul wrote to the Ephesians, his letter was addressed "to the saints which are at Ephesus" (Eph. 1:1).*

*Consequently, if you want a saint to pray for you, you should find a Christian and ask him to join you in prayer. Any time you try to contact people who have died, it is a form of spiritism. The Bible repeatedly condemns any attempt to commune with the dead (Isaiah 8:19-20) . . . .*

*. . . I am sure, after reading this, that some will say, "But what about the miracles which have been performed by the intercession of the saints?"*

*This consists of statues that weep, form tears on faces, or produce (alleged) miracles. The Virgin of Lourdes is the most publicized of these.*

*Actually, there is absolutely* nothing *in the Word of God that even* hints *at such a thing. God has never healed or performed miracles or done any type of good works through inanimate objects except in the case of Paul's handkerchiefs and aprons as described in Acts 19:12. And this one isolated case is* not *an example of worshiping or venerating an idol or image.*

*If one were to visit Lourdes today, he would be appalled by the carnival atmosphere. This is, of course, totally foreign to the Word of God, and the* work *of God.* There are no miracles at Lourdes, no healing or cures — or anything else of this nature. There may be emotional reactions, but that's as far as it goes.

*. . . Many accept false religions that promise healing and other benefits. Satan cooperates with these religions, which he himself has founded to deceive men. He can even bring about a withdrawal of the sickness from people without God being involved in the process. Such people naturally think they are in the true religion. They reject Christ and see no need of getting saved from sin or following Christianity. They will be damned for doing so, Satan having won their souls.*

*One of the major works of Satan is the work of deception, and in this vein, along with other efforts, he is leading much of the world astray.*

*Yes, we do believe in miracles. We believe in healing. We believe that God answers prayer. But we believe that it comes in a Biblical way.*

*God uses living men and women to pray for individuals who are sick (James 5:14). And He does answer prayer — when it is offered according to His Holy Word.*

*The worship of saints and images has absolutely no foundation in the Word of God. It is an excursion into superstition and paganism which will further enfold its web of deceit around the followers of Catholicism.*

*The Evangelist*, January 1986

The above, which pretends to present what the Roman Catholic Church teaches and proclaims regarding saints and images, completely misrepresents the faith. It presents, rather what the fundamentalist would like people to think the Roman Catholic Church teaches and practices. It represents accusations made for centuries, answered hundreds of times, but which fundamentalists refuse to accept as they mistrust the Catholic Church when it states it own teachings. Fundamentalists continue to prompt wrong concepts of what the Church teaches on these matters. They promote what they claim the Church teaches and believes rather than what the Catholic Church actually teaches.

As presented earlier, nothing can be so dangerous as a half-truth. Fundamentalists who present their concepts of the Roman Catholic religion frequently present half-truths. This gives a note of credibility to their misrepresentations to the uninformed or confused and results in making Catholic teachings seem ridiculous.

It is to be noted that the Catholic Church is fully aware that "saints" is a name generally given in the New Testament (Col. 1:2). However, the custom developed very early among Christians of restricting the title to persons who were eminent for holiness. Anyone with faith, living in the grace of Jesus Christ is a saint in the general sense. In a more strict sense, and as commonly used, "saints" refers to those who distinguish themselves by heroic virtue during life and whom the Church honors in a special way, either by her ordinary universal teaching authority or by a solemn declaration called canonization. Canonization does not mean that the Catholic Church on earth "makes a saint" or puts a saint in heaven, as is commonly declared by the secular media and as described by fundamentalists. The Church simply declares what God has already done. The person is already in heaven, but not because of the process of the canonization. The Church's official recognition of sanctity implies that the person is now in heavenly glory. Saints may be publicly invoked everywhere in the Church. Their virtues during their lives on earth, or their deaths as martyrs are a witness to Christ and an example to the

Christian faithful. They lived the Christ-life in an exceptional way.

There are millions of persons — saints — in heaven. Few are ever canonized. The relatively few that are canonized are presented to the faithful not simply that we may invoke their intercession with God but because they are presented for models for living the Christ-life. I know of no Church teaching that says that we *must* address prayers to, or through, each canonized saint, or that we must kneel before them. It is spiritually advantageous to study the lives of saints who can inspire us with their heroism in living the Christian life. Some Catholics are inclined more than others to invoke certain saints. As a matter of fact, I dare say that the author of this book, like most Catholics, does not know the lives of most of the canonized saints or even their names, except of those of more universal significance or whose lives inspired and served the cause of Christianity in one's own country or local Church.

The value of honoring the members of one's country, state or community whose contributions have been especially valuable for the common good and whose lives are an inspiration to others is easily recognized. Every civilized society has done this. Ought we not do the same among the "saints" of God as the New Testament speaks of them?

It is not only Catholics who honor saints. Millions of Christians other than Roman Catholics do likewise, including Anglicans (Episcopalians) and Orthodox Christians. Lutherans, as do Catholics, set aside November 1st each year to honor all the saints in heaven. All Saints Day is a time to honor those millions of our brothers and sisters who lived in faith and died in the faith and grace of Jesus Christ. We do not know the names or lives of most of them, but they are nonetheless our brothers and sisters in Jesus Christ. They have been victorious in the trial which we are still undergoing. They now "see God face to face, even as He is."

After I saw a hugh number, impossible for anyone to count, of people from every nation, race, tribe and language; they were standing in front of the throne and in front of the Lamb, dressed in white robes and holding palms in their hands. They shouted in a loud voice, "Salvation to our God, who sits on the throne, and to the Lamb." And all the angels who were standing in a circle round the throne, surrounding the elders and the four living creatures, prostrated themselves before the throne, and touched the ground with their foreheads, worshiping God with these words:

Amen, praise and glory and wisdom,
Thanksgiving and honor and power and strength
to our God for ever and ever. Amen.

... These are the people who have been through the great trial; they have washed their robes white again in the blood of the Lamb. That is why they are standing in front of God's throne and serving him day and night in his sanctuary; and the One who sits on the throne will spread his tent over them. They will never hunger or thirst again; sun and scorching wind will never plague them, because the Lamb who is at the heart of the throne will be their shepherd and will guide them to springs of living water; and God will wipe away all tears from their eyes (Rev. 7:9-17).

It is the *intercession of the saints* that the Catholic Church approves. This means that those persons in heaven may be invoked to pray for us and they, too, go to God the Father through the one essential Mediator, Jesus Christ. They are not mediators equal to our Lord and Savior, Jesus Christ. Fundamentalists present them as if Catholics replace the unique mediatorship of Jesus Christ. This is a serious misrepresentation of Catholic teaching, which carefully adheres to the essential role of Jesus as Mediator for every kind of prayer sent forth to God.

God is not less honored in his saints when their intercession with and *through* Jesus is sought. God is more glorified. When speaking of the Last Judgment, 2 Thessalonians 1 tells of some who "will be punished with eternal ruin (v. 9) "away from the face of the Lord and the glory of His power," and tells also of those who were faithful "when on that day He shall come to be glorified in His saints ... " (v. 10). The Apostle Paul immediately continues with,

To this end also we pray always for you, that our God may make you worthy of His calling, and may fulfill with power every good purpose and work of faith, that the name of our Lord Jesus Christ may be glorified in you, and you in Him, according to the grace of our God and the Lord Jesus Christ. (2 Thess. 1:11-12).

St. Paul obviously believes in the power of prayer of those upon earth to bring souls to heaven, where they will be saints who glorify God forever. What is to prevent souls, once in heaven, before the throne where they glorify God forever, and are perfected in the light of glory in the love of God, to continue to pray for their brothers and sisters upon earth? Is their charity now less in heaven that they should have no care about the salvation of their brothers and sisters still upon earth, yet undergoing the trial?

The book of Daniel gives us an account of Susanna, the young wife wrongly accused of adultery by the two lustful elders. This virtuous woman, who lived according to the law of Moses, was about to be put to death.

She cried out as loud as she could, "Eternal God, you know all secrets and everything before it happens; you know that they have given false evidence against me. And now I must die, innocent as I am of everything their malice has invented against me." The Lord heard her cry and, as she was being led away to die, He roused the Holy Spirit residing in a young boy called Daniel who began to shout, "I am innocent of this woman's death" (Daniel 13:42-46).

The spirit of Daniel proved the innocence of Susanna and the wickedness of the evil judges. This is found only in the Greek version of the Bible. Even if some not of the Catholic faith do not accept this as part of the Bible, this passage illustrates the belief of peoples before the coming of Christ. That is that God at times works through the spirit of others. Always, however, the answer to every prayer comes ultimately from God.

When the fundamentalist already mentioned, who is adept at drawing individuals at random from the crowd of anonymous millions of Catholics, presents the views of one or two of them as official Catholic teachings, it is hoped that the average reader can detect his absurdity and unfairness. A man on the street who calls himself "Catholic" is not always a good representative for the voice of Catholicism. We see this in the fundamentalist's claim that Catholics approach the saints through God.

Pray tell, what is so unreasonable about approaching saints, living on this earth or already in God's presence in heaven, to reach God? There is nothing in fact we can do, whether of the natural or supernatural level, except through the power of God. The Apostle St. Paul said, "it is in Him that we live, and move, and exist" (Acts 17:28). Jesus is Himself the King of Saints. All prayers go to the Father through the human nature of the King of Saints. The Apostle Paul tells us that as we await "the glory which is destined to be disclosed for us, . . . we have the first-fruits of the Spirit" (Romans 8:18-25).

Finally, the third Person of the Blessed Trinity actually prays within us.

And as well as this, the Spirit too comes to help us in our weakness, for, when we do not know how to pray properly, then the Spirit personally makes our petitions for us in groans that cannot be put into words; and He who can see into all hearts knows what the Spirit means because the prayers that the Spirit makes for God's holy people are always in accordance with the mind of God (Romans 8:26-27).

As members of Christ's body, which we are, and which the Apostle Paul attests to repeatedly in the Scriptures, it is in Christ Jesus that we pray and it is Christ Jesus Who prays within us when we adore, thank, petition or ask forgiveness. We do not even know at times how to pray properly or what are our needs. If open to the action of the Holy Spirit, the Spirit Himself prays within us, says the Apostle Paul. "Nobody is able to say, 'Jesus is Lord' except in the Holy Spirit" (1 Cor. 12:3).

When the fundamentalist quoted speaks about an impossibility of a finite saint hearing the prayers of not simply two or three people but even "multiplied thousands who are praying at the same time," he is restricting the power of the saints who live in God's heavenly glory with the limitations we have on this earth. At the end of the world, at the Last Judgment, "all nations will be assembled before Him [Jesus] and He will separate people one from another as the shepherd separates sheep from the goats . . . ." (Matt. 25:31ff). The justice of God will be revealed "when the Son of Man comes in His glory, escorted by all the angels." The mercy of God will be revealed and made manifest unto the glory of God for those who are saved. All shall recognize God's justice in those who are lost because they did not in repentance avail themselves in faith and love of God's mercy. All shall know God's decisions. With four billion people living upon the earth at this moment and all who have and shall live gathered together for the Last Judgment, it will not take years to reveal God's justice and mercy to all. In a moment the power of God can infuse knowledge into the souls of billions of individuals.

In eternity our bodies will not be tied down to the limitations of space and time such as we know it. The resurrected body of Jesus Christ passed through doors. It came and went, appearing and disappearing in a moment. His was a glorified body. Our resurrected bodies will have such spiritual qualities as did the risen body of Jesus. So too the mind, in glory beholding God "face to face as He is" shares in the unimaginable glory of God, shares in His knowledge and love. Any saint of heaven that is aware of us still upon earth, is aware through the power of God. Sharing in heavenly glory, the souls in heaven at this moment (who await their bodies) could, through the power of God absorb the thoughts, the prayers, of any number of people upon earth. Every one of the more than four billion people now upon earth is less than a drop of the reality of Infinity.

Let us not put limitations upon God's powers and what He can do for those He loves in a special manner and for whom He has put before His face in glory.

It is of the mysterious wisdom of God that we talk, the wisdom that was hidden, which God predestined to be for our glory before the ages began. None of the rulers of the age recognized it; for if they had recognized it, they would not have crucified the Lord of glory; but it is as Scripture says: What no eye has seen and no ear has heard, what the mind of man cannot visualize; all that God has prepared for those who love Him ... (1 Cor. 2:7-9).

When it is said that the intercession of Jesus Christ is all that is necessary and we do not need the prayers of others, such is contrary to Sacred Scripture. St. James, after the Ascension of Christ into heaven, called for prayers for the salvation of others. Scripture approves of secondary mediators, but always in, with and through Jesus Christ. In Acts 12:5 the Christians offered prayer without ceasing for St. Peter who was in prison. In Hebrews 13:18 the Apostle wrote, "Pray for us ... " These people on earth are secondary mediators with Christ, the essential Mediator. How can their prayers with Christ be not possible for others, once they are in heaven in the presence of the Christ of glory, sharing in His life, where He lives, as Scripture says, "to make intercession for us?"

When the early Catholic Church Christianized pagan practices it was not continuing heathen beliefs in false gods, etc. It was replacing what was invalid with a valid Christian practice.

The ancient catacombs of Rome have inscriptions, still seen today, showing that the first Christians believed in the intercession of the saints — those who had died in faith or even as martyrs. There is abundant testimony that they venerated their remains, even offering the Holy Eucharistic celebration over their graves from which arose the practice to the present day of Catholic altars containing relics of martyrs to the faith. Altar stones or small flat stones consecrated by a bishop contain a hollowed-out cavity with relics of two canonized martyrs, a practice inherited from early Christians and a demonstration of the faith in the communion of saints, which the Apostles' Creed mentions. There is a spiritual union with the saints still upon earth with those in heavenly glory, a union in Christ the Vine.

Under Augustus, a temple had been dedicated by Agrippa to all the pagan gods; it was thus given the name Pantheon. Between 607 and 610 Pope Boniface IV translated to the Pantheon numerous remains of martyrs taken from the catacombs. On May 13, 610, this Pope dedicated this new Christian basilica to St. Mary and the martyrs. Later on, the temple was consecrated to St. Mary and all the saints. In various parts of the Christian world there was already a feast in commemoration of all the saints celebrated on various dates. The feast of All Saints was first celebrated on May 13. Pope Gregory III (731-41) changed the date to November 1. Pope Gregory IV later extended the feast to the whole Church. The feast of All Saints therefore recalls the triumph of Christ over the false pagan deities, which is just the opposite of what the fundamentalist quoted earlier claims is the position of the Catholic Church.

Christmas itself is the Christianizing of a pagan rite. How many Christians of whatever denomination would object to celebrating the birth of our Savior? Christmas replaced a pagan rite of lights in the depths of winter's darkness. The Feast of Christmas on December 25 coincides with the ancient pagan feast in which the winter solstice was celebrated in honor of the birth of the sun, which they deified. The Church therefore Christianized this pagan rite, at first in Rome, in the fourth century. It is in the midst of darkness, when nights are longest (but when each day begins to get a little longer,) symbolic of that which darkens the soul, that the Church observes the birth of the Son of God as man who is the "light of the world." In this way the Church said, "Behold the true 'Light of the world, your Savior.' "

This is the beauty of authentic Christianity. It makes all things holy. Christ came in the "fullness of time" as God's Word informs us, "born of a woman." The world was ripe for its Savior. Without knowing it, the world was longing for a Savior.

The Apostle Paul was seeking to Christianize pagan practices when he made his speech before the council of the Areopagus. "Men of Athens, I have seen for myself how extremely scrupulous you are in all religious matters, because, as I strolled around looking at your sacred monuments, I noticed among other things an altar inscribed: 'To An Unknown God.' In fact, the unknown God you revere is the one I proclaim to you ... " (Acts 17:23).

Fundamentalists will agree that miracles can and do happen. So does the Catholic Church. Unfortunately, fundamentalists are often reluctant to look objectively at miracles that have been declared authentic by the Catholic Church, such as the image of Our Lady of Guadalupe, imprinted on a cloak in Mexico City, or the miracle on May 13, 1917 at Fatima, Portugal when between seventy and one hundred thousand people witnessed the appearance of the spinning of the sun, among other things.

When the fundamentalist already mentioned declares that "there are no miracles at Lourdes, no healings or cures — or anything else of this nature" he is speaking without investigation and doubtlessly is threatened by the reported cures and the phenomena of Lourdes which has drawn millions each year. The extraordinary supernatural happenings associated with Lourdes and Fatima are a special threat to fundamentalists who declare the Catholic Church unbiblical and even that the Catholic Church cannot save anyone and that unless people come out of such churches and accept the Word of God they cannot be saved. In the same way that the miracles, the works of Jesus, those recorded in the Bible and those not recorded (John 21:24-25) served to bring people to faith in Jesus, so fundamentalists fear that miracles reported as occurring in the Catholic Church will bring people to faith in it as the true Church of Jesus Christ.

Lourdes is a world famous shrine in honor of the Immaculate Conception of Mary in the region of Hautes-Pyrénées in France. In 1858, the Blessed Virgin Mary appeared eighteen times at Massabielle, at the grotto near Lourdes to Bernadette Soubirous, a 14 year-old peasant girl. On the occasion of one of the apparitions a spring suddenly appeared and miraculous healings were soon reported by those who bathed in or applied the water. Pilgrims soon began to come to the spot. After a study, the Church declared in 1862 that the apparitions were worthy of human faith. A church was built above the grotto. Between 1883 and 1901 a magnificent Church in honor of Our Lady of the Rosary was built.

Lourdes has a medical bureau established to investigate the character of reported cures. Doctors associated with the bureau are not all Catholic; indeed some have not even been Christian. Not all reported cures can be thoroughly investigated nor need they be. The Church does *not* declare every reported cure miraculous — only those which medical specialists say are unexplainable by medical science. Relatively few have thus been authenticated. Only the unusual cases have been investigated by the medical team. Instantaneous cures, such as the sudden replacement of bones and muscles, are beyond human understanding.

The healings generally take place after the people have been immersed in the waters of the spring, or during the blessing with the monstrance with the Blessed Sacrament carried in procession. Not all cures are physical. Many report marvelous conversions and graces in the spiritual life. When God performs miracles His ultimate end is to bring men to faith and eternal salvation, not simply to grant physical cures for their own sake. What is more, the Church does not demand that we have even human faith in the cures authenticated by the Lourdes or any other medical bureau. In fact, Lourdes, Fatima,

Guadalupe, etc. are not of divine faith. The Church after careful investigation merely declares in certain cases that we may put *human* faith in the extraordinary happenings which cannot be explained. Note the clear distinction between *divine* faith and *human* faith. Catholics *must* have *divine* faith if they are to be considered Catholic regarding the miracles of Jesus Christ recorded in the Bible under divine inspiration. Catholics *may* have *human* faith in miracles reported since the days of Christ and the Apostles upon earth. They are not required to have even human faith if not convinced.

There is a modern prejudice against the supernatural in the modern world. Fundamentalists seem willing to admit miracles can happen, only not in the Catholic Church. The modern world on the other hand has a prejudice against miracles under all circumstances. It was this prejudice against the supernatural, which had the brilliant Dr. Alexis Carrel expelled from the University of Lyons for admitting a miracle at Lourdes. It was the famous author, Arnold Lunn, who wrote,

> The sudden and overwhelming success of Darwinism was due not to the positive arguments in its favor, but to the negative prejudice against the intrusion of the Creator into the work of creation — as is, indeed, admitted by leading Darwinists (*The Third Day*, ch. 14).

What is true is true, and cannot be explained away by prejudice or the insecurity of fundamentalists who cannot trace their origins back two thousand years. Truth does not demand our approval to remain true. Whether fundamenalists believe in Guadalupe, Lourdes or Fatima does not affect the miracles in the least. They still stand on their own merits, regardless of what a person may say, with an almost neurotic fear, about what might be true.

Whether fundamentalists, Catholics or anyone else, believe it or not, it is documented that a cloak with a miraculously painted portrait of Mary has existed in central Mexico, in a suburb of Mexico City, since 1531 and can be seen to the present day. The cloth, made of cactus fiber, should have turned to dust within twenty years, even sooner under the climatic conditions it was kept for its first century. Yet it hangs together more than four hundred and fifty years later with a marvelously beautiful portrait whose colors and stroke-free "painting" cannot be scientifically explained under present-day scientific scrutiny. Fundamentalists without faith in the teachings of the Catholic Church would find the miracle of Guadalupe difficult to accept as the reported happenings in connection with the bestowal of the cloth whose preservation itself is a miracle, even without considering the miraculous image, presented to us by a converted Indian man who said the Virgin Mother spoke things which reaffirm Catholic teachings.

As Jesus worked miracles to bring mankind to faith in the Word of God, so too, miracles today are designed to bring faith in certain messages from heaven. Admittedly there are many reported miracles and apparitions which are false. Indeed, most reported miracles and apparitions are never acted upon by Church authorities but rather discouraged and even proclaimed unworthy of human faith. " ... The deeds my Father has given me to perform, these same deeds of mine testify that the Father has sent me" (John 5:36). " ... As He was approaching the downward slope of the Mount of Olives, the whole group of disciples joyfully began to praise God at the top of their voices for all the miracles they had seen" (Luke 19:37). "If I am not doing My Father's work, there is no need to believe Me; but if I am doing it, then even if you refuse to believe in Me, at least believe in the work I do; then you will know for certain that the Father is in Me and I am in the Father" (John 10:37-38).

The bishop of Mexico City required a sign from the Virgin Mother Mary when the native Aztec Indian, 51-year-old Juan Diego, a recent convert, proclaimed that the beautiful Lady from heaven wanted a church built on the hillside in the country near Mexico City. Bishop Zumarraga got the sign which he demanded. The world then got one of its principal shrines of Christendom.

Juan Diego said that Mary had said,

> You must know, and be very certain in your heart, my son, that I am truly the eternal Virgin, holy Mother of the True God, Lord of heaven and Lord of the earth.

Let not the word "eternal" disturb you, for Mary was created in time. "Eternal life" was the term used by Jesus Christ to describe the state of endless happiness enjoyed by the just in heaven (Matt. 25:46; Mark 9:44; Luke 18:30; John 17:3). It means both everlasting duration and also fullness of life.

What would the fundamentalist mentioned say about x-rays of deteriorated bones taken before going to Lourdes, bathing in the waters and being blessed by the Real Presence of Jesus Christ in the Most Blessed Sacrament and then to see x-rays of the very same bones a short time later after the Lourdes' encounter now restored, miraculously created in an instant? Such documentation exists.

What would fundamentalists say about the miracle of the spinning of the sun at Fatima at exactly 12 noon, Oct. 13th, 1917? The miraculous event was foretold months in advance by the beautiful Lady from heaven. A miracle would take place at an exact location, day and hour. It was witnessed by at least seventy thousand people present and seen for over thirty miles around the Cova da Iria in the parish of Fatima, Portugal. For thirteen consecutive years up to the writing of this book, I have spent much time annually in Fatima, meeting leading characters associated with the miraculous events. I have met witnesses to the spinning of the sun miracle. I have interviewed leading authorities on Fatima, including the official historian and theologian on the events of Fatima. I have written several books* after doing much research on the miraculous events of Fatima. The message of Fatima has been summarized as a reaffirmation of the Gospels by every Pope since the Church has approved of the miraculous events of 1917. The message is one of a call to faith in the Blessed Trinity, to faith in Jesus Christ as Savior; the message is a call to repentance and love.

Here is how the non-believer thinks: With an unyielding prejudice against the miraculous, miracles prove nothing because miracles just do not happen. Miracles do not happen because they cannot happen. "The resurrection of Jesus cannot be a miraculous proof," wrote the most influential of Biblical form critics. The Resurrection of Jesus mentioned in the Bible, he said, meant only that the followers of Jesus continued to have faith in Christ the Lord whose Body stayed lifeless in the tomb. There was a kind of resurrection of Jesus in the faith of His followers, but not a resurrection of the physical Body of Jesus. Rudolf Bultmann won fame in our century for that kind of exegesis, however much an infamous kind of fame.

One finds the inconsistent and contradictory in the anti-supernaturalists, in those whose minds are made up: "miracles can't happen." Such inconsistencies and prejudice are found too in fundamentalists when they claim, "miracles can and do happen but never in the Catholic Church." We see the inconsistency in the famous Biblical form critic who wrote, "Conclusive knowledge is impossible in any science or philosophy" and then concluded that science had positively disproved miracles.*

Many accounts could be documented for one who seriously desired to investigate the claims of Lourdes. The French naturalist,

---

* *Rediscovering Fatima*, Our Sunday Visitor, Inc., Box 920, Huntington, Ind. 46750; *Fatima Today*, Christendom Publications, Route 3, Box 87, Front Royal, Va. 22630.

Emile Zola, became interested in a patient, Marie Lemarchand, who was suffering from the ravages of lupus who was on her way to Lourdes in hope of a cure. The novelist met the patient. This is what he wrote:

> The cartilage of the nose was almost eaten away, the mouth was drawn all on one side by the swollen condition of her upper lip, the whole a frightful, distorted mass of matter and oozing blood.

Emile Zola's description did not include everything, for he did not know what Dr. d'Hombres knew. Both of Marie's lungs were affected. She had putrid sores on one of her legs and the symptoms were not responding to professional treatment.

Emile Zola himself went along to Lourdes to witness the outcome. He doubtlessly thought of what a frustration and disappointment awaited Marie, for miracles do not happen. And here, this poor woman, was banking her future on a miracle.

Marie Lemarchand would be immersed in the ever-running waters at the base of the Grotto of Massabielle, where in 1858, while a crowd of people watched, Bernadette, at the bidding of the vision of Mary, dug into the floor of the cave with her fingers. A trickle of water started. It grew to a torrent. It now continues to pour our twenty-seven thousand gallons a day.

Frustration would follow but it would not be that of Marie Lemarchand, but of Emile Zola. Marie would prove to be subjected to the Lourdes medical bureau established in 1882 to test the authenticity of the cures. The doctors, as noted, included unbelievers as well as believers and any doctor is welcome to take part in the examination of alleged cures. As many as five hundred medical men, of all faiths or none, have taken advantage of the invitation each year. Though many cures are claimed by pilgrims, no cure is regarded as miraculous if science can show any natural explanation of it. Here lies the ridiculous, the inconsistencies of unbelievers who say "science has proven miracles do not happen." Pray tell, how can that be? If natural science proves something natural in cause, how does it have the equipment to prove miracles do not happen when at times it must admit it can find no natural cause? How can the finding of no natural cause be proof against the miraculous?

The case of Marie Lemarchand was to prove to be one of those

---

* *Kerygma and Myth* (W.H. Bartsch, London and New York, 1961). Cf. *The New Columbia Encyclopedia*: Bultmann, Rudolf Karl (Columbia University Press, New York and London, 1975).

ole instant cures of a most serious condition in the gans of the body. What is more, a French naturalist there to witness it. It reminds one of the un-believing ɔ came to Fatima on May 13, 1917, the day the Lady ᴧad told the three children she would perform a miracle at ᴦ all may believe." They came to expose the nonsense of the reportel pparitions but witnessed for themselves the miracle of the sun seen by more than seventy thousand other companions.

The president of the medical bureau at Lourdes, once all the experts had signed an affidavit of their finds, brought the cured patient Marie to Zola. It frustrated him so greatly, that he said, "No! I do not want to look at her." He turned his gaze away and added, "She is still too ugly." He was referring to her new layer of skin on her now normal cheeks, which had a reddish tint. Others saw it as a healthy glow in one cured instantly.

This confirmed naturalist, who had boasted of respecting facts, refused to respect this factual cure. He did not conceal his disappointment in the miracle. His final retort to the eminent surgeon was, "Were I to see all the sick at Lourdes cured, I would not believe in a miracle."

There are none so blind as those who will not see. Jesus gave the disciples warnings about the yeast of the Parisees and the yeast of Herod. "Are your minds closed? Have you eyes and do not see, ears and do not hear?" (Mark 8:18-19). Jesus also said, "Can one blind person guide another?" (Luke 6:39).

"My mind is made up, don't confuse me with facts" is the attitude of one who will not believe in miracles. It is the attitude of those whose minds are closed to two thousand years of Catholicism. Dr. Alexis Carrel, the eventual winner of the Nobel prize, was expelled from the faculty of the University of Lyons by its own members for no other reason than that he also had accompanied a dying patient to Lourdes, and there, after her baths in the fountain, after her immersion in the waters as mentioned in the Scriptures, he had the courage of his convictions to declare the girl cured and to pronounce the cure a natural impossibility.

And at a time when academic freedom and the right to it was more and more coming into vogue, right at the center of prestigious learning, at the university, it was declared through the expulsion of Dr. Alexis Carrel that there are certain things we will not permit to be the truth, namely evidence of the supernatural. Some thirty years later, Dr. Carrel published *Man the Unknown*,* in which he admits that he began

---

* *Man the Unknown* (Harper & Bros., New York, 1936).

examining miraculous cures "at a time when it was dangerous for his future career to become interested in such a subject."

The book in which Dr. Carrel carefully wrote of how he accompanied a dying patient to Lourdes did not get published until six years after his death. In *The Voyage to Lourdes*, he tells how he watched the dying patient closely at the grotto and then in the hospital had her reexamined to reassure himself of the miracle. In this book he gave 18-year-old Marie Bailly the fictitious name of Marie Ferrand, the name by which she is now generally known. As the author and narrator he used the name Lerrac, his own name spelled backwards. He wrote the manuscript in 1903 hoping to publish it in his lifetime. He used this manner of identification to avoid another outburst of indignation.

Can there be a less scientific attitude than those who boast of not even wanting to investigate the evidence in favor of miracles? Denial of the reality and possibility of miracles opens the door for the denial and doubting of the supernatural and a transcendent Creator.

Fundamentalists are believers. They just don't go far enough. The wonders they behold in the Bible happen yet today, and in the Catholic Church, too. Fundamentalists cannot believe in the Catholic Church. What G. K. Chesterton said of agnostics* can apply to fundamentalists, too, in regard to their lack of belief in the Catholic Church.

The ordinary agnostic has got all his facts wrong. He is a non-believer for a multitude of reasons; but they are untrue reasons. He doubts because the Middle Ages were barbaric, but they weren't; because Darwinism is demonstrated, but it isn't; because miracles do not happen, but they do.

Many people who witnessed the public miracles of Jesus Christ, our Lord God and Savior, as these miracles are recorded in Sacred Scripture were not convinced of the supernatural power and authority of Jesus in union with the Father. They had closed their minds to Jesus and thus to the proofs — His works, which He said were His credentials. Their bad wills, their closed minds, brought sorrow to the human heart of Jesus Christ. Jesus expressed His sorrow through Abraham that, "Neither will they be convinced if someone should rise from the dead" (Luke 16:31). The fact is, they did not believe Jesus even after He arose from the dead. They remained dishonest after His Resurrection and offered money to the soldiers standing guard at Jesus' tomb to say His disciples stole His body away.

How does the non-believer think? Remember, Sacred Scripture

---

* (*Orthodoxy*, ch. IX (Dodd, Mead & Company, New York, 1908).

repeatedly equates Jesus and His Church as one. St. Paul the Apostle repeatedly calls the Church the "body of Christ." When Saul, before his conversion to St. Paul, who subsequently writes much of the New Testament, was on the road to Damascus to throw Christians into prison, the Lord in a blinding light strikes him down with the words, "Saul, Saul, why do you persecute Me?" St. Paul never forgot that word "Me." Jesus identified Himself with His followers. Well, how does the non-believer think? He thinks of the Catholic Church today in the same way that non-believers thought of Jesus when He was physically upon the earth.

If one is appalled by the "carnival atmosphere" around some religious shrines, it should first be noted that the selling of most religious articles or souvenirs is not under the sponsorship of the Church. I remember well at Lourdes briefly visiting one of the shops to take home a small memento, and after the purchase being told by a guide that the saleswoman was not Christian. The actual grounds of religious shrines like Lourdes and Fatima are places of prayer and solemn religious processions. There will always be of merchants who will snatch the opportunity at most any place in the world, if possible, to set up their shops wherever great numbers of people converse.

The author of this book for many years has led groups of youthful pilgrims each year to Fatima, up to two hundred each summer. He has spent between one month and six weeks annually at Fatima where the Mother of Jesus appeared in 1917 with a message for the world. The diocese in which Fatima is located was careful as soon as the apparitions were approved (after thirteen years of investigation) to obtain sufficient land around the site of the apparitions to make space available for pilgrims, prayerful processions, a hospital, a basilica (church), a retreat house, etc.

It is possible to go to Lourdes, Fatima, Guadalupe, etc. and spend one's time preoccupied with souvenir shops rather than time in quiet reflection, prayer and study. Admittedly, some come to these places more as sightseers than pious pilgrims. I have discovered youths at Fatima from Holland, hitchhiking across Europe and who shared with me that they did not believe in God. I asked them what they knew about the accounts of Fatima. All they knew was that some "mysterious light" has been reportedly, seen there in 1917. They knew nothing about the accounts written by Sister Lucia, one of the three children who lives as a Carmelite nun.

The miracle of the sun, witnessed by over seventy thousand people, was a natural disturbance which was not detected by any scientific instrument, which normally would have recorded such disturbances. Such a phenomenon is an indication that it was supernatural. Its report had drifted down to these Holland youths as a "mysterious light." These youths, however, felt that there was a natural explanation which scientists had not yet been able to explain.

What would also have to be explained was the sudden dryness after it rained heavily all the night of October 12, 1917 and through the morning hours of the 13th. The crowds who had come despite the rain stayed. Suddenly, at exactly 12 noon, true sun time, not war time, which the Portuguese clocks registered, it stopped raining. The clouds swung back and the miracle of the sun was witnessed. The phenomena of the sun came down upon the people in three successive plunges, returning to its place of orbit overhead each time, before resuming its spinning and plunging toward the earth as a giant Catherine wheel. When the spinning of the sun was completed, the people who had stood in rain and mud for hours — in water ankle-deep in places — suddenly found themselves and the ground perfectly dry.

The message of Fatima contained a reaffirmation of Biblical revelations concerning the existence of angels, the Mystery of Three Persons in One God, the Providence of God, which directs and governs the world and presides over the events of human history; the Omnipotence and Omniscience of God Who knows and realizes all things; God the Rewarder Who rewards or punishes; the reality of heaven, hell and purgatory, the Real Presence of Jesus Christ in the Most Blessed Sacrament, the necessity and value of Holy Communion; the necessity of a holy life for true happiness even on this earth as well as for eternity; the loves of the Hearts of Jesus and Mary for people still upon earth; the need for the sanctification of the family, etc.

I could not help but think, as these Holland youths sat outside the Church at Fatima in a pensive mood, that somehow they had been drawn there by God. I prayed that they would one day come to the faith. They did not know exactly why they themselves had come. They had the greatest respect for natural science which had become their god. I could only pray that their being drawn to Fatima and their observing the faithful prayers and practices of others that it would occasion their submission to the God above and all around us.

The author of this book has known of Catholics who have gone to Fatima, obviously without due preparation, without the prayerful dispositions of a pilgrim, who commented, "Fatima was too commercialized" and "there was nothing there." On the contrary, I've spent up to six weeks at a time at Fatima without noticing the commercial aspects of merchants who have built their small stores on the outlying areas around the places of the apparitions. In fact, the first few years in traveling to Fatima I was unaware of the commercial areas surrounding the sanctuary of Fatima. The same is true at Lourdes. Time, I've felt, is too precious to search for any carnival atmosphere. Time is needed for prayerful reflection.

One who comes to a religious sanctuary without a spirit of penance and prayer, without humble faith — unless that person is deeply touched by conversion — will see only externals. Fatima, as Lourdes, is not found in buildings, in statues, or in the landscape, but essentially in opening one's heart in faith, hope and love to divine action. The spirit of Fatima is the spirit of the Gospels. This is availabe anywhere in the world, of course. But, as seen in the Scriptures, there are certain places where God has worked in a special way.

There have obviously been cases of individuals who have attempted to gain attention by producing statues that have shed tears or blood; such are deliberate attempts to deceive. The Church does not promote reports of weeping statues. The secular press has repeatedly picked up such reports. On occasion it has been shown that fraud was involved. The Catholic Church need not apologize for the deceit or unbalance of a few individuals. Even when no natural explanation can be given, the Church does not require our faith, even human faith, in statues that have shed tears or bled. It is not a part of the Catholic faith.

The escort of the International Fatima statue, Louis Kaczmarek, is a personal friend of mine. He has gone around the world more than once with the image of the Mother of Jesus. On occasion it has shed tears which cannot be explained. Analysis has shown the tears to be genuine human tears, of salt content, etc. Yet, neither my faith in Jesus nor my devotion to the Mother of God depend upon that statue or reports of it shedding tears. Nor does the faith and devotion of its escort. Louis has written a book of his experiences with the statue.*

When the fundamentalist already mentioned says, "God has never healed or performed miracles or done any type of good works through inanimate objects except in the case of Paul's handkerchiefs and aprons as described in Acts 19:12" he is admitting that there is Biblical evidence for God working through what the Church calls "sacramentals."

Sacramentals (this is not the same as the seven Sacraments), are

---

* *The Wonders She Performs*, Trinity Communications, P.O. Box 3610, Manassas, Va. 22110.

objects or actions that the Church uses for spiritual reasons. Examples would be crucifixes, blessed candles, scapulars, medals, rosaries, holy pictures and statues of Christ, Mary, saints and angels, blessed palms and ashes, etc. The Church teaches that these objects have no power in themselves. All spiritual power comes ultimately from God Himself. The efficacy of the use of sacramentals does not depend on the rite itself or the object itself, but on the faith and love of the faithful in prayerful petition and praise. The validity of words, actions, objects, and gestures involved in these things draw from the personal dispositions of faith, hope and love of the individual and on the prayers of the whole Mystical Body of Christ relying on the infinite merits of Jesus Christ.

It has been approximately two thousand years since Jesus Christ came to this earth; how can anyone say that in all the centuries since the Incarnation and Redemption God has never used objects except Paul's handkerchiefs and aprons?

> So remarkable were the miracles worked by God at Paul's hands that handkerchiefs or aprons which had touched him were taken to the sick, and they were cured of their illnesses, and the evil spirits came out of them (Acts 19:12).

Occasionally there have been as already noted miraculous cures reported by those who with faith in Jesus Christ were immersed into the waters at Lourdes. The use of cures by bathing in waters is not foreign to accounts in either the Old or New Testaments of the Bible. There is the account in 2 Kings, chapter 5, of Naaman being cured from a virulent skin disease. Naaman was instructed by the prophet Elisha,

> "Go and bathe seven times in the Jordan, and your flesh will become clean once more." But Naaman was indignant and went off, saying, "Here was I, thinking he would be sure to come out to me, and stand there, and call on the name of Yahweh his God, and wave his hand over the spot and cure the part that was diseased. Surely, Abana and Parpar, the rivers of Damascus, are better than any water in Israel? Could I not bathe in them and become clean?" And he turned round and went off in a rage. But his servants approached him and said, "Father, if the prophet had asked you to do something difficult, would you not have done it? All the more reason, then, when he says to you, 'Bathe here and you will become clean.' " So he went down and immersed himself seven times in the Jordan, as Elisha had told him to do. And his flesh became clean once more like the flesh

of a little child (2 Kings 5:10-19).

Our Lord Jesus Christ spoke of this cure of Naaman. "And in the prophet Elisha's time there were many sufferings from virulent skin diseases in Israel, but none of these was cured — only Naaman the Syrian" (Luke 4:27).

Chapter 5 of John tells of the pool called Bethesda in Jerusalem which had five porticos:

> and under these were crowds of sick people, blind, lame, paralyzed. One man there had an illness which had lasted thirty-eight years, and when Jesus saw him lying there and knew he had been in that condition for a long time, He said, "Do you want to be well again?" "Sir," replied the sick man, "I have no one to put me into the pool when the water is disturbed; and while I am still on the way, someone else gets down there before me." Jesus said, "Get up, pick up your sleeping-mat and walk around." The man was cured at once, and he picked up his mat and started to walk around (vv. 1-9).

In John 9 we see Jesus healing a blind man, using two materials, a paste and the waters of Siloam:

> ... He spat on the ground, made a paste with the spittle, put this over the eyes of the blind man, and said to him, "Go and wash in the Pool of Siloam (the name means 'one who has been sent')." So he went off and washed and came back able to see (vv. 6-7).

There was also a woman who had suffered from a hemorrhage for twelve years, and "after long and painful treatment under various doctors, she had spent all she had without being any better for it ...." She had great faith in Jesus. Her faith was so strong in Jesus that touching His *garments* would suffice for healing.

> She had heard about Jesus, and she came up through the crowd and touched his cloak from behind, thinking, "If I can just touch his clothes, I shall be saved." And at once the source of the bleeding dried up and she felt in herself that she was cured of her complaint ... (Mark 5:25-34).

There is surely a sufficient number of miraculous healings in the Bible in which objects play an important role — contrary to the opinion that there is no Biblical basis for God working through objects. The curing waters of Lourdes, and, although lesser known, that of Fatima, is certainly not without precedent in Sacred Scripture.

The Marian shrines of the world are Christ-centered. The Rosary itself, when properly understood, is Christ-centered. (See questions in final chapter). Every major Marian shrine of the Catholic world is centered on Jesus Christ and the worship of the Blessed Trinity in, with and through Jesus Christ in the Eucharistic Liturgy. Jesus takes precedence over every devotion conducted at these shrines. There is no question of rejecting or replacing Jesus Christ. Jesus is always central to authentic Marian devotion or it is not authentic. Mary and the saints now in heaven are the greatest victories of Jesus Christ.

It was surely of the saints who have passed from this world into the eternal glory of the just, as reflected in Christ who obtained it for them, that St. Paul wrote in the second epistle to the Thessalonians:

> Indeed it is just on the part of God to repay with affliction those who afflict you, and to give you who are afflicted rest with us at the revelation of the Lord Jesus, who will come from heaven with the angels of His power, in flaming fire, to inflict punishment on those who do not know God, and who do not obey the Gospel of our Lord Jesus Christ. These will be punished with eternal ruin, away from the face of the Lord and the glory of His power, when on that day He shall come to be glorified in His saints, and to be marvelled at in all those who have believed. For our testimony before you has been believed. (2 Thes. 1:6-10).

St. Paul is speaking here of the *parousia*, or Second Coming of Christ (cf. Matt. 24, 30f). God is "glorified in his saints" in heaven, as indicated here, and it will be manifested to all at the end of the world. Yet, God is glorified in His holy ones who even at this moment are in heaven giving Him glory, something which we all hope to do eternally.

Most Christians of the world recite the Apostles' Creed which, it is believed, was handed down by the Apostles as a formula for belief, in twelve articles, containing the fundamental doctrines of Christianity. In it, one professes faith in "the communion of saints." This communion of the saints means that the faithful on earth are in communion with those who have left this world in faith and divine charity (grace). As the saints (Christians upon earth) should honor one another, so in the Apostles' Creed we profess to continue honoring those glorified members of the Church, now in heaven, by invoking their prayers and striving to imitate their virtues. We do not worship them as we do not worship the saints still living upon the earth.

When Mary prophesied that "all ages to come shall call me blessed" (Luke 1:48) she was speaking under the influence of the Holy Spirit, saying that we would honor her even after she had died and left this world. After Jesus we honor Mary in a special way, more than other saints, because God has honored her above all. Is this prophecy in Sacred Scripture not a call to honor the Queen of Saints, as we must adore as well the King of Saints, Jesus Christ?

As previously noted, the early Church had first to clearly establish in the mind of early Christians that Jesus was true God and true man. The first converts had come in many cases from paganism and from Jews for whom the Incarnation, God become man, crucified, was quite a "stumbling block." The devotion to Mary and the other saints gained attention as Christianity was accepted and spread. But the veneration of Mary and the other saints was by no means something that began only after several centuries, even as late as the fifth century, as is sometimes claimed. We have already shown that the catacombs give evidence yet today that the first Christians honored the remains of early Christian martyrs and sought the intercession of their brethren who had gone to their death believing and practicing the faith in Jesus Christ. The many inscriptions in the Roman catacombs of the first Christians leave no doubt that the first Christians cultivated with great piety the memory of the dead. Vatican II states:

> The Church has always believed that the Apostles, and Christ's martyrs who had given the supreme witness of faith and charity by the shedding of their blood, are quite closely joined with us in Christ. She has always venerated them with special devotion, together with the Blessed Virgin Mary and the holy angels. The Church too has devoutly implored the aid of their intercession. To these were soon added those who had imitated Christ's virginity and poverty more exactly, and finally others whom the outstanding practice of the Christian virtues and the divine charisms recommended to the pious devotion and initiation of the faithful.
>
> (*Dogmatic Constitution on the Church,*
> *Lumen Gentium,* Vatican II, n. 50).

> In the earthly liturgy, by way of foretaste, we share in that heavenly liturgy which is celebrated in the holy city of Jerusalem toward which we journey as pilgrims, and in which Christ is sitting at the right hand of God, a minister of the sanctuary and of the true tabernacle (cf. Apoc. 21:2; Col. 3:1; Heb. 8:2); we sing a hymn to the Lord's glory with all the warriors of the heavenly army; venerating the memory of the saints, we hope for some part and fellowship with them; we eagerly await the Savior, our Lord Jesus Christ, until He, our life, shall appear and we too will appear with Him in glory. (cf. Phil. 3:20; Col. 3:4).
>
> (*Constitution on the Sacred Liturgy,* Vatican II, n. 8).

The saints have been traditionally honored in the Church and their authentic relics and images held in veneration. For the feasts of the saints proclaim the wonderful works of Christ in His servants, and display to the faithful fitting examples for their imitation.

Lest the feasts of the saints, however, take precedence over the feasts which commemorate the very mysteries of salvation, many of them should be left to be celebrated by a particular church or nation or religious community; only those should be extended to the universal Church which commemorate saints who are truly of universal significance.

(*Constitution on the Sacred Liturgy*, Vatican II, n. 111).

Let the people be instructed that our communion with those in heaven provided that it is understood in the more adequate light of faith, in no way weakens, but conversely, more thoroughly enriches the supreme worship we give to God the Father, through Christ in the Spirit.

(*Lumen Gentium*, Vatican II, n. 51)

The three shepherd children of Fatima (from left):
Jacinta, Lucia, and Francisco

A little boy stands before the statue of Francisco, one of the seers at Fatima. (Fatima Family Shrine, Alexandria, South Dakota)

"... for behold, henceforth all generations shall call me blessed."
(Luke 1:48)

# CHAPTER 8

# Mary, The Mother of God

The title of this chapter was used as the title of an article on Catholicism in the magazine, *The Evangelist*, except that it had a question mark at the end. Below are extensive quotes indicating how fundamentalists view both Mary and Catholic concepts of Mary.

> *A former Catholic priest wrote, "I can personally testify to the fact that the Jesus Christ I knew, loved, and served as a Roman Catholic is not the same Jesus Christ I know, love, and serve today. The Jesus I once knew was a wafer of bread and a cup of wine — He had a mother called Mary who stood between Him and me. I couldn't get through to Him except through her, and He couldn't get through to me except through her. In other words, my religion back then was tantamount to — let's say — Buddhism or the Muslim religion. There was no difference, objectively speaking, between me as a Catholic priest, and a Moslem priest, for example."*

"These are some of the saddest words I've ever read," continues the article in *The Evangelist*, a fundamentalist publication sent throughout the U.S.A.

> *In this article, I want to look at Mary as the Catholic sees her, Mary as the mediator between Jesus Christ and man, and Mary as the Bible describes her ... . Catholics feel that Mary occupies a unique and tremendously influential position as a result of her role as Christ's human mother. They are taught that they can safely entrust all their problems to her. She provides the spiritual key to salvation of the soul and to receiving miraculous answers to prayers concerning more earthly problems.*

*Catholics* are *taught (although they will deny this) that Mary is to be given worship equal to God — and higher than that afforded the angels and saints. She is to be addressed as "My Mother." ...*

*No. Mary is* not *the mother of God. Mary was the mother of the human being, Jesus. Mary served a biological function that was necessary to bring about a* unique *situation. The* preexistent *Son of God was to take on* human *form. As He walked the earth (in human form) He was very God and very man. His "God" component had always been. While Mary was essential to harbor His developing* human *form (for nine months) she had* nothing whatsoever to do with his Godly being! *Mary was, therefore, the mother of Jesus, the man. She was* not, *by any stretch of the imagination, the "Mother of God."*

*God has no mother. If one understands the incarnation, one understands that God, while never ceasing to be God, became completely* man ... .

*The Bible tells us that the Angel Gabriel was sent from God to a virgin named Mary. Luke 1:28 states:*

*"And the angel came in unto her, and said, Hail, thou art highly favoured, the Lord is with thee: blessed art thou among women."*

*Using this passage, the Catholic Church has altered the words to read: "Hail, Mary,* full of grace' ... .

*The unbiblical worship of Mary has its perverted foundation in the insupportable misnomer, "Mother of God." The* correct *scriptural description of Mary is the simple Biblical expression, "Mother of Jesus, our Lord." ...*

*The doctrine of the Immaculate Conception implies that for Mary to be born without original sin, her mother had to also be a sinless virgin. The only alternative is that God granted her a unique immunity to the all-pervasive original sin that is an inescapable element of the human condition.*

*To be frank, Roman Catholic theologians lamely defend their assertion of the Immaculate Conception by saying that "God could have done it" or "it was fitting that He should do so — and therefore He did it."*

*But of course if God had decided on such a course, it would have meant that He was replacing the plan of salvation described in the Bible with a totally new concept. If this had*

happened, we would have a quadrinity inste.
ty. *God's Word would have then stated that the*
*sists of God the Father, God the Son, God the Holy*
*Mary, the Mother of God. The Bible does not so state,*
*then conclude that this aberrant doctrine is* not of Go

*In 1950, Pope Pius XII pronounced the doctrine of the*
*sumption of Mary." This states that Mary, at the comple. n*
*of her earthly life, was bodily taken up into heaven without*
*knowing death. Oddly enough, this mystical belief had been*
*a peripheral precept within the Catholic Church since the Mid-*
*dle Ages, but was only given official certification in 1950. There*
*was a* great *deal of resistance to the issuance of this doctrine by*
*Pius XII, but he insisted that it was his infallible right to declare*
*such a "fact."*

*Fundamentally, the worship of Mary originated with the wor-*
*ship of "The Queen of Heaven" — a pagan deity. It seems that*
*the Roman Church — in altering its doctrines to conform*
*to those formerly observed by conscripted pagans — saw that it*
*would be politically desirable to supply the populace with*
*a satisfying parallel figure within their newly imposed*
*Christian religion.*

*The image of mother and child had been a primary object of*
*Babylonian worship for centuries before the birth of Christ.*
*From Babylon, this spread to the ends of the earth. The original*
*mother figure in this tableau was Semiramis — the personifica-*
*tion of unbridled lust and sexual gratification. And once we*
*start to study the worship practices of heathen nations, we find*
*amazing similarities embraced over wide areas and through*
*long periods of time . . . .*

*Incredibly, the Catholic position is that no grace flows from*
*God to any person without passing through the good offices*
*of Mary! . . .*

*The Roman cult of Mary erects a barrier between the individ-*
*ual and the Trinity. It confuses the Catholic believer's percep-*
*tion of the work and functions of the individual members of the*
*Godhead. It robs Christ of His unique creatorship . . . .*

*No man can come to me, except the Father which hath sent*
*me draw him" (John 6:43-44) . . . .*

*So, according to the Bible, Mary has* no *role to play in the*
*salvation of a soul.*

*I go back once again to our quote from a former Catholic*

*priest: The Jesus I once knew was a wafer of bread and a cup of wine, and He had a mother called Mary who stood between Him and me . . . ." Does this statement sound like* he *was "led to Christ by Mary"? . . .*

*In ascribing the Immaculate Conception to Mary, the Catholic Church has, in effect, declared her divine, and thus renders her worship that* should *be reserved only for Deity. By their constant reference to her, worship is afforded.*

*Yes, Catholics* do *worship Mary. To be tragically concise, most Catholics don't understand the worship of God the Father or of His Son, Jesus Christ. Their real focus and conception of worship is to Mary. And of course their perception of worshipping God is the worship of God* through *Mary. Everything* must go through Mary *to God — and everything must* come from *God through Mary.*

*To be brutally frank, there is very little mention of Mary within the word of God . . . .*

*In Luke 1:38, Mary called herself* "the handmaiden of the Lord." *This describes the beautiful humility that she had, and is a statement that might well be studied by Catholic theologians.*

However, there is a tremendous difference between "the handmaiden of the Lord" and "the Mother of God."

*Mary herself, in Luke 1:47 refutes the Catholic Immaculate Conception doctrine because she said, "And my spirit hath rejoiced in God my Savior." This statement totally discounts the theory of an Immaculate Conception and the Catholic contention that Mary was ever without sin. If God was her Savior, then she must have needed salvation, which presupposes some history of normal human sin.* No Scripture even hints that Mary was sinless.

*This false cult of Mary worship is another effort by Satan, who knows that one cannot completely accept Christ as long as he retains heretical concepts of Mary. And, incidentally, Luke's statement in 1:28 quotes God's words as being,* "Blessed art thou among women." *It does not say,* "Blessed are thou above women ... ."

*Jesus Christ is our only intercessor. There is no hint or suggestion in the Word of God that Mary should or would occupy such a role. Whenever Mary is inserted into the role of intercessor (as she is by the Catholic Church, to intercede with her Son Jesus*

*Christ on behalf of individuals on earth), this, in effect, robs Christ of the rightful position He earned through His tremendous sacrifice on Calvary. He paid the full price on that cross with the shedding of His precious blood.*

*Christ alone is worthy to make intercession for us. Christ alone paid the price. Mary did not suffer and die on the cross. She did not shed her blood. And neither does Christ need an assistant to motivate Him to make intercession for the saints. He's perfectly capable of performing this duty Himself as He ever sits at the right hand of God, making intercession for us (Romans 8:34).*

*There is no hint in the Bible that Christ will have a "staff" to assist Him, nor that Mary has any role to perform in such a position. There is no need for additonal mediators or motivators.*

We blaspheme when we imply that Jesus Christ would not satisfactorily accomplish His eternal job without permission from His earthly mother . . . .

*The Roman Catholic position is that God the Father and His Son, Jesus Christ, are, through normal human efforts, unreachable. By extension, they then propose that since Christ's mother is available, that petitions delivered by her will not be ignored . . . .*

*The Evangelist,* December 1985
(original emphases indicated in roman type in the above)

The above was quoted at length to acquaint the reader with the attacks of fundamentalists against Catholic teachings regarding the Blessed Virgin Mary. Most of their attacks have been included with perhaps the exception of their denial of the perpetual virginity of Mary, claiming she had other children.

What can be especially dangerous are half-truths. The reader is led to think that the Church teaches differently about Jesus and Mary than it actually does. The fundamentalists who pass themselves off as understanding even better than Catholics what the Catholic Church teaches about Mary would have us think that the Church is replacing Christ Jesus as the one essential Mediator between God and mankind with other mediators and intercessors, especially replaced by Mary. They present the Catholic teaching as claiming that Mary merited her own priviliges and took away from the universal saving role of Jesus Christ. The Catholic Church teaches just the opposite.

Not all Protestants share the extreme views of Mary that some fundamentalists promote in attempting to discredit Catholic Marian devotion. Eastern Orthodox Christians, who number in the millions, have a devotion to Mary very similar to Roman Catholics. Many Lutherans and Anglicans have high convictions about Mary. An excellent book on meditating the mysteries of the Rosary was written by a Methodist minister, J. Neville Ward, *Five for Sorrow, Ten for Joy.*

There are many Roman Catholic priests today who are converted from various Protestant denominations. Some were Protestant ministers. I am personally acquainted with priests who belonged to non-Catholic denominations. I've never known any such priest to attack their former faith. On the other hand, former priests have been welcomed into some pulpits not favorable to Catholicism. They are quoted in publications attacking the Catholic Church as they misrepresent their former Catholic faith. There have been many incidences where devout Catholic people and loyal priests have accepted invitations open to the public where a "former priest" would speak of his experiences as a Catholic. Seeing priests in the audience has usually caused such speakers misrepresenting Catholicism to break down or become extremely nervous in their delivery. Some years ago the Catholic press carried a report of a "former priest" speaking in a local fundamentalistic church. Five area priests sat in the front row. The "former priest" found the pressure too great as he beheld the priests before him. He shouted, "Why do you persecute me?" The priests had not said a word.

One can sympathize with a "former priest" who loses his perspective or who found the demands of life too great. While much could be written about their rejection of God's grace, there is also the possibility of serious psychological problems beyond the control of some people thus afflicted. Priests are human and are subject to the same attacks of mind and body as are lay people. There have been priests who have betrayed our Divine Lord Jesus Christ for years and then received the grace to "come back home." The author of this book once had the privilege of personally hearing from a priest returned to his Father's House who wrote of his great sorrow and need to do penance. One cannot but help admire their humility and rejoice with their reclaimed grace as one does with Peter who denied our Lord Jesus Christ three times in His darkest hour and then later wept and made a three-fold profession of faith and love after Jesus' Resurrection (John 21:1-19).

One can have the greatest compassion for a priest that falls due to human weakness. What is more tragic is when the fall is of pride and the priest misrepresents Catholic teachings. The two thousand year history of the Church has taught that at times intellectual pride has led some theologians, priests, and religious as well as laity, astray and into darkness. There have been cases of bitterness when one did not feel he was treated fairly enough and revolted against the bishop or religious superior and then, begrudgingly struck out against the Church. There have been cases of human weakness followed by pride in the attempt to justify one's life of immorality. God is ultimately the Judge. It is not for any of us to judge the soul of another regarding their eternal salvation. It is obviously equally tragic when a "former priest" deliberately misrepresents his Church, and thereby misrepresents Jesus Christ.

It has never occurred to this writer in talking to priests who were members of other denominations even to suggest that they say or think anything derogatory about their former faith. Knowing that it has been, rather, a case of a fuller flowering from the bud of Christianity as they formerly knew it, I simply had cause to rejoice — not that they had turned their back on anything; they had not. They simply found fulfillment.

Mention is made here of "former priests" for in the writings of fundamentalists occasional use is made of these men who are presented as their "best evidence of what the Catholic Church actually teaches." In reality, it is the worst evidence and usually dishonest. "Former priests" is put in parentheses because in reality there is no such thing as a "former priest." According to Catholic doctrine, once a priest, always a priest for all eternity.

There have been other defectors from the faith. Did Judas have faith? There was nothing wrong with what Jesus, our Lord, God and Savior taught. Judas followed our Lord and heard His teachings during the three years of His public ministry. He obviously witnessed the many miracles of Jesus Christ. Judas was at the Last Supper when Jesus instituted the Holy Eucharist but left early to betray our Divine Lord. The long account of Jesus concerning the Passover of the Bread of Life recorded in the sixth chapter of St. John's Gospel ends with these words,

> "Did I not choose the Twelve of you? Yet one of you is a devil."
> He meant Judas son of Simon Iscariot, since this was the man, one of the Twelve, who was to betray Him (vv. 70-71).

Do we use Judas as evidence against Jesus or the early Church? Our Divine Lord obviously knew there would be other Judases and just as we can point no finger against Jesus or the early Church because one of the Twelve betrayed Him, neither is it valid to do so with those who betray our Lord and His Church today.

If the "former priest" is honest in what he wrote, he never had the Christian faith of any kind, for neither Buddhists, nor Muslims believe in Jesus Christ as Lord, God, and Savior. They do not believe that God became man in Jesus Christ, Who redeemed us by His death on the Cross. The Catholic Church does not teach that Jesus is a "wafer of bread and a cup of wine." Such is nonsense.

The late Archbishop Fulton J. Sheen once told of an experience he had while conducting a retreat for priests. One priest came to the archbishop claiming a theological problem concerning Catholic teaching on the Holy Eucharist. "Well, I'll explain it to you," said Archbishop Sheen as he went through the Sacred Scriptures pointing out foreshadowings of the Holy Eucharist in the Old Testament and fulfillment in the New Testament. The archbishop carefully explained the Scriptures and the doctrines of Catholicism concerning the Eucharist. Later the priest came back to the Archbishop claiming he still had a theological problem concerning the Eucharist. "Well, I'll explain it again," said Archbishop Sheen. "Let me try it this way ... " as he again explained the Catholic doctrine drawing from the Scriptures and the constant teachings of the Church through the centuries. The priest responded to all this with, "I still don't see it. I still am having a theological problem." Archbishop Sheen looked at the priest and said, "Your problem is not theological. Is it a blonde or a brunette?" The priest said, "I resent that." "You think it over," said the archbishop. A few hours later the priest returned and said to Archbishop Sheen, "It's a blonde."

This mistrust of the fundamentalist for the testimony of *true* Catholics is seen in the fundamentalist's admission that Catholics themselves deny that they give Mary equal worship with God. Their implication is: no matter what individual Catholics say or the Church says it teaches, it actually teaches something else. Jimmy Swaggert, who wrote this accusation, is not an ignorant man. It is difficult to believe he is sincere in such rash accusations. Rather, he is merely attempting to lead Catholics out of the Church by confusing them, while keeping others out of the two-thousand-year-old Church founded by Jesus Christ.

The Catholic Church condemns the adoration of anyone except God Himself. Worship given to God is adoration. Veneration is generally the word used when directed to the angels, saints, and to Mary. Worship can be used in the general sense to include both the adoration given God and veneration given the angels and saints. But even when worship is used in the sense of veneration, to say Catholics give equal worship (veneration) to God and to Mary is not only a false-hood but echoes what the Catholic Church in reality condemns. An-gels and saints are honored for their sanctity. They are asked to inter-cede before the Divine Majesty. We are asked to imitate them in their love and service of God as they lived the Christian life. If the angels and saints — that includes Mary, too — go to the Father on our behalf, they too must go through the one essential Mediator, Jesus Christ. They are not tied down to our limitations of space or time and in an in-stant many can be praising the Blessed Trinity in all its infinite glory and at the same time invoking the Triune God through the humanity of Jesus Christ.

We can certainly go to the Father, in the unity of the Holy Spirit through the humanity of Jesus Christ, Mediator, without the need to think of Mary, the angels or saints.

What the fundamentalist does in the above quoted article is to di-vide the humanity of Christ from His divinity. Fundamentalists are so disturbed with the title "Mother of God" and can feel comfortable only with "Mother of Jesus" and present Mary's role as giving birth only to the human nature of Jesus Christ. What happens to the Person of Jesus Christ which is the Second Person of the Most Blessed Trinity? Was Jesus not a Person? Did Mary give birth to a human nature that was not a person? If so, she would have given birth to a monstrosity.

Jesus Christ is true God and true man. The creed, which was handed down from the early Church and used at Sunday Mass puts it this way:

> We believe in one Lord, Jesus Christ, the only Son of God, eternal-ly begotten of the Father, God from God, Light from Light, true God from true God, begotten, not made, one in being with the Father. Through Him all things were made. For us men and for our salvation He came down from heaven: by the power of the Holy Spirit He was born of the Virgin Mary, and became man . . . .

The attack on Catholicism quoted at the beginning of this chapter says, "God had no mother . . . . God . . . became completely *man* . . . ." Is Jesus "completely" man? If by "completely" here is meant that Jesus in His divine Person is wholly God the Son and He took on a true human nature, we would agree. One must distinguish between the eternal divine Person of Jesus, which always was and will be, and the created human *nature*. What the fundamentalists are saying is that Mary is mother of the human nature of Jesus Christ but not of His di-vine Person. But there is only one Person in Jesus Christ, the Second Person of the Blessed Trinity. In Jesus Christ there is a human *nature* but not a human *person*. The Angel Gabriel, in explaining to Mary that she would conceive the Christ Child by the power of the Holy Spirit added, "And so the child will be holy and will be called Son of God" (Luke 1:35). The Child, which would be the Son of God, would also be the Son of Mary. That is why Jesus referred to Himself for the most part as "Son of Man." He became Son of Man by becoming Son of Mary through the power of the Holy Spirit.

Mary did not become the Mother of God the Father or of God the Holy Spirit, although as the highly favored daughter of God the Father, she did become the Spouse of the Holy Spirit in order to be the Mother of God the Son.

Jesus Christ is true man and the true Son of God. Jesus Christ took to Himself a real physical body, not a phantom body. The Son of God assumed not only a real human body but also a rational human soul. Christ was and is truly generated by the Father from all eternity, and in time, was born of the Virgin Mary in His human nature. When Mary had just conceived the Christ Child, she was told by the angel that her aged cousin Elizabeth "has conceived a son, and she whom people called barren is now in her sixth month" (Luke 1:36). The passage continues,

> Mary set out at that time and went as quickly as she could into the hill country to a town in Judah. She went into Zechariah's house and greeted Elizabeth. Now it happened that as soon as Elizabeth heard Mary's greeting, the child leapt in her womb and Elizabeth was filled with the Holy Spirit. She gave a loud cry and said, "Of all women you are the most blessed, and blessed is the fruit of your womb. Why should I be honoured with a visit from the mother of my Lord?" (Luke 1:39-43).

Notice that Elizabeth, under the influence of the Holy Spirit, called Mary, who had only recently conceived the Christ Child, "the mother of my Lord." "Lord" is the title commonly used for God in the Old Testament (Adonai). It is commonly applied to Christ in the New Testament (Kyrios). The consistent way that St. Paul as well as other New Testament writers use the term for Christ indicates that they regarded Him as God. "The mother of my Lord" is certainly the equivalent of "mother of my God." To say there is nothing in Scripture to indicate that Mary became God's mother is unbiblical.

The majority of Christians in the world accept the term "Mother of God," including millions of Orthodox, which are mostly in the eastern part of the world. The very use of the term "Mother of God" protects the divinity of Jesus Christ. When the Catholic Church at the Council of Ephesus in 431 A.D. defined that Mary is truly the Mother of God, the main concern of the Church was not to render greater glory to Mary. The dispute concerned protecting the truth that Jesus Christ is truly divine, the Son of God, the Second Person of the Blessed Trinity. Did Mary give birth to a Person who is divine? If so, Jesus is God and Mary is His Mother.

The fundamentalist, who usually knows nothing of scholastic philosophy and thinks more in contemporary meanings and languages interpreted literally, fails to grasp what the Church is saying and feels threatened and supposes the Church is downgrading Christ and elevating Mary to divinity. Such a conclusion is totally false. Compared to the Person of Jesus Christ Who is divine — God Himself — Mary is less than an atom. The Person of Jesus is infinite and uncreated. The person of Mary is finite and created in time. The Person of Jesus is from eternity. The person of Mary was created about two thousand years ago.

There is one *Person* in Jesus Christ. That Person is God the Son. There are two *natures* in Jesus Christ, the divine nature and the human nature. The divine and human natures of Jesus Christ are "hypostatically" united, that is, they are joined to each other in one divine Person, the Second Person of the eternal and Most Blessed Trinity. Such is the teaching of the Church. To say that Mary is not the Mother of God is to say that she is not the Mother of the Person to whom she gave birth. That infant Jesus in the womb of Mary, that Child she conceived and carried for nine months in her womb and finally gave birth to, indeed had a human nature united to the very Person of the Son of God. To deny that Mary gave birth to this divine Person is to deny belief in the divinity of Jesus Christ, as some have done who have thought of themselves as Christians. Essential to being a Christian is a professed faith in Jesus Christ as Lord, God and Savior, the Second Person of the Three Persons in One God. There were not two persons in the Son of Man, Jesus Christ. He is one divine Person.

Notice that in the criticism of Catholic doctrine in the beginning of this chapter regarding Mary as the Mother of God is the typical fundamentalist position:

> *While Mary was essential to harbor His developing human form (for nine months) she had nothing whatsoever to do with His Godly being! Mary was, therefore, the mother of Jesus, the man. She was not, by any stretch of the imagination, the "Mother of God."*

That statement falls into the trap of Nestorianism, a fifth-century heresy that held that there were two distinct persons in the Incarnate Christ, one human and the other divine, as against the teaching of the Church, which is that Christ was a *divine Person* who assumed a *human nature.* Obviously Jesus was and is a person. To say that Mary is not the Mother of God the Son but only of Jesus is equivalent to saying that Jesus was a human person, because Mary had to be the Mother of a person. This is the error of Nestorianism, rejected by Christians over 1,550 years ago.

The heresy of Nestorianism took its name from Nestorius (died c. 451), a native of Germanicia in Syria, and later Bishop of Constantinople. Nestorianism was condemned by the ecumenical Council of Ephesus in 431, a Council which hundreds of millions of Orthodox accept to this day. While fundamentalists are prone to deny the authority of Councils of the Church, even those of early centuries, we nonetheless present the problem of Nestorianism as a repetition of what can develop when Christians today pick up the Bible and privately interpret it, ignoring the wisdom of the centuries and the guidance of the Holy Spirit shown to earlier Christians and accepted by most Christians.

Nestorius postulated two separated persons in Christ. When he came to describe their union, he could not have them joined ontologically (in their being) or hypostatically (constituting one person), but only morally or psychologically. They would be united only by a perfect agreement of two wills in Christ, and by a harmonious communication of their respective activities. This harmony of wills (*eudoxia*) and the communion of action to which it gives rise are, according to Nestorious, what form the composite personality (*henosia*) of Christ.

In the Nestorian idea we cannot speak of a true communication of idioms, i.e., that while the two natures of Christ are distinct the attributes of one may be predicated of the other in view of their union in one person of Christ. Therefore it could not be said that God was born, that He was crucified or died. The conclusion would be that Mary is not the Mother of God, but had given birth to a man whose human personality was somehow conjoined to the Word of God. Christ Jesus in that case would not have been the Son of God.

Those who followed the error of Nestorius continued to propagate their views. The confusion which resulted produced among the people a heresy that contributed to the success of Islamism in the seventh century.*

It was the great convert John Cardinal Newman who in the last century pointed out that the early Fathers of the Church spoke of Mary because it was important to tell her story in order to know Christ's. It was the Council of Ephesus (431) that condemned Nestorianism. That Council gave Mary the title, Mother of the Son of God made Man. The concern of first importance was to recognize faith in the real unity of the divine and human natures in the *one* divine Person of Jesus Christ. As a consequence of it being recognized as the official position of faith that there is but one Person in Jesus Christ, the Divine Person of the Son of God, Mary is seen to be the Mother of God.

The Catholic Church has not altered words of the Bible when it prays, "Hail Mary, full of grace." It is merely borrowing from the Bible in the formulation of a prayer. Catholic editions of the Bible record the Angel from heaven addressing the Woman chosen to be the Mother of the Messiah, not as "Mary" but as "full of grace." "*Gratia plena*" (full of grace), a special name given this Woman by heaven, is one of the references used to explain how it is divinely revealed that Mary was conceived free of Original Sin. The Church came to realize ever more clearly that it was divinely revealed that "full of grace," a name given to a virgin, could not be given to anyone who was sinful or had ever been in sin. Biblical names describe the very nature of a person, and the name "full of grace" gives the very nature in which Mary was created.

Various modern English translations of Luke 1:28-29 are in use. Examples are, "Rejoice, you who enjoy God's favour! The Lord is with you" (*New Jerusalem Bible*). "Rejoice, O highly favored daughter! The Lord is with you" (*The New American Bible*). "Hail, full of grace, the Lord is with thee. Blessed art thou among women" (*Douay and Confraternity versions*). Whatever version is used, including non-Catholic editions, as quoted in the introduction, the validity of Mary's special grace still holds. Both Catholic and other Christian translations have it, "highly favored daughter," which scholars see as describing Mary to be the recipient of the divine favor, i.e., of the sanctifying power of

---

* Islamism, or Mohammedanism, is a religion practiced by millions even today in southeastern Europe, Asia Minor, Arabia, Persia, India, North Africa and parts of Asia. It was founded by Mohammed, a native of Arabia, and is a mixture of paganism, Christianity, and Judaism. It looks at Christ as a prophet but not as divine. It honors Mary and accepts the Immaculate Conception.

God, in view of her office as Mother of the Messiah, which the Angel announced.

However translated, "Full of grace" or "Hail, thou that art highly favoured," the title recognizes the perfect union of Mary's will with the will of God. This fullness of grace in Mary, so full that she is conceived immaculate, is dependent on the infinite merits of Jesus Christ. According to Catholic teachings, Mary did not merit her own great privileges. Jesus is Mary's Savior, too. Jesus merited Mary's privileges, too, including her having been conceived without original sin and never having committed the slightest sin during her entire life upon earth.

There is no grace in Mary that does not have its source in the Author of divine life for men, Jesus Christ. Just as all grace we receive comes from and through Jesus Christ, so it is with Mary. Any grace that we receive through Mary's intercession with Jesus comes not from herself but from the humanity of her divine Son which is one with the Father. "I give them eternal life; they will never be lost and no one will ever steal them from my hand. The Father, for what He has given me, is greater than anyone, and no one can steal anything from the Father's hand. The Father and I are one" (John 10:28-30).

Mary is a creature formed by the hand of God. She is a willing instrument in the plan of God whereby God the Father, through the overshadowing of the Holy Spirit (Luke 1:35) gives the world His Son for our salvation. It is always God become man we are encountering in Jesus Christ. In Mary we encounter the one whom God used to become man so that we might become like God, sharing His divine life. When Jesus said, "I am the way, and the truth, and the Life; no one comes to the Father, but by me" (John 14:6), He included Mary. When Jesus said, "I am the vine, you are the branches. He who abides in Me, and I in him, he it is that bears much fruit, for apart from Me you can do nothing" (John 15:5), He included His Mother as well.

One of the most popular spiritual writers among Catholics in the past century concerning Mary is St. Louis de Montfort. He began his *True Devotion to the Blessed Virgin* with these words,

> I behold, with the entire Church, that, in comparison with the infinite majesty of the Most High God, Mary is no more than a mere creature formed by His hand; that, in the light of such a comparison, she is less than an atom — no more, that she is nothing, since only He Who Is has existence as of Himself.

Consequently, this great Lord, eternally independent and sufficient unto Himself, had absolutely no need — and still has no need — of the Blessed Virgin for the fulfillment of His designs and for the manifestation of His glory. He has merely to wish, and all is fulfilled.

This introduction by Father Louis de Montfort correctly represents the position of the Catholic Church regarding Mary. He has been canonized by the Church. A lengthy investigation must be undertaken before anyone is canonized, that is, declared to have lived a very holy life and died in God's grace and gone to heaven. If the person in question wrote, his or her writings are closely scrutinized to make certain the writings were in harmony with the teachings of the Church. The above quoted paragraph would certainly have fallen under that scrutiny, for St. Louis De Montfort is considered one of the greatest of saints known for his devotion to Mary. His book, *True Devotion*, is his best known book throughout the world.

It is significant that in attacking Catholic teaching regarding the intercessory power of Mary with her Divine Son, Jesus Christ, fundamentalists at times willingly acknowledge explicit mention of Mary in Sacred Scripture. But they seem to ignore her presence and intercessory influence with Jesus at the wedding feast of Cana. The account in *The Evangelist*, quoted at the beginning of this chapter, was followed by:

> *In the second chapter of John, she asked Jesus to perform His first public miracle at Cana (Obviously, because of the confidence with which she approached the situation, she knew His capabilities.) Oddly enough, in Mark 3, Matthew 12, and Luke 8, she seems either opposed to His ministry or at least harboring some confusion about His mission. In John 19, it talks about how she stood at the foot of the cross and observed with great sorrow the death of her Son — her Saviour and our Saviour — the Lord Jesus Christ.*

(The sentence with parentheses above is as it appears in *The Evangelist* article.)

It is not an insignificant factor that Mary is present at important moments in the Savior's life upon earth. She must be present at the Annunciation when the Word was made flesh and dwelt among men (Luke 1). Mary is only "betrothed" (v. 27) and does not have conjugal relations, a semitic sense of "know." Genesis, the very first book of the Bible, records that when Adam and Eve had just fallen and God promised salvation, a "woman" is mentioned:

Then Yahweh God said to the snake,
  "Because you have done this,
Accursed be you
of all animals wild and tame!
On your belly you will go
and on dust you will feed
as long as you live.
I shall put enmity
between you and the woman,
and between your offspring and hers;
it will bruise your head
and you will strike its heel."

(Genesis 3:14-15)

The Hebrew text, in proclaiming that the offspring of the snake is henceforth at enmity with the woman's descendants, opposes the human race to the devil and his "seed," his posterity, and hints at ultimate victory. It is the first glimmer of salvation and is often called the *proto-evangelium* (first Gospel). In the Old Testament, revelation was gradual and God's people did not fully and clearly understand it throughout the centuries. Upon fullfilment of the Great Promise and completion of Divine Revelation, it is known that the offspring is Jesus Christ, our Lord and Savior, and the woman is His Mother Mary. It is significant that Jesus calls His Mother, "Woman." She is the Woman whose offspring would be at enmity with the devil and whose child would defeat the forces of evil.

The Greek version of the *proto-evangelium* uses the masculine pronoun "he," not "it" will bruise. This ascribes the victory not to the woman's descendants in general but to a son of the woman in particular. This is why the early Fathers of the Church gave this text of Genesis a Messianic interpretation, the promise of a Messiah who would save mankind from sin. The Latin version has the feminine pronoun, "she" will bruise and since, in the Messianic interpretation of the text, the Messiah and His mother appear together, the pronoun has been taken to refer to Mary. At any rate, the woman is certainly Mary. Her Child is certainly Jesus Christ, God incarnate, Who crushes the head of the serpent.

Isaiah 7:14 is a clearer and fuller unfolding of the revelation about a Messiah to come who would save the people and St. Matthew 1:23 will leave no doubt in our minds that the text is a prophecy of the virginal conception of Jesus.

Yahweh spoke to Ahaz again and said:
"Ask Yahweh your God for a sign,
either in the depths of Sheol or in the heights above.
But Ahaz said, "I will not ask. I will not put Yahweh to the test."
He then said: ...
"The Lord will give you a sign in any case:
It is this: the young woman is with child
and will give birth to a son
whom she will call Immanuel ... .

(Isaiah 7:10-15)

The Greek text reads "the virgin" which is more explicit than the Hebrew which uses "almah" meaning either a young girl or a young, recently married woman. The Greek is an important witness to an early Jewish interpretation, later adopted by the evangelist Matthew (1:23), who tells of Joseph betrothed to Mary "but before they came to live together she was found to be with child" (v. 18). St. Matthew tells then of the virginal fatherhood of Joseph regarding the Christ child, whose name "Immanuel" means "God-is-with-us" (21-25).

When fundamentalists say there is little of Mary in Scripture what is needed is a rereading and meditation on Sacred Scripture again with Mary in mind. Although neither she nor Jesus are mentioned explicitly through the pages of both the Old and New Testament they are implicitly there; Mary appears at times implicitly in prophecy in the Old Testament as "Woman" and "Virgin" or "Young Woman." Mary is always inseparable from her Son whom we learn explicitly in time, in the New Testament, to be our Lord and Savior, Jesus Christ. Mary's role always revolves around and gravitates toward her and our Saviour, Jesus Christ.

Obviously it was the will of God that the Mother of Jesus interceded with her Son and God's Son to advance the Messiah's hour in working His first public miracle, in which His disciples were brought to faith. " ... The mother of Jesus said to him, 'They have no wine.' Jesus said, 'Woman, what do you want from me? My hour has not come yet.' His mother said to the servants, *'Do whatever He tells you.'* " (John 2:1-12). The account is well known to people acquainted with the Bible. It ends with Jesus changing water in six stone water jars, each holding twenty or thirty gallons, into the best wine. "This was the first of Jesus' signs; it was at Cana in Galilee. He revealed His glory, and His disciples believed in Him. After this He went down to Capernaum with His mother and His brothers and His disciples, but they stayed there only a few days."

Our Lord and Savior works His first public miracle at the request of His Mother. Mary's intervention is a prophetic symbol of that hour of Jesus' glorification and later of His return to the Father's right hand. Its approach is noted by John the evangelist, 7:30; 8:20; 12:23, 27; 13:1; 17:1; 19:27. This "hour" is set by the Father and cannot be anticipated, yet, here it is prophetically symbolized, with Mary involved. Mary is always inseparable from Jesus in the Scriptures. How powerful is the intercession of the Mother of Jesus when He, as it were, advances His hour symbolically, and in divine providence works it at the request of His Mother, who first notices the embarrassment about to take place, the need for the happiness of the wedding couple, and whose power of intercession with the Son of God made man brings about His first miracle, thus bringing faith to the Apostles. The Word of God records nothing by accident. All is recorded under the inspiration of the Holy Spirit. Included in the powerful lessons present here is the influence of Mary with Jesus.

When the fundamentalist says that Mary "seems either opposed to His ministry or at least harbors some confusion about His mission" in Mark 3, Matthew 12, and Luke 8, this amounts to contradicting the Word of God as recorded in Luke 1 where the Angel Gabriel calls her "full of grace." Enjoying God's favor, being full of grace, is the fruit of a will fully joined to God's will. Having a will at harmony with God's will is what brings holiness. To suggest that Mary could have been opposed to Jesus' ministry is to deny her holiness and the words of Scripture.

It is significant that the three evangelists Matthew, Mark, and Luke all considered the event in question important to record when there was obviously so much else they could have recorded. John assures us that "there was much else that Jesus did, if it were written down in detail, I do not suppose the world itself would hold all the books that would be written" (John 21:25). The event that the fundamentalist already mentioned refers to, when he mentions Mary's opposition or confusion about Christ's ministry, concerns the time Mary and their relatives stood outside and were anxious to have a word with Jesus when He was speaking to the crowds. A man told Jesus that "His mother and His brothers" (Matt. 12:46-50) were waiting outside. Jesus stretched out His hands towards His disciples and said: "Here are my mother and my brothers. Anyone who does the will of my Father in heaven is my brother and sister and mother." St. Luke quotes our Lord this way: "My mother and my brothers are those who hear the Word of

God and put it into practice" (Luke 8:21).

The Catholic Church has always taught that the essential greatness of Mary is not because she served simply a biological function to bring forth the Savior. Her greatness was because of her great faith and her grace. She accepted the will of God and put it into practice. The early Fathers of the Church, referring to Sacred Scripture, taught that Mary conceived the Word of God in her Heart before she did in her womb. Jesus Christ was not putting His mother down when He spoke as He did. The words of Christ reveal that the greatness of Mary was not due to physical relations simply but to her faith in God's word and doing God's will.

Luke 11:27-28 tells us more.

> It happened that as He was speaking, a woman in the crowd raised her voice and said, "Blessed the womb that bore you and the breasts that fed you!" But He replied, "More blessed still are those who hear the Word of God and keep it!"

Those who live according to the preaching of Jesus truly belong to the family of God. If we hear the Word of God in faith and keep it, it takes hold in us and Christ lives in us by faith, by grace. The Apostle Paul wrote, "For me to live is Christ: and to die is gain" (Phil. 1:21). In Galatians 2:20 the Apostle wrote of being alive in God saying, "Yet it is no longer I, but Christ living in me."

Jesus Christ was telling His listeners that even more important than biologically bringing forth the Messiah was to have faith in that Word of God made flesh. He was not saying that Mary did not have faith or grace. He was not denying her holiness.

If you are going to praise anyone, praise them for the right reason. Mary's blessedness or anyone else's consists in believing the Word of God and keeping it. Was not that the message of the Holy Spirit speaking through Elizabeth shortly after Mary conceived the Christ Child when she went to visit Elizabeth?

> Now it happened that as soon as Elizabeth heard Mary's greeting the child leapt in her womb and Elizabeth was filled with the Holy Spirit. She gave a loud cry and said, "Of all women you are the most blessed, and blessed is the fruit of your womb. Why should I be honoured with a visit from the mother of my Lord? Look, the moment your greeting reached my ears, the child in my womb leapt for joy. Yes, blessed is she who believed that the promise made her by the Lord would be fulfilled."

And Mary said:

My soul proclaims the greatness of the Lord
and my spirit rejoices in God my Savior;
because He has looked upon the humiliation of his servant.
Yes, from now onwards all generations will call me blessed,
because He Who is mighty has done great things for me,
and Holy is His name,
and His faithful love extends age after age
to those who fear Him.
He has used the power of His arm,
He has routed the arrogant of heart.
He has pulled down princes from their thrones
and raised high the lowly.
He has filled the starving with good things,
sent the rich away empty.
He has come to the help of Israel His servant,
mindful of His faithful love
— according to the promise He made to our ancestors —
of His mercy to Abraham and to his descendants forever.

Mary stayed with her some three months and then went home.

(Luke 1:40-56)

The Catholic Church, in harmony with the Scriptures, praises Mary for her great faith. As Abraham was the man of faith in the Old Testament, Mary is the Woman of faith in the New Testament. Notice that Elizabeth, under the influence of the Holy Spirit, does not praise Mary because of a biological function but proclaims "blessed is the fruit of your womb" and "blessed is she who believed."

As the above paragraphs were being written a good mother of a family phoned because her daughter who was away at college had joined an ecumenical Bible discussion club. She had been invited there by her Catholic boyfriend. Obviously the controlled approach was of the fundamentalists. The Catholic girl was becoming quite involved with the discussions and when her mother questioned her involvement, the girl shot back, "Where does it say in the Bible that Mary was holy?" The fundamentalists claim there is little mention of Mary in the Bible. How easy it is to not see what one does not prefer to see. A man convinced against his will is of the same opinion still. The unsuspecting Catholic who is guided through the Bible by the fundamentalist can be easily deceived when an enthusiastic zeal is behind the isolation and interpretation of texts out of context and apart from the intention of the authors used by the Holy Spirit, and apart, consequently, of the Holy Spirit Himself.

When the fundamentalist quoted admits the "beautiful humility" Mary had and that it "might well be studied by Catholic theologians," I can say that as a Catholic priest I well agree. Spiritual writers and theologians in the Catholic Church have studied and meditated on Mary's humility for two thousand years. There must be an emptying of self so that one's spirit can be filled with God, with grace. It is this humility of Mary, not ascribing greatness to herself but to the Lord, while rejoicing in God her Savior, hearing and acting on the Word of God perfectly, that is the key to Mary's holiness. The favorite Marian prayer of the Church through the centuries has been the Magnificat (Luke 1:46-56) quoted above. That prayer is prayed each day by hundreds of thousands of priests, religious and laity the world over in the Catholic Church as they pray the Divine Office or Liturgy of the Hours at Vespers each day.

Yes, indeed, Jesus is Mary's Savior. The Church does not deny that but rather teaches it. Jesus is the Universal Savior. That includes His own Mother. The faith of the Church in Mary being conceived immaculate, that is, without original sin and never having committed the slightest sin goes back to the origins of Christianity. The early Church Fathers wrote of it but not as explicitly as later centuries. This does not mean that they did not believe in the perfect holiness of Mary at every moment of her existence. The early Greek and Latin Fathers professed implicitly the Immaculate Conception. They said she was most perfect in purity of morals and holiness of life.

St. Ephrem (c. 306-73) addressed Jesus and Mary with these words: "You and Your mother are the only ones who are totally beautiful in every way. For in You, O Lord, there is no stain, and in Your mother no stain." The spiritual writers and Fathers of the first centuries of Christianity described Mary as the antithesis of Eve. St. Ephrem said, "Mary and Eve (were) two people without guilt. Later one became the cause of our death, the other cause of our life."

Faith in the Immaculate Conception was always implicitly believed in the Church and contained in the Scriptures: Genesis 3, the Woman whose nature is to be at enmity with the devil; Isaiah 7, the young woman bringing forth a Child Who is "God-is-with-us"; Luke 1, Mary is "full of grace" and "of all women the most blessed" and blessed because of her faith, and whose very soul proclaims the greatness of the Lord, etc.

To be *explicitly* declared a dogma of faith, the Immaculate Conception had to be clarified. It had to be clarified how Mary could be conceived from the first instant of her existence without original sin and yet have Jesus Christ, her Son, for her Savior. God is not bound by time. Everything is always in the mind of God. With God there is no time. In chapter 31 of Jeremiah when Yahweh announces the New Covenant under which Christians live today, God says "I have loved you with an everlasting love" (v. 3). Each one of us was always in the mind of God. With God there is no past or future. All is now. When the time came, God brought forth each one of us always in His mind.

" . . . When the completion of the time came, God sent his Son, born of woman" (Gal. 4:4). From all eternity this was in the mind of God, in the eternal counsels of the Most Blessed Trinity, that in the fullness of time the Second Person of the Trinity would become man, born of a woman. Together with that eternal knowledge of Christ Jesus, was the woman through which this would be accomplished by the overshadowing of the Holy Spirit (Luke 1:35). Each one of us has always been present and loved in the eternal mind of God. God loves us according to our holiness which is in accordance with our response in faith and love to the Word of God. Loving Jesus Christ the God-Man, the Blessed Trinity eternally loved the Woman with whom He is inseparable in Divine Revelation as the Scriptures so well testify. Christ is the New Adam, or Second Adam as the early Fathers saw Him and inseparable from the Woman Mary, whom they called the New Eve or Second Eve.

It was the Franciscan John Duns Scotus (c. 1264-1308) who introduced, not a new doctrine, but a clarification of the sinlessness of Mary. He spoke of the pre-redemption in order to reconcile Mary's freedom from original sin with her conception before the coming of Jesus Christ, Lord and Savior. By a prevenient grace, a grace God gives which is not limited by time, Mary was perfectly redeemed at the moment of her conception. Her conception and her perfect redemption in virtue of the infinite merits of Jesus Christ coincided.

Pope Pius IX's solemn definition made in 1854 was not the beginning of a new teaching but a clarification of an old teaching. In the definition of the Church's faith he wrote:

> The most holy Virgin Mary was, in the first moment of her conception, by a unique gift of grace and privilege of almighty God, in view of the merits of Jesus Christ the Redeemer of mankind, preserved free from all stain of original sin.

This freedom from sin was unmerited. It was a free gift of God, a special grace, a privilege from the law which no other created person has received. (Remember the Person of Christ was not created, but eternal.) The title heaven gave her, "Full of Grace," could never be given to any creature who was ever in sin. Genesis 3 already saw that her very nature would be to be opposed to the devil as she brought forth the Savior.

When the fundamentalist mentioned says that Roman Catholic theologians "lamely defend their assertion of the Immaculate Conception by saying 'God *could* have done it ... and therefore He did it,'" he ignores the Scriptural references Catholic writers have used. By no means does the Church present fittingness as an essential argumentation for the Immaculate Conception. It is not the best or sufficient proof. It is simply true that it is fitting that God became man from a Woman who was perfectly sinless, for it was her intellect and will that made the decision to accept the will and request of God. God eminently respects the free will of everyone, including the Woman chosen to be the Mother of Jesus. It was not forced upon her. Mary had a decision to make and as the prudent Virgin, she was not questioning to avoid God's will but questioning to understand God's will when she asked, "But how can this come about, since I have no knowledge of man?" (Luke 1:35). When heaven's Messenger explained that Mary would preserve her virginity, the Blessed Virgin answered without hesitation to God's will, "You see before you the Lord's servant, let it happen to me as you have said" (Luke 1:38).

The claim of the fundamentalist already quoted that the doctrine of the Immaculate Conception makes of God "a quadrinity instead of the Trinity" is a *non sequitur*. There is a lack of logic and a failure to understand what the Catholic Church teaches. As stated earlier, in defining Mary as the Mother of God, the Council of Ephesus was more concerned about defending the teaching of Christ's divinity than Mary's greatness. If the Islamic religion, for example, which honors Mary's Immaculate Conception, had also recognized her as the Mother of God, then Islamism or Mohammedanism today would be able to accept Christ not simply as a prophet but as God become man.

The fundamentalist's claim that the Assumption of Mary, body and soul, into heaven was only given official certification in 1950 and had been a peripheral precept within the Catholic Church since the Middle Ages, is simply untrue. The statement that there was a "*great*" (emphasis not ours) deal of resistance to the issuance of this doctrine by Pius XII is also false.

Belief in the Assumption of Mary into heaven existed from the early centuries. It is true that in the beginning of the infant Church all attention was centered on the figure of Jesus, around Whom all other mysteries revolved. Not even Christmas was celebrated at first. Rather,

Easter was the big feast and every Sunday seen as a little Easter. The Resurrection was the supreme proof that Jesus is Lord, God and Savior. As it was accepted by Christians that Jesus was indeed the Word of God, the Son of God made flesh, attention gradually focused more at understanding the Woman through whom, by the Holy Spirit, this was accomplished. With the divinity of Christ Jesus firmly established, Christians could turn attention to studying other consequent mysteries revealed by God in Christ.

Some thirty years after Mary's death, St. John the Apostle, who for at least sixteen years was Mary's companion, and who took her into his own home at the command of Christ from the Cross (John 19:27), described his vision of "a woman clothed with the sun, with the moon under her feet, and crowned with twelve stars" (Rev. 12:1). This "woman" is understood to be a figure of the Church, and also of Mary, who is a perfect figure of the Church. The person in the vision is ascribed to be "Lady Mary," as even the Moslems speak of her to this day.

Why was Mary assumed? Corruption of the body into dust is the penalty of sin. The Bible recounts instances of those who, by virtue of their holiness and God's divine favor, escaped corruption; Enoch and Eliah, who left the earth before death; Lazarus, whom Christ called from the tomb; and the saints, who came forth from the grave after Jesus' death on the Cross on Good Friday. Mary had no sin, and thus God bestowed upon her the grace of freedom from earthly corruption of her body. Furthermore, being inseparable from her Son, Jesus Christ, her bodily assumption is the natural counterpart of Christ's Ascension into heaven. The Church speaks of Christ's Ascension, for He is God and ascended with His own power. Mary is not God and is therefore said to be *assumed*.

The Feast of Mary's Assumption into heaven was celebrated by the Church as early as 400 A.D (Epiphanius). The day was called by early Christians "Mary's *dormitio*, or transition" (Mary's going to sleep, her passing or transition).

At the Council of Chalcedon in 451, the Church had to deal with a different problem than the Council of Ephesus, which preceded it by 20 years. The Council of Ephesus was concerned with the *divinity* of Christ and had condemned Nestorianism, which denied the real unity of the divine and human natures in the Person of Jesus Christ. The Council of Chalcedon then condemned Monophysitism, also called Eutychianism, which denied the *humanity* of Christ by holding that Jesus had only one, the divine, nature. At the Council of Chalcedon, St. Juvenal, Bishop of Jerusalem, spoke of Mary's death and the account was repeated by St. John Damascene (780). Records have been passed down verifying a unity of faith in the Assumption as understood today with Christians of early centuries. The bishop of Jerusalem repeated what had been passed down through the first few centuries.

St. John Damascene wrote this about Mary's death:

Mary died near Coenaculum in Jerusalem and was buried at Gethsemane, where Sts. Joachim and Anna and Joseph were buried. At her death, after three days the song of the Angels came to an end. Thomas, the only Apostle then absent, arrived, and desired to see and venerate the body in which God had dwelt. The Apostles opened the tomb but did not find the sacred deposit. Seeing only the linen which had enveloped the body of Mary, and from which a sweet odor arose, they closed the sepulchre. Astonished at the miracle, they could have but one thought: that He who has been pleased to become incarnate in the chaste womb of the Virgin Mary and to be born of her, being the Word of God and the Lord of glory and having already preserved the virginity of His Mother, had also willed to preserve from corruption her immaculate body after death, and to translate it to heaven before the general and universal resurrection.

While the exact place and manner of Mary's death and Assumption is not part of divine faith for Catholics as is her Assumption itself, these accounts surely testify to the faith of the early Christians that God, in the case of Mary, as in the case of Jesus Christ Whom He raised from the dead, did not "allow your holy one to see corruption" (Acts 2:27).

When Pope Pius XII defined the Assumption of Mary into heaven he did not meet opposition from Catholics. In fact, most Catholics were surprised when it was defined solemnly for they had always observed it as a holy day, together with Christians as early as 400 A.D. A liturgical feast existed even then and by the time of Pope St. Sergius I (born in Syria and Pope from December 15, 687 until September 8, 701), the Feast of the Assumption was one of the principal celebrations in Rome, with an impressive procession starting from the Church of St. Hadrian. It was even then a holy day of obligation for Catholics. Before solemnly defining what Catholics already believed, Pope Pius XII wrote to all the Catholic bishops of the world to determine their faith and that of their people regarding Mary's Assumption and all they virtually unanimously expressed the belief that this was part of the Divine Revelation.

When the fundamentalist quoted earlier says the "worship" of

Mary originated with a pagan deity and was taken up by the Church for political reasons this is simply an attempt to discredit veneration of Mary. Veneration of Mary begins with the Word of God, the Word made flesh by the power of the Holy Spirit, conceived and born of Mary as Sacred Scripture describes. Catholic veneration of Mary is simply fulfilling the prophecy of the words spoken by Mary under the inspiration of the Holy Spirit in her Magnificat, in which her soul proclaims the greatness of God. "Yes, from now onwards all generations will call me blessed" (Luke 1:48). Elizabeth, "filled with the Holy Spirit ... gave a loud cry and said, 'Of all women you are the most blessed' " (Luke 1:42). Heaven's Angel Gabriel certainly venerated Mary in the address, "Hail, full of grace" (Luke 1:28).

Catholics are doing what God's Word proclaims in Scripture in venerating Mary as blessed because of her faith. The declaration of the blessedness of Mary will continue among "all generations" until the end of the world, and then for all eternity in heaven. It is those who fail to do so who are not being true to Sacred Scripture. When they work to downgrade the holiness of Mary they are working in opposition to the Word of God. They are discrediting the Mother of Jesus and this is certainly not pleasing to our Lord and Savior. No one wants the truth distorted about one's mother, especially the Mother of the Holy One, the Mother of the holy Child who would "be called Son of God" (Luke 1:36). When Sacred Scripture calls Mary's Child "son of God" and the Son is equal to the Father and the Holy Spirit, how can it be said, as the fundamentalist says, "she was *not*, by any stretch of the imagination, the 'Mother of God?' " It is, rather, stretching the imagination to deny Who Mary's Child is and make her the mother of only part of Jesus and to claim Jesus as being both a human person and a divine person.

Why is it so incredible to the fundamentalist to see Mary willing the salvation of every one of us? Mary is not the Savior. She is not the one essential Mediator. She is not the Source of grace, our sharing in the divine life. But she is the Mother of "the Author of life" (Acts 3:15). She is the Mother of the "author and finisher of faith, Jesus, who for the joy set before him, endured a cross, despising shame, and sits at the right hand of the throne of God" (Heb. 12:2). She is the Mother of the One of whom it is written: "God sent His Son, born of a woman" (Gal. 4:4). Mary is the one who said "yes" (*fiat*) to God when finally in the fullness of time, mankind was asked in her person to accept the Savior. Not only does Mary always answer "yes" to God's will and accept His Word, but she ponders words concerning Jesus in her heart. See Luke 2:20, where Mary ponders in her heart all that the shepherds told concerning what the angels said and sang the night Jesus was born.

St. Luke ends the second chapter of his Gospel with the account of the Child Jesus in the Temple at the age of twelve after Mary and Joseph lost Him for three days. When they found Him, "His mother said to Him, 'Son, why have you done this to us? See how worried your father and I have been, looking for you' " (v. 48). The reply of Jesus reminds both Joseph and Mary that He has a relationship surpassing human family ties. In the presence of His virginal foster father, Jesus acclaims that God is His father (cf. 10:22; 22:29; Jn. 20:17). The account ends as Jesus,

> went down with them and came to Nazareth and lived under their authority. His mother stored up all these things in her heart. And Jesus increased in wisdom, in stature, and in favour with God and with people" (v. 51-52).

The Gospel account of God's Word is careful to tell us more than once that Mary "pondered," "stored up" in her heart the things said and done by the Word of God made flesh.

We may and should pray for one another upon earth. The words of Sacred Scripture are abundantly clear recommending prayers for our needs and as a community. "Give *us* this day our daily bread and lead *us* not into temptation ... ." We were taught by our Divine Lord Himself in answer to the request of how to pray, to pray for our own needs and those of others. Notice that our Lord uses the plural "us."

"For where two or three meet in my name, I am there among them" (Matt. 18:20). While Jesus here is praising community prayer upon earth, He is not isolating us from the prayers offered in heaven. God's will is done in heaven, too. "Thy will be done on earth as it is in heaven." Those in heaven are concerned about what happens upon earth. "I tell you, there will be more rejoicing in heaven over one sinner repenting than over ninety-nine upright people who have no need of repentance" (Luke 15:7). Prayer has four ends: praise, thanksgiving, reparation and petition. The essential and eternal prayer of all in heaven will doubtlessly be praise, rendering glory to God. But if the saints of earth who have passed into glory could not also pray for us in God's presence as they did upon earth, their power of influence, of intercession would be less in God's glory than while upon sinful earth.

When Mary is spoken of as the mediatrix of grace, she is not replacing the essential role of Christ as the one essential Mediator and Author of life (grace). The Church is saying that Mary intercedes with and through Jesus for the salvation of all. Should not every one of us do the same? The author of this book, whatever grace he may have, is less than a spark of the flame of Jesus' heart, and the faith he has is infinitesimal compared to Mary, the Woman of faith of the New Testament, and yet, I do not hesitate to say that my intercession daily is for the salvation of all. Now Mary, whose nature is "full of grace," does God's will perfectly, now in heaven as once upon earth, as God's specially chosen and favored one. Given that fullness of grace through no merits of her own but only out of God's own goodness and love, that Woman at enmity with the devil surely wills and prays for the salvation of all. The fundamentalist, however, fears that somehow Mary's universal intercession detracts from Jesus, the Head of the Church, the Mystical Body of Jesus. On the contrary, when she prays for mankind, Mary, too, draws from the infinite treasury of His Sacred Person.

The contrary is true also when the fundamentalist sees Mary as a barrier between the individual and the Trinity. To the devout Catholic who knows his faith and the role of Mary, this Woman is rather the first disciple of Christ; she is the Woman of faith, the creature of God privileged to be "full of grace." Mary is the one whose example teaches us the perfect response to God's Will, the willingness to always say "yes" to God. Mary is the favorite Daughter of God the Father, the Mother of the Son made man, and the Spouse of the Holy Spirit. True devotion to Mary for the informed Catholic is Trinitarian and Christological and illumines the authentic Christian life. Mary's life, centered on and in Jesus Christ, is a life that directs us to her Son Jesus and thereby to the Trinity. The Catholic whose devotion to Mary is balanced hears Mary say as she said at the wedding feast of Cana, "Do whatever He tells you."

The fundamentalist, who does not understand secondary intercessors with Christ, will quote "except the Father which hath sent Me draw him" as a proof that since all must go to the Father through Christ, Mary can have no role to play in the salvation of a soul. With that logic no mother upon earth need pray for the salvation of her children since only Jesus can draw them to the Father.

In Colossians 1, the Apostle St. Paul speaks of making up for the sufferings lacking in Christ. "What is lacking of the sufferings of Christ I fill up in my flesh for His body, which is the Church" (vv. 24-25). The Apostles and their successors certainly have a role to play in the salvation of souls. So do parents as regards their children. All salvation comes from and through Jesus Christ. But Jesus does not work in isolation. Jesus is the Head of the Body of His Church, of which we are members and the Holy Spirit the Soul. The merits of Jesus Christ for our salvation were infinite, and nothing was lacking in that. What is lacking at times are the prayers and sacrifices of the members of the Body of Christ — i.e., you and me. Our prayers and sacrifices can be meritorious only insofar as they are in union with Jesus and draw from Him. So too it is with Mary. As Mary was a willing cooperator with Jesus upon earth while in no way displacing His unique Mediatorship, so in heaven through her intercession she cooperates with Jesus in the distribution of His graces, not as an equal but as a secondary intercessor, the one next closest to her Divine Son.

When the fundamentalist says that since Jesus was Mary's Saviour, "she must have needed salvation, which presupposes some history of normal human sin," he is not acknowledging that the Catholic Church teaches that Mary was a descendant of Adam and Eve like us all and therefore rightfully should have been conceived in original sin. But because her very nature was being "full of grace," her salvation was so perfectly realized that the moment of Mary's creation coincided with the moment of her redemption in virtue of the future merits of Jesus Christ. There would be no need of "normal human sin" for Mary to need a Savior. She would not have to commit personal actual sin. Being a descendant of our first parents sufficed for her need of redemption.

The fundamentalist says,

> *Christ alone is worthy to make intercession for us . . . . Mary did not suffer and die on the cross . . . . And neither did Christ need an assistant to motivate Him to make intercession for the saints.*

While it is true that Christ's infinite merits were sufficient in themselves, it is not for us to decide other than what God has done. Christ could have broken into this world as a full-grown man without the need to be born of Mary, without the need to flee into Egypt after being born under difficult conditions in a cave. Nor should we dismiss Mary's suffering. It was not easy to learn of the slaughter of the innocents because of her Child. Nor was it easy to see Christ's own people reject Him, or for her to see Him crucified and dying on the Cross as a common criminal.

The aged Simeon, who had been promised "by the Holy Spirit that he would not see death until he had set eyes on the Christ of the Lord" (Luke 2:26), prophesied to Mary His Mother that "a sword will pierce your soul too" (Luke 2:35). Mary certainly suffered with Her Son as He hung on the Cross — not physically, but mentally, and spiritually. What good mother would not, if she could, change places with a son in such suffering? What mother does not suffer when she sees her children suffer? Mary is not redeeming us in the same manner as is her Son, who is God, but she is suffering with Him. Her sufferings and prayers were not a waste or only for herself. Such sufferings, as mentioned before, supply what is wanting in the sufferings of Christ. In Mary, the first disciple of Christ, we have one who is perfectly pleasing to her Son and therefore to His Father. If Christ is alone worthy to make intercession for us, as the fundamentalist says, then none of us can ever make intercession for one another. But we can — in, with and through Jesus Christ. That is the way Mary does it.

If "there is no hint in the Bible that Christ will have a 'staff' to assist Him," then why did Jesus establish the college of Apostles and command them to preach to the ends of the world, and why did He give them His very own authority?

> All authority in heaven and on earth has been given to me. Go, therefore, make disciples of all nations; baptize them in the name of the Father and of the Son and of the Holy Spirit, and teach them to observe all the commands I gave you. And look, I am with you always; yes, to the end of time (Matt. 28:19-20).

Obviously the God-Man decided that He wanted "additional mediators or motivators." When the fundamentalist accuses the Catholic Church of not being Biblical in its doctrine, it is rather the fundamentalist who is not being Biblical.

It is not simply the prayers of Mary and the saints that help Catholics; it is their living of the Christian life, their example. Where there are abuses in understanding the position of the Church that need to be corrected, the fault does not lie with the teachings of the Church. What large religious body will not have some members misrepresent its own teachings? Pope John Paul II once told bishops to make sure that popular devotions don't degenerate into "superstition." The Pope said,

> The best remedy against the ever possible deviations is to permeate these manifestations of popular piety with the word of the Gospel . . . . Devotions to the saints, expressed in feast days, images, processions and so many other forms of piety, should not be reduced to merely seeking protection of material goods or bodily health . . . . The saints must first of all be presented to the faithful as models of how to live and as imitators of Christ.

Cardinal Newman, a great English convert to Catholicism, had a strong devotion to Mary. This distinguished convert, whose love for Mary was so warm, was appalled at the excesses of some authors who sought to enhance devotion to Mary by exaggeration. Presenting Mary as the *sole* refuge of sinners, as *the* merciful one, and Jesus Christ as merely the God of Justice is simply being disloyal to both Mary and Christ. "Sentiments such as these," wrote the Cardinal, " . . . seem to me like a bad dream. I could not have conceived them to be said .... I will have nothing to do with statements which can only be explained by being explained away."

The Church indeed speaks of Mary as Mother of Mercy, as the refuge of sinners, but always in terms of Jesus Christ, always as dependent on the merits of Jesus Christ, never as inseparable from Jesus Christ. The teachings about Mary are beautiful enough without the need for exaggerations. A good analogy is the sun and the moon. The sun represents Jesus, the Son of God made man. The moon represents Mary, who receives all her light from the sun.

CHAPTER 9

# Is Catholicism Christianity?
# The Search for True Christianity

The question form of the title of this chapter may surprise sincere Catholics and many Christians of mainline Protestant churches. The fact is that many in fundamentalistic camps would not consider Roman Catholics as Christians. In saying this we must give recognition again that there is a wide variety of fundamentalists. Not all have this narrow view. Some of them have a very limited knowledge and some are very scholarly; some of them are violently anti-Catholic and others are not anti-Catholic at all. It is especially those who are anti-Catholic who hold the narrow view. Their number is not small. There are countless fundamentalists who believe Catholics have never been exposed to the light of Sacred Scripture, that they do not enjoy intellectual freedom. They are convinced that if Catholics once read the Bible with an open mind and with the freedom of intellectual inquiry, they would never continue being Catholics.

The author once had a minister of a fundamentalist faith at his rectory door early on a Saturday morning, with his 7-year-old daughter at his side, who said, that "We love to evangelize Catholics." It was obvious that the man did not believe this priest had any knowledge or faith in the Good News of the New Testament. One can conclude what he thought of the average Catholic. Knowing nothing about me, he saw a need to bring me to Jesus Christ. Asking why he had his seven-year-old daughter out so early on a Saturday morning, the answer came, "We believe in teaching our children the art of evangelizing very early in life."

The fundamentalist who does not believe that Catholicism is authentic Christianity is moved with an intense zeal to save Catholics from damnation and bring them freedom. The Bible gives Catholics freedom if only they could discover its light, at least according to the interpretation of the particular fundamentalist who is speaking.

This freedom, fundamentalists will say, began with the Protestant Reformation, which destroyed the great power that Catholic priests and bishops had, thus liberating people from an autocratic hierarchy. Protestantism, according to fundamentalists, meant a purifying of the ministerial office of its evils, thus freeing people concerning how and where we meet our Lord in prayer. According to some, the Protestant Reformation even has caused a purification of family life. Likewise, those who left the yoke of Catholicism were freed from the papacy, which some even regard as the Antichrist, the "seven-headed, ten-horned beast" while the Roman Catholic Church is "Satan's organization."

The anti-Catholic fundamentalist has heard many strange things about the Catholic Church, what happens in it, and often has a list of "authoritative sources" to prove his points, all the way from former priests to nameless former Catholics. The fundamentalist will refer to these people in his attack upon the Catholic Church, saying that they expose the Church's "evils," now that they "came to the light of the Gospel."

Concerning another kind of apostasy, it is interesting to note that some dissenters, who are still in the Church, strike out today against the it, accusing their own Church in the same terms that anti-Catholics have long done so. Such as, the Church has a "totalitarian character," does not permit intellectual freedom, dissent, etc. A closer look reveals that such dissenters have in fact lost the Catholic faith, while protesting that they will remain within the Church in order to change it. Why do they wait — what they desire already exists outside the Catholic Church. It would be honest to declare themselves no longer Catholic if they reject Catholicism. The fullness of true faith can be lost from a neglect of prayer, a lack of humility, a compromise with the world in a life of sensuality, etc.

If these who call themselves "Catholic" had authentic Catholic faith they would believe that the Catholic Church possesses the fullness of true faith as the Mystical Body of Christ, has the Holy Spirit as Soul and Spirit of Truth and therefore cannot err or change its dogmatic positions on faith and morals. Jesus Christ cannot change. The Church is the extension of the Incarnate Christ into time and space and "Jesus Christ is the same yesterday, today, and forever" (Heb. 13:8).

To reject consciously and deliberately any of the dogmas of Catholicism is to put oneself automatically outside the Catholic Church.

Sociologists take surveys and tell us about a certain number who answered their questions and "considered themselves good Catholics" even though they don't go to Confession, do not obey Church teachings because they do not accept them, do not go to weekly Mass, believe remarriage after divorce is all right before God, approve of artificial birth control and abortion, etc. Willingness to help the poor in some surveys is the main criterion in determining whether one is a good Catholic. The author would have to agree that such people who call themselves "Catholic" are hardly Christian.

The official Catholic Church has never abandoned the teachings of the Gospel. There was a laxity of many of her members and priests that resulted in the Protestant Revolt at the beginning of the sixteenth century. Volumes could be written on the history of Europe at the time, and the many circumstances that contributed to the disruption of Christian unity. There is a laxity today, there are dissenters today, but the Catholic Church of Jesus Christ still exists and can never be destroyed. The Reformers of the sixteenth century were not united. They fought each other's teachings and divided among themselves again and again. The forming of new denominations has continued since that century to the present day. Among those who accept the Bible as the sole rule of faith, there is little agreement as to what the Bible means. The Protestant Reformation abolished the priestly office, denied the special powers which Jesus gave to the Apostles, who were the first bishops and priests of His Church. Ministry in Protestant churches was limited to preaching the Word of God and the administration of some of the Sacraments, e.g., Baptism.

The Catholic Church teaches that anyone may baptize, something which, however, should be done only in an emergency when no priest or bishop is available. Since an ordained priest is not needed for valid Baptism the Church recognizes Protestant Baptism if the minister intends what Jesus Christ intended by the Sacrament when He instituted it and provided the Sacrament is administered properly while pouring water and invoking the Father, Son and Holy Spirit.

Protestantism reduced the priesthood of Jesus Christ to a mere function, denying the special sacramental powers and character of Holy Orders. The Catholic Church teaches that an indelible mark of the priesthood of Jesus Christ is imprinted on the soul of the man ordained by the bishop. Typical Protestantism would attribute no special supernatural powers to their ordained ministers. For that matter, where the Apostolic Chain has been broken, neither does the Catholic Church attribute any special powers of Christ to Protestant ministers.

If the Catholic clergy at the time of the Protestant Reformation had been living the priestly life which Jesus and the Church expected of them, the disaster of the Protestant Revolt would never have occurred. The same could be said today. If all priests and religious were living and teaching the Catholic faith as the official Catholic Church requires, many confused "Catholics," some of whom have fallen into fundamentalism, would not be confused or leave the Catholic Church, the true Church of Jesus Christ. Religious and priests who are not true to Catholicism keep others from recognizing the true face of Catholicism. The priestly and religious life is a terrible responsibility before God. There were holy religious and priests at the time of the Protestant Reformation in the sixteenth century. Jesus would never permit the mark of holiness to disappear entirely from his Church. When disunity came, the very holy priests and religious stayed with the Catholic Church and worked to develop holiness in all its members. A much needed counter-reformation took place within the Catholic Church to purify these abuses.

The Reformation did not purify the ministry within the Catholic Church. The Catholic Church called the Council of Trent to bring about better formation of future candidates for the priesthood, and the elimination of abuses.

The Protestant Reformation did have the effect of challenging the Catholic Church to bring about, where needed, the purification of its clergy and members. Roman Catholics are perfectly free to seek union with Jesus Christ in private prayer, in private reading of the Bible, even in group study of the Bible but sincere Catholics will look to the teaching Church, the Pope and bishops in union with the Pope, for any final official interpretation of God's Word. This does not mean individual Catholics are not free to interpret. It simply means that individual Catholics know they have no guarantee that the Holy Spirit will infallibly guide them. Such infallibility is reserved for the official teaching Church under certain conditions. (This is explained more in the next chapter).

The Protestant Reformation did not bring about a purification of family life, as some have claimed, nor have those who call themselves dissenting Catholics today done so. Loose ideas of marriage, easy divorce and remarriage, the widespread plague of contraceptive birth control, and now millions of abortions — all have their roots in the evils which brought about the Protestant Revolt of the sixteenth century. Such liberal thinking has affected some who call themselves "Catholic" today. These advocate dissension within the Church, and call for easy divorce, remarriage, contraception, etc.

The sanctification of the family is to be found in living an authentic Catholic life, not in dissension. In fact, in order to survive today, Catholic families must be heroic, even to the point of martyrdom. Ordinary Catholic families cannot survive. Catholic families which live the strict Catholic life of sanctification will survive in the future. The parents cannot be ordinary parents in their personal holiness nor in educating and forming their children for this to happen. Surveys of what Catholics believe are meaningless as far as the teachings of the Church go. Many are "Catholic" in name only.

A Christian is a person who is baptized into Jesus Christ. He is one who believes in the essentials of the Christian faith, notably as found in the Apostles' Creed. A Christian believes in the Blessed Trinity, three Persons in one God and that the Second Person, the Son, became Man, died on the Cross for our salvation, rose again from the dead and ascended into heaven where He lives with God the Father in the unity of the Holy Spirit.

A Catholic Christian further accepts the teachings of the Roman Catholic Church, participates in the Eucharistic liturgy and the Sacraments of Catholic Christianity, and gives allegiance to the Pope and those bishops who are in union with the Pope as Bishop of Rome and visible head of the universal Church. The Catholic Church believes that Jesus Christ is the invisible Head of the Church, that Jesus will always be Head and that this Church is the Mystical Body of Christ which can never be destroyed (Matt. 16:19).

The sincere Catholic Christian believes that the Bible is the inspired and holy Word of God, an inspired record of the revelations made to mankind by God about Himself and His will for men. He believes in the inerrancy of the Bible. But he also believes that while we are encouraged to study the Bible for ourselves, as individuals we have no assurance that our individual interpretation will always be according to the mind and will of God.

If each individual's interpretation was true and divinely guided we would not have over eighteen thousand Christian denominations in the world. The sincere Catholic Christian believes he needs the hierarchy, namely the Pope and bishops in union with the Pope in order to keep in true faith and to interpret the Bible correctly when there is a need for an official interpretation.

The Roman Catholic, then, while accepting the Bible as the inerrant and inspired holy Word of God, does not accept the Bible as the sole Christian rule of faith. The Catholic Christian cannot separate Jesus from the Bible any more than he can separate Jesus from the

Church. The Church is, as St. Paul says in the Bible at least sixty-four times, "the body of Christ." The Bible is a Church book, written by Church men, for the Church's use. It was written under the inspiration of the Holy Spirit. The Holy Spirit is the Soul of the Church, the Primary Author of the Bible. That same Holy Spirit which was the Primary Author is the Primary Guide of the Church in interpreting through the centuries what His Word means.

The Catholic Christian then accepts the Bible in accepting the Church. He accepts the Church as the "body of Christ" and its tradition, that is, the teachings of Jesus Christ, the revealed Word of God handed down through the centuries. The Church, the Bible, and Tradition are all authorities to the Catholic Christian as following from one Source, God. If properly understood, the Bible without the Church loses its authority from God. These three sources are not in opposition; they are like currents of Truth flowing from one Source, God. As the individual who reads the Bible frequently grows in understanding the realities of God's Word, so too, and vastly more so, the Catholic Church, which authentic history attests, has had approximately two thousand years to meditate and grow in understanding under the guidance of the Holy Spirit. To appreciate what this means we must believe that the Catholic Church is a divine organism, the "body of Christ," never dying, always living and developing on earth, and inseparable with Jesus Christ, its Head, in heaven.

The word tradition (Gk. *paradosis*, Lt. *traditio*) means literally that which has been "handed over" or "passed on." In the New Testament the word tradition is often used in reference to customs, practices, and teachings. Jesus criticized the scribes and Pharisees for setting aside God's commandment for the sake of their own human traditions (Mark 7:1-13; Matt. 15:1-5). St. Paul used the word tradition to refer to his instructions to the community at Thessalonica (2 Thes. 2:15) and in the sense of his rules of conduct, from which no member of the community should deviate (2 Thes. 3:6).

The Apostle Paul refers to both the Eucharistic institution narrative (1 Cor. 11:23) and to an early summary of the entire Gospel (1 Cor. 15:3-4) as objects of tradition. This is a far more primary and fundamental meaning of tradition. Tradition in its most basic sense refers to the living faith experience of the Christian community. St. Paul is using formulas or expressions which have already become fixed in a particular liturgical tradition when he writes of the institution of the Holy Eucharist. At the same time there is an immediacy in his language "I received from the Lord what I handed on to you" which reflects this primary meaning of tradition. It is used in the sense of the

Lord's presence in the midst of His people. St. Paul is not simply speaking about a memory of the historical Jesus. St. Paul was not converted until after the ascension of our Lord. For him "to receive from the Lord" is often "to receive from the community, the Church, the "body of Christ."

Tradition in the primary sense is the Church community's shared experience of the Lord through faith. In a secondary sense, tradition is the handing on — in different ways — of that faith experience. Officially, the tradition is expressed in the worship and Sacraments of the community, in those written works recognized by the Church as inspired or Sacred Scriptures, and in the formal definitions and creeds formulated by the Church's teaching authority. The living faith experience of the Lord of the Church community always occurs prior to any of the various forms through which it may come to expression. Otherwise there would be nothing to express, no faith to proclaim, no life to celebrate. Sacred Scripture therefore is the living tradition of the community or Church coming into written expression. Because the Church recognized the inspired nature of the Scriptures, they constitute the primary or normative expression of the Church's faith. We see from this how closely wedded are the Scriptures and Tradition since Sacred Scripture is the recorded living tradition of the early Church.

Jesus did not say that the Apostles would understand everything He taught in the full immediately, at the very moment He spoke it with no possibility of development of understanding the faith.

These things I have spoken to you while yet dwelling with you. But the Advocate, the Holy Spirit, whom the Father will send in my name, He will teach you all things, and bring to your mind whatever I have said to you (John 14:26).

The Catholic Church in its official position on Tradition, a word frequently misunderstood by those who attack Catholicism, has given its official position in the Second Vatican Council's *Dogmatic Constitution on Divine Revelation*. Below are just a few quotes:

And so the apostolic preaching, which is expressed in a special way in the inspired books, was to be preserved by a continuous succession of preachers until the end of time. Therefore the Apostles, handing on what they themselves had received, warn the faithful to hold fast to the traditions which they have learned either by word of mouth or by letter (cf. 2 Thes. 2:15), and to fight in defense of the faith handed on once and for all (cf. Jude 3). Now what was handed on by the Apostles includes everything which contributes to the holiness of life, and the increase in faith of the People of God; and so the Church, in her teaching, life, and worship, perpetuates and hands on to all generations all that she herself is, all that she believes.

This tradition which comes from the Apostles develops in the Church with the help of the Holy Spirit. For there is a growth in the understanding of the realities and the words which have been handed down. This happens through the contemplation and study made by believers, who treasure these things in their hearts (cf. Luke 2:19, 51), through the intimate understanding of spiritual things they experience, and through the preaching of those who have received through episcopal succession the sure gift of truth. For, as the centuries succeed one another, the Church constantly moves forward toward the fullness of divine truth until the words of God reach their complete fulfillment in her . . . . .

Sacred Tradition and Sacred Scripture form one sacred deposit of the Word of God, which is committed to the Church. Holding fast to this deposit, the entire holy people united with their shepherds remain always steadfast in the teaching of the Apostles, in the common life, in the breaking of the bread, and in prayer (cf. Acts 2, 42, Greek text), so that in holding to practicing, and professing the heritage of the faith, there results on the parts of the bishops and faithful a remarkable common effort.

The task of authentically interpreting the Word of God, whether written or handed on, has been entrusted exclusively to the living teaching office of the Church, whose authority is exercised in the name of Jesus Christ. This teaching office is not above the Word of God, but serves it, teaching only what has been handed on, listening to it devoutly, guarding it scrupulously, and explaining it faithfully by divine commission and with the help of the Holy Spirit; it draws from this one deposit of faith everything which it presents for belief as divinely revealed.

It is clear, therefore, that Sacred Tradition, Sacred Scripture, and the teaching authority of the Church, in accord with God's most wise design, are so linked and joined together that one cannot stand without the others, and that all together and each in its own way under the action of the one Holy Spirit contribute effectively to the salvation of souls (See 8, 9, 10).

A fundamentalist with little education can quote the Bible easily and proficiently. But that is not enough. Exegesis (correct interpretation) is essential. One needs to match his interpretation with the wisdom of the ages and the wisdom of the Holy Spirit which as Soul of the Church guides it in truth, as Jesus promised "unto the end of the world." It is essential to accept Jesus' wholly revealed truth, not part of it.

It is worth repeating. Each generation ought not start anew with only the Bible, the dead printed words of the text, which is but a translation of a translation, many times over, without any of the original texts, which have long ago turned to dust. The original Bible texts, written on scrolls, were destroyed. But the Church, which Jesus promised would remain forever, continues to preserve the divinely inspired written Word of God. This points again to the fact that the Bible, the Church, and Tradition are not to be separated but have God as their one Source.

## THE CATHOLIC CHURCH IS THE BODY OF CHRIST.

Those who sincerely and with an open mind study the Bible and the traditional teachings of the Church from the first century on will discover, if they have faith in Jesus Christ and the Bible as the inspired Word of God, that the Roman Catholic Church is the "body of Christ" which Saint Paul the Apostle mentions repeatedly in the New Testament. The intrinsic nature of the Church is that it is a divine organism, a supernatural body. This divine body of the Church is the Mystical Body of Christ Himself. Mystically, Christ's faithfull, who possess the fullness of true faith, which is found in authentic Roman Catholicism, make up the members of Christ's Church-body, whereas Jesus Christ as Head of this Church-body reigns eternally in heaven. The ancient Catholic Church, the same Church of the first century, the same Church of Pentecost Sunday, the same Church of the twentieth century, passing into the twenty-first, and which will be here until the end of time according to the promise of Jesus Christ, is in fact the body of Christ; and this truth is taught in many parts of the Bible. Some of the obvious Biblical passages are found below:

> . . . Again, He is the head of His body, the Church; He, who is the beginning, the firstborn from the dead, that in all things He may have the first place. For it has pleased God the Father that in Him all His fullness should dwell, and that through Him He should reconcile to Himself all things, whether on the earth or in the heavens, making peace through the blood of His Cross. (Col. 1:18-20).

> Do you not know that your bodies are members of Christ? (1 Cor, 6:15).

But as it is, there are indeed many members, yet but one body ... Now you are the body of Christ, member for member. And God indeed has placed some in the Church, first Apostles, secondly prophets, thirdly teachers; after that miracles, then gifts of healing, services of help, power of administration, and the speaking of various tongues. Are all Apostles? Are all prophets? Are all teachers? Are all workers of miracles? Do all have the gift of healing? Do all speak with tongues? Do all interpret? Yet strive after the greater gifts." (1 Cor. 12:20-26)

... Because we are members of His body, made from His flesh and from His bones ... (Eph. 5:30).

For just as in one body we have many members, yet all the members have not the same function, so we, the many, are one body in Christ but severally members one of another. But we have gifts differing according to the grace that has been given us ... (Romans 12:6).

The Church as "the body of Christ" is made up of millions of the faithful who have been baptized into Jesus Christ and profess "one faith, one Lord, one Baptism." The indelible mark of Jesus Christ from Baptism is printed upon their souls for all eternity; they participate in the divine nature, as St. Peter wrote in his Epistle; they "share in the life of God," as Scripture testifies again and again.

The Church is not simply an organization, a natural body of people. It is a divine organism, the Mystical Body of Christ. Jesus Christ is the Head. The Holy Spirit is the Soul. The faithful are the members of this body.

Jesus Christ did not intend that Christians be divided into hundreds of denominations with different interpretations of the faith. In fact, there are today thousands of churches claiming to interpret the Bible correctly. Jesus intended that there be one Church. Knowing that His followers would tend to divide due to sin, pride, etc., our divine and loving Savior prayed for unity in His Church at the Last Supper, the night before He died. We shall see that it is the reason Jesus appointed St. Peter as the first Pope, to preserve unity in His followers, as seen in His prayer:

... Sanctify them in the truth. Your word is truth. Even as you have sent me into the world, so I also have sent them into the world. And for them I sanctify myself, that they also may be sanctified in truth.

Yet not for these only do I pray, but for those also who through their word are to believe in Me, that all may be one, even as You,

Father, in Me and I in you; that they also may be one in Us, that the world may believe that You have sent Me. And the glory that You have given Me, I have given them, that they may be one, even as We are one: I in them and You in Me: that they may be perfected in unity, and that the world may know that You have sent Me, and that You have loved them even as you have loved Me . . .
(John 17:17-23).

Only the Roman Catholic Church has existed in the world since Jesus Christ established His Church upon the earth and sent together with the Father the Holy Spirit on that first Pentecost Sunday. " . . . the gates of hell shall not prevail against it." If that original Church disappeared, or became corrupt, as many Protestants claim, and Martin Luther and others came along to purify it and restore the Church of Jesus Christ to its original truth and integrity, then Jesus Christ did not keep His promise, "the gates of hell shall not prevail against it."

Jesus Christ had clearly promised His Church that its Soul, the Spirit of Truth, the Sanctifier, would remain with it, keeping it in the Truth forever, and that He, the Head, Jesus Christ, Lord, God and Savior, would be with His Church until the end of the world.

Many New Testament references could be used to point out Jesus' promise of the Holy Spirit to keep His Church always in the truth. For example,

I will ask the Father and He will give you another Advocate to dwell with you forever, the Spirit of Truth whom the world cannot receive, because it neither sees Him nor knows Him. But you shall know Him, because He will dwell with you, and be in you (John 14:16-17).

St. Matthew closes his Gospel with Jesus, just before His Ascension to the Father, speaking to the remaining eleven Apostles. (Judas had committed suicide as the world's first bad priest.) The Lord Jesus commissions the Apostles to make the Church *Catholic*, which means universal, for all nations.

But the eleven disciples went into Galilee, to the mountain where Jesus had directed them to go. And when they saw Him they worshipped Him; but some doubted. And Jesus drew near and spoke to them saying, "All power in heaven and on earth has been given to me. Go, therefore, and make disciples of all nations, baptizing them in the name of the Father, and of the Son, and of the Holy Spirit, teaching them to observe all that I have commanded you; and behold, I am with you all days, even unto the consummation of the world" (Matt. 28:16-20).

Where do any one of the hundreds of Protestant churches, fundamentalist or otherwise, end up, or start, if they attempt to trace their history, their roots, back to Jesus' Ascension and the descent of the Holy Spirit? The origins of some are only a few years in the past. If any claims to be the original Protestant church, they can only trace their roots to the sixteenth century. Have they purified a corrupt church? What about the absolute promise of Jesus Christ? Jesus is not God if He did not keep His promise that the Church He built upon Peter would never be destroyed (Matt. 16:19). To deny that Jesus Christ is God incarnate, the Lord, God and Savior is to be no kind of Christian at all.

Jesus speaks of only *one* Church. The Church He founded must be true, for Jesus is Truth itself:

... There shall be one fold and one shepherd (John 10:16).

[Be] careful to preserve the unity of the Spirit in the bond of peace: one body and one Spirit, even as you were called in one hope of your calling; one Lord, one faith, one Baptism; one God and Father of all, Who is above all, and throughout all, and in all (Eph. 4:3-6).

Now I exhort you, brethren, that you watch those who cause dissensions and scandals contrary to the doctrine that you have learned, and avoid them. For such do not serve Christ our Lord but their own belly, and by smooth words and flattery deceive the hearts of the simple. For your submission to the faith has been published everywhere. I rejoice therefore over you. Yet I would have you wise as to what is good, and guileless as to what is evil. But the God of peace will speedily crush Satan under your feet. The grace of our Lord Jesus Christ be with you (Rom. 16:17-20).

Note that even Christians from the time shortly after Jesus Christ was upon earth in His physical body, there were those who caused dissension. The use of "smooth words" to lead others astray is still present among some even today who claim to be Catholic. Satan will ever attempt to bring disunity to the Church as he has from the beginning, being as Scripture said, "the father of liars" and the "spirit of disunity."

Christ's true Church is made up of a single unified body — unified in every respect: in organization, in faith, in worship. This is the way Jesus Christ constituted His Church as His own body to be upon earth. That there are attempts to destroy this unity should not surprise us. Jesus foresaw it and prayed for unity. That Jesus intended His Church to be "one faith ... one body ... " is glaringly evident in Sacred Scripture if one can read it without prejudice, without using the

Scriptures to attempt to prove one's pre-determined conclusions.

St. Cyprian in the third century wrote:

> God is one and Christ is one, and one is His Church, and the
> faith is one, and one His people welded together by the glue of
> concord into a solid unity of body. Unity cannot be rent asunder,
> nor can the one body of the Church, through the division of its
> structure, be divided into separate pieces (St. Cyprian, O*n the Uni-
> ty of the Church*, chapter 23).

In the third century, Tertullian wrote, "We are a society with a single religious feeling, a single unity of discipline, a single bond of hope"
(*Apology*, 39, 1). In the fourth century, St. Hilary wrote,

> In the Scriptures our people are shown to be made one; so that
> just as many grains collected into one and ground and mingled
> together, make one loaf, so in Christ, who is the heavenly Bread,
> we know that there is one body, in which our whole company is
> joined and united (*Treatise* 62, 13).

Protestant Christians, however good and sincere, are not members
of a Christian unity, a single body in the sense Jesus Christ intended
and the Bible clearly describes. They may be members of a certain
Christian cooperative, an inter-denominational association, one of
hundreds of denominations or Christian bodies, each with a different
name, and at variance in belief, in government, and in some form of
worship.

To the extent that all Protestants profess Jesus Christ as Lord and
Savior, profess to preach His Gospel, and desire the salvation of souls,
there is a common identity between them. The Catholic Church does
not wish to discount the good and truth that is in these various Christian denominations. However, there is not among them a fullness of
true faith and unity in Christ concerning agreement on what constitutes Christ's whole Gospel. They are in disagreement over what is required for eternal salvation.

There are many examples of their lack of unity: One Protestant
body holds that there is no place in Christian worship for altar or liturgy. Some fundamentalists are heard publicly discrediting any Christians who hold to a liturgy. Liturgy, in fact, refers to the official public
worship of the Church as distinguished from private devotions. In the
Catholic Church "Divine Liturgy" is the special title for the Holy Eucharist, or what is commonly called "the Mass." In the Old Testament,
there were religious duties performed by priests and Levites in the
Temple, especially those related to the sacrifice.

Fundamentalist preachers spend much time, if not exclusively, in preaching their private interpretation of the Word of God. That is to say, preaching is front and center of their worship. No need for liturgy, therefore no need for altar. Such is, they claim, in contradiction to the New Testament religion of Jesus Christ that grew out of Old Testament faith and worship. All we read in the Old Covenant Temple worship was a preparation for the coming of Jesus Christ and the New Covenant worship.

Some Protestant churches hold that Sacraments, even Baptism, should be withheld from infants and small children. Some "Modernist Catholics," dissenters, that is, put themselves outside of the official Catholic stream of faith in proclaiming that Baptism should be delayed. As we shall see in the next chapter, Jesus gave His Church the Pope as final and highest authority in the Church to speak in His Name when people question the Catholic faith and its practices. Catholics are free to reject them, but in rejecting official Catholic positions they place themselves outside the Catholic Church.

Some Protestant churches hold the view that one becomes cleansed of sin and certain of salvation once he accepts Jesus Christ as his personal Savior. Another holds that membership in Christ's Church is limited to a select few, and if one of the select few falls away from God's grace, no amount of repentance can restore him. Members of such a denomination will even be heard to say, "I know I am saved. I am not a sinner. I will never sin. If I ever sinned I know I could never be forgiven or saved again ...."

Another church the independent view that Saturday, not Sunday, is the Lord's Day. Others hold that the powers of church administration reside not with the clergy but with the laity of the local congregation and it is the congregation that gives certain individuals the call to the ministry. (The Catholic Church, however, teaches that the call to the priesthood is a call from Jesus Christ affirmed by the bishop who speaks for Jesus Christ and through whose ministry the powers of Jesus Christ are bestowed on the one ordained). Concerning the Holy Eucharist, there are countless interpretations of the meaning of the Holy Eucharist among Protestant Christians. Many more examples of divisions could be given.

With such division there is not "one faith ... one body." Such is not the unity in Christ which our Savior and the Founder of the Church intended and for which He prayed. Such is not the perfect oneness in Christ for salvation which is the Will of Jesus Christ, Son of God, Savior.

The above is not to mark off fundamentalists and various

Protestant denominations as lost. But such disunity is not the Will of Jesus Christ. It is not the perfect means to salvation and the worship of the Father, in, with and through Jesus Christ.

## THE SEARCH FOR CHRIST'S TRUE CHURCH

Protestants who read this book and come to the conclusion that they must seek a more perfect unity as intended by God can ponder well the words of Jesus,

> Ask, and it shall be given to you; seek, and you shall find; knock, and it shall be opened to you. For everyone who asks, receives, and he who seeks, finds; and to him who knocks, it shall be opened ... (Matt. 7:7).

In speaking with Christians not in full union with the Catholic Church but who were interested in inquiry classes on the Catholic faith, the author has frequently advised them to pray to pray to Jesus Christ for guidance in this way: "Lord Jesus, lead me to the fullness of true faith. Lead me to see and accept faith in You as You intended when You came upon the earth, taught the Good News, and called all to unity under one Lord, in one faith, in one Baptism."

I remember a young man who refused to pray in this manner. My experience is that if a person sincerely prays for Jesus Christ to lead himself according to His will in seeking truth in Christ, and seriously investigates the Catholic Church from reliable sources, he will finally come to seek membership in the Catholic Church.

The glorified body of Jesus Christ in heaven and His Mystical Body on earth have never been and can never be a disjointed body. To be joined to Christ's true body on earth, having available a share in its bountiful grace as Jesus intends through the Sacrifice of the Mass and all the Sacraments which Jesus instituted, we must be a formal member in good faith and in grace in the One, Holy, Catholic and Apostolic Church. Then, as the Apostle Paul said, we are a member of Christ's body, of His flesh and of His bones (Eph. 5:30).

## TO BE "BORN AGAIN"

To come to this realization with deeper faith and with a desire to live one's Baptismal vows is indeed to be born again. A person can be baptized only once. In this instance the expression "born again" is used in a more general sense, compared to that of an instant change. It means coming to grasp vividly, strongly, and deeply what happened at our Sacramental Baptism. It's like a deeper conversion. The result is that a person consciously lives his or her Baptismal vows daily and always.

We are first born again in Jesus Christ at our Baptism. Every baptized person upon the earth, whoever administers the Sacrament, Protestant or Catholic, provided the ritual was administered with water flowing properly or dipping properly, using at the same time the Trinitarian formula, is sanctified in the Lord Jesus Christ unto everlasting life. At that time an agreement is made by the person being baptized, either personally or through a sponsor, to belong entirely to Christ. Jesus Christ in turn promises to bless the new Christian with a lifetime of divine grace as necessary for the everlasting life of heaven.

Sacramental Baptism removes all guilt of original and personal sin. In this Sacrament Jesus Christ also removes all punishment due to sin, temporal and eternal. This is to say if one were baptized and immediately departed this world thereafter he or she would be immediately admitted to heaven. Sanctifying grace is granted the soul. This means the soul shares in the life of God and the Blessed Trinity comes to dwell in the person as in a temple. The supernatural virtues of faith, hope and charity and the gifts of the Holy Spirit mentioned in Sacred Scripture are granted the soul. By Baptism a person is incorporated into Jesus Christ, the glorified Christ and the Mystical Body of Christ, for they are one.

The baptized soul is imprinted with the Baptismal character of Christ which enables a person to receive the other Sacraments, to participate in the priesthood of Christ through the divine liturgy, (the priesthood of the baptized), and to grow in the likeness of Christ through personal sanctification. Baptism enables a person to be sanctified in his struggle with concupiscence and gives him the title to rise in a glorified body on the last day. In summary, this is the teaching of the Catholic Church about Baptism.

Now when the reality of being born again into Jesus Christ at Baptism becomes a constant guiding light of daily living, a rising from a dead faith to a living exciting faith, then that person is "born again." This is to say that he or she actually begins to live one's Baptism, one's life in Christ.

## IN SEARCH OF UNITY IN THE BODY OF CHRIST

Jesus spoke of the unity which would distinguish the body of His faithful people. We must search for it. The author of this book went through a certain search as he approached manhood to reaffirm in his own mind that he was in fact in that unified Church of Jesus Christ which our Lord, God and Savior placed upon the earth with the promise that it would never be destroyed. Many others, not born of Catholic parents, have searched and become Catholics. For some it is a long, slow, laborious search that requires many sacrifices.

It is a sad note in modern history, that some baptized into this Mystical Body of Christ, the Catholic Church, have never recognized the true face of Catholicism. Some have been swept astray by the zeal of fundamentalists, or of a strong personality, or the world, the flesh and the devil, and left this unified Mystical Body of Christ, the Catholic Church, without realizing what they left. As the late John Cardinal Wright once said, "Some who have left the Catholic Church never had the Catholic faith." No one who was rightfully educated and formed in authentic Catholicism ever left and actually found the means to a holier life in Jesus Christ. The means our Lord established is His one true Church.

The author once had a recent convert to Catholicism travel over fifteen hundred miles to see him. Not only was the man a convert to Catholicism, but a convert from a sinful life that had landed him in prison. His time in prison was well used. He studied not only Sacred Scripture but ancient and modern philosophers and theologians, including Aristole, Plato, Socrates, the early Church Fathers, modern philosophers and those writers which advocated "God is dead."

After he came into faith in Jesus Christ, the next step in his long search was to discover that the Roman Catholic Church had to be the Church of Jesus Christ. He did not start with this as a preconceived conclusion. He arrived at it with prayer, work and sacrifice.

Released from prison, he sought a priest for instructions to be received into the Catholic Church. He was unfortunate in first meeting two "modernist priests and a modernist nun" who watered down Catholicism and did not present to him the truths of Catholicism he had discovered. Finally, a third priest presented to him the true face of Catholicism and he was finally baptized into the Roman Catholic Church.

This man, in his great desire to discover how he could share with others his experience of conversion to the true faith in its fullness, and his new membership in the true body of Christ, drove half-way across the United States to spend a couple days with the author. He wanted to share his true faith with others. Eternal life is worth it.

If necessary, you should search through every history of Christian church development that can be found. Be as comprehensive and as objective in your search as possible because in your own conscience you can only live with the truth, the absolute truth. Jesus Christ is Truth. "I am the Way, the Truth and the Life" (John 14:6).

Go to all the reliable history books and encyclopedias and compare these volumes with the Holy Bible and you will find holy unity in the Roman Catholic Church. To recognize the true faith of Catholicism is to discover Jesus Christ fully. Do not be discouraged by "modernist Catholics" who in reality are not Catholic. In your study of two thousand years of Catholic Christianity you will learn that from the very first years of Christ's Church to the present, the devil has not been inactive in attempting to destroy Christ's Church, to mix error with truth in clever and smooth words in order to destroy the Church of Jesus Christ. While some temporary success have been realized, while entire families, or individuals here and there can separate, while history has known even entire countries at time to be lost to the fullness of true Catholic faith, there is an never ultimate and complete success on the part of the evil one.

Ultimately, Christ is the victor and his true Church comes back more vibrant than ever in some part of the world. Often, once those who in their search have been led to discover that the Roman Catholic Church is the Church of unity in Christ fulfilling Bible prophecy, there are still natural problems to overcome. Oftentimes, even though a person becomes intellectually convinced, there is need of the convincing of one's emotions, and conquering one's feelings, which may have been trained for years to oppose Catholicism.

There also may be opposition from others who have not gone through an honest, open, objective, prayerful search. Others may even consider one's conversion to Catholicism the damnation of his soul.

There will be questions about Catholic doctrine, Catholic dogmatism, Catholic authoritarianism, etc., to answer in one's mind. Long-nurtured suspicions may still have to be settled peacefully. This is why prayer is so important in order to keep open to God's merciful grace.

## CHRIST'S CHURCH IS A TEACHING, NOT JUST A LEARNING CHURCH.

One will learn from reading Sacred Scripture that Christ's true Church is not simply a "learning" Church, but a teaching church. One can discover from the Bible that Christ's one true Church is an infallible teacher. It is not permitted by Jesus Christ to teach error. It has the Holy Spirit for its Soul; the same Holy Spirit that served to keep the Bible inerrant keeps the Church out of error in its official dogmatic teachings. Reading Matthew 28:18-20 again in the light of deeper discoveries brings home to one's conscience

that Jesus clearly gave a teaching mission to his Church. "Go therefore, teach all nations; baptizing them ...".

The teaching mission of Christ's Church is seen also in our Lord's
statement to the Apostles, "As the Father has sent Me, I also send you"
(John 20:21). It is clear that the Church as the body of Christ is to be no
less a teacher than Jesus Christ, "the Teacher." Jesus did not give this
teaching authority to every baptized member of his Church. *Some* have
been placed in the body of Christ as teachers, wrote the Apostle Paul.
(1 Cor. 12:28-29). (The infallibility of the Church's dogmatic teachings
will be considered in the chapter on the Pope).

In the fifth century, Saint Augustine wrote,

> The Catholic Church is the work of Divine Providence, achieved
> through the prophecies of the prophets, through the Incarnation
> and the teaching of Christ, through the journeys of the Apostles,
> through the suffering, the crosses, the blood and death of the
> martyrs, through the admirable lives of the saints, and in all these,
> at opportune times, through miracles worthy of such great deeds
> and virtues. When, then we see so much help on God's part, so
> much progress and so much fruit, shall we hesitate to bury
> ourselves in the bosom of that Church? For starting from the
> apostolic chair down through successions of bishops, even unto
> the open confession of all mankind, it has possessed the crown of
> teaching authority (*De Utilitate Credendi*).

St. Ignatius of Antioch was a disciple of the Apostle John, who
wrote so gloriously in the Bible about unity in Christ and the spirit of
unity and union in Christ as vine and branches (John 15). St. Ignatius
lived from the first to the second century. This is what he wrote in the
second century:

> Ignatius, also called Theophorus, to the Church that has found
> mercy in the transcendent Majesty of the Most High Father and
> of Jesus Christ, His only Son; the Church by the will of Him who
> willed all things, beloved and illuminated through the faith and
> love of Jesus Christ our God; presiding in the chief place of the
> Roman territory ... presiding in love, maintaining the law of
> Christ, and bearer of the Father's name: her do I therefore salute
> in the name of Jesus Christ." (Introduction — *To the Church of
> Rome*).

A person who sincerely and prayerfully searches will see that
these statements of the primitive Christian Fathers concerning the
teaching Church of Jesus Christ speak of the Catholic Church. But to
such a person, nurtured on anti-Catholic slogans and misconceptions,

becomes convinced of the unity found in official Catholicism, (we are not talking about dissenters who in no way speak for the official Catholic Church), there may still remain questions such as: "Why does the Catholic Church suppress the Bible, or bypass the Bible and draw upon tradition for some of its articles of faith?"

One who honestly searches and investigates from direct and reliable Catholic sources will discover that those statements are totally false. Admittedly, some "Catholics" who have fallen into the trap of Fundamentalism will in their new zeal actually convince themselves that such is the case. In fact, every Mass contains Scriptural readings. Each Sunday's Mass at present contains three Scriptural readings, drawing from both the Old and New Testament. The Church has had Scriptural readings as part of the Divine Liturgy (the Mass) from the first centuries. The first part of the Mass is the Liturgy of the Word of God. Next is the Liturgy of the Eucharist. It is entirely Scriptural.

One who sincerely searches the teachings of Catholicism ought not trust sources from some denomination which justifies its existence by attacking Roman Catholicism. These churches were founded more than fifteen hundred years after Christ, and some nearly two thousand years after Jesus Christ was born into this world, lived, taught, and died for us on the Cross. If you want to know what the Republican Party advocates, go to that party, not the Democrats, and vice-versa. The same with the Catholic Church, which has been upon the earth since the days of Jesus Christ. Go to it, not a dissenter who is attempting to change what the Church is; not to Protestant denomination, however sincere a particular denomination may consider itself to be.

Catholic reverence for the Bible is as old as the Bible itself. It should be obvious to the reader by now that Jesus Christ founded the Church, promised it the Holy Spirit of Truth as its Soul. Jesus did not write or promise a book. It was the Catholic Church founded by Jesus Christ that first determined the canon of Sacred Scripture. Once the Church had the complete Bible, in the fourth century, reverence for this Book as the recorded or written Word of God has been great in the Catholic Liturgy.

"Catholics have their church. We have the Bible, God's Word." That is what many Protestants have been brought up to believe. Those especially of the fundamentalist variety think Catholics are taught not to read the Bible. Some even hold that Catholics are not permitted to read the Bible. In fact, however, Catholics are encouraged in sermons, in letters from their bishops, and in Papal encyclicals to read the Bible and are told of the spiritual good that can come from keeping a Bible in the home, ideally spending some time in daily meditation on its content.

Pope Pius XII wrote in the encyclical letter, *On the Promotion of Biblical Studies,*

> For the Sacred Books were not given by God to men to satisfy their curiosity or to provide them with material for study and research, but, as the Apostle observes, in order that these Divine Oracles might "instruct us to salvation, by the faith, which is in Christ Jesus," and "that the man of God may be perfect, furnished to every good work." Bishops should help excite and foster among Catholics a greater knowledge of and love for the Sacred Books. Let them favor, therefore, and lend help to those pious associations whose aim is to spread copies of the Sacred Letters, especially of the Gospels, among the faithful, and to procure by every means that in Christian families the same be read daily with piety and devotion... for, as St. Jerome, the Doctor of Stridon, says: "To ignore the Scripture is to ignore Christ."

Does the Catholic Church *bypass* the Bible when she bases some of her articles of faith on Tradition? This allegation is also without foundation. For those who lack understanding of the nature of the Church as a divine organism, Christ's Mystical Body, but look purely and simply to written words in a book which the world did not have for the first few hundred years as we have it today, it may seem so. Careful study will show otherwise.

## THE BIBLE AND TRADITION

The Bible itself actually states that some of the teachings of Jesus Christ were committed to Tradition. The Bible speaks of certain teachings being handed down by word of mouth rather than by letter. The Bible actually states that these teachings are no less important for having been committed to the Church in its living tradition which is also guided by the Holy Spirit, "the Spirit of Truth." Consider the following:

> Therefore, brothers, stand firm. Hold fast to the traditions you received from us, either by our word or by letter (2 Thess. 2:15).
> We command you, brothers, in the name of the Lord Jesus Christ, to avoid any brother who wanders from the straight path and does not follow the tradition you received from us (2 Thess. 3:6).

The Apostle St. Paul is specifically stating that the letter, (or the Bible which did not yet exist as we have it today) is not the only criteria of Christian truth. The early Church had Scriptures which were not yet bound together in the canon. This had to wait several centuries and then have an authority to approve it as authentic. That authority so declaring was the Church founded by Jesus Christ, the Catholic Church whose chief Bishop lived at Rome.

St. Paul is clearly giving credence to Tradition, namely the unwritten Word of God, handed down. He is telling us that both letter and tradition are of equal importance to the faith of Christians. Likewise, the words of John, the beloved disciple of Christ, gives evidence that not all that Jesus taught was written down:

> It is this same disciple who is the witness to these things; it is he who wrote them down and his testimony, we know, is true. There are still many other things that Jesus did, yet if they were written about in detail, I doubt there would be room enough in the entire world to hold the books to record them (John 21:24, 25).

The Apostles and their disciples set about doing primarily what Jesus had ordered them to do, to preach and baptize and organize the Church in the far-flung mission field, the nations of the known world at the time. Had they stopped to write down all of Our Lord's doings and teachings, they could not have carried out his command to take the teachings of Christ to all nations. But how do we know that the tradition which forms the basis of part of Catholic doctrine is the Tradition, the unrecorded teachings of Jesus Christ, mentioned in the Bible? Again, to answer this question in one's search there is needed objective research and reasoning. For this, we have the testimonies of the primitive Christian Fathers.

## THE EARLY CHURCH FATHERS

St. Athanasius wrote in the fourth century,

> But it will hardly be out of place to investigate likewise the ancient traditions, and the doctrines and faith of the Catholic Church, which the Lord communicated, the Apostles proclaimed, and the Fathers preserved; for on this has the Church been founded.

St. Augustine wrote in the fifth century: "These traditions of the Christian name, therefore, so numerous, so powerful, and most dear, justly keep a believing man in the Catholic Church."

If one goes back over the mainstream of Christian belief and practice since Christianity began, one will discover in his search that all the other ancient and semi-ancient Christian churches, Coptic, Greek Orthodox, and Russian Orthodox, have consistently held to the same tradition-based doctrines of the Roman Catholic Church. This is evidence that the acceptance of them was universal prior to the revolt and advent of Protestantism in 1517.

## WHAT ARE THE TRADITIONS MENTIONED IN THE BIBLE?

An excellent question that those outside the Catholic Church do not ask (unless they are in the process of honest search on their way into the Catholic Church) is this: "If the tradition which forms the basis of part of Catholic doctrine is not the tradition mentioned in the Bible, what has become of it? Have some of Christ's teachings become extinct?" The answer is that Christ promised the Spirit of Truth and to be with us until the end of the world. After suffering the ignominy of the Cross to plant His truth in the world, Jesus Christ would not permit any part of His teachings to become extinct. "Heaven and earth shall pass away, but my words shall not pass away," said Jesus. (Mark 13:31).

Many who have prayerfully and objectively searched have concluded that Catholic Tradition is Bible Tradition. In basing part of her doctrine on the unwritten Tradition the Catholic Church has, in fact, complied with the Bible's recorded teachings. For example, the Catholic practice of praying to God through the intercession of Mary and the saints is part of the traditions referred to in the Bible. Otherwise, why were beliefs such as these so precious to early Christians? Consider the ancient Marian Prayer of St. Ephraim, an illustrious deacon of the fourth century:

> O Virgin Lady, immaculate Mother of God, my lady most glorious, most gracious, much purer than the sun's splendor, budding staff of Aaron, you appeared as a true staff, and the flower is your Son our true Christ, my God and Maker. You bore God and the Word according to the flesh, preserving your virginity before childbirth, a virgin after childbirth, and we have been reconciled with Christ, God your Son.

## CATHOLIC TRADITION IS BIBLE TRADITION.

Volumes could be filled quoting Bible passage after Bible passage, Church Father after Church Father, giving evidence that Catholic Tradition is Bible Tradition, part and parcel of the deposit of faith given to the Church by its Founder, Jesus Christ, Son of God, Savior. Doubtlessly some people who are truly searching will read this book. As a matter of fact, the author received help in writing this book from people who made the search and ended up devout Catholics. They will tell you that habit is a mighty force. Because of habit, a person is capable of resisting some of the strongest logical persuasions. Habit can play tricks on the mind. It anesthetizes the mind. It creates the illusion that custom, somehow, is a profound truth in itself and for some mysterious reason can transcend all other truths. One can be certain, too, that the Evil Spirit is not helping a person in his or her search. Therefore, it is essential that one pray earnestly and humbly. It is important, too, that one be open to one's good holy Guardian Angel, and ask his assistance for the light of truth.

## BUT I AM AN IRREVOCABLE PROTESTANT BY TRADITION.

It is easy to convince oneself that one is a Protestant by the irrevocable force of family traditon. How can one disown one's family? One can convince oneself that he is a Protestant "by nature," certainly by inheritance. Many people who have not searched in this way would be deeply hurt if you converted. God is all love and does not expect that, you tell yourself. He will understand — the "natural" thing to do is to remain a Protestant. The conscience, however — once one has come this far — is not easily quieted. There are suggestions to the mind that God is all mercy and will make allowances at the Judgment if one loved God with one's whole heart and soul and repented of all sins committed. After all, I am baptized, you may say.

## CONVERSION IS AN ACT OF GOD REQUIRING GRACE.

But there is the grace of God. It would seem that one who comes this far in the search, and still resists, is praying, "Not your will, Lord, but *mine* be done." What about the Apostolic Chain, broken for Protestants whereby their ministers do not have the special indelible mark of Christ from Holy Orders upon their souls? How will a Protestant who has a minister who has not been ordained by a bishop who is a successor of the Apostles in an unbroken line for two thousand years, how will that Protestant ever be able to eat the Bread of Life, to receive the Lord's Body and Blood, Soul and Divinity in Holy Communion which Jesus said is necessary for salvation?

## DOES GOD REALLY EXPECT SOMETHING SO HEROIC?

God is just. He judges us according to our good will and knowledge. Therefore, he makes allowances for a person who does not know, through no fault of his own, that the Catholic Church is the one true Church. So, can I be saved if I *know* where his true Church is to be found, but refuse to join? If I know the Catholic Church is the true Church of Jesus Christ, do I not therefore know the will of Jesus for me? One who makes as thorough a search as suggested in this chapter will certainly have read the Documents of Vatican II of the Roman Catholic Church. The words of *Lumen Gentium*, the *Dogmatic Constitution on the Church*, will surely demand respect:

> This sacred Synod turns its attention first to the Catholic faithful. Basing itself upon Sacred Scripture and tradition, it teaches that the Church, now sojourning on earth as an exile, is necessary for salvation. For Christ, made present to us in His Body, which is the Church, is the one Mediator and the unique Way of salvation. In explicit terms He Himself affirmed the necessity of faith and Baptism (cf. Mk. 16:16; Jn. 3:5) and thereby affirmed also the necessity of the Church, for through Baptism as through a door men enter the Church. Whosoever, therefore, knowing that the Catholic Church was made necessary by God through Jesus Christ would refuse to enter her or to remain in her could not be saved" (n. 14).

## JESUS SAID I MUST EAT THE BREAD OF LIFE.

If you open the Bible, Jesus Christ will speak you straight out of the pages:

> I am the bread of life. Your fathers ate the manna in the desert, and have died. This is the bread that comes down from heaven, so that if anyone eat of it he will not die. I am the living bread that has come down from heaven. If anyone eats of this bread he shall live forever; and the bread that I will give is my flesh for the life of the world . . . .
>
> Amen, amen, I say to you, unless you eat the flesh of the Son of Man, and drink his blood, you shall not have life in you. He who eats my flesh and drinks my blood has life everlasting and I will raise him up on the last day. For my flesh is food indeed, and my blood is drink indeed. He who eats my flesh, and drinks my blood, abides in me and I in him. As the living Father has sent me, and as I live because of the Father, so he who eats Me, he also shall live because of me. . . . (John 6:48-59).

## CHRIST'S WORDS ON THE EUCHARIST HAVE NO FIGURATIVE SENSE.

Christ will no longer seem to speak figuratively to one who has made the search in the direction of the long journey home to one's Father's house. The bread Jesus speaks of is not merely symbolic or representative. Can symbolic bread be called "living" bread? Can symbolic bread vivify and impart divine life to the soul for everlasting life? Can dead vegetable substance be representative of the living Son of God made man? Is God's power so limited that Jesus could not give us his Body to eat and his Blood to drink, just as He is recorded as saying He was doing and as the Catholic Church has taught and believed for two thousand years?

In interpreting the Bible we must interpret the whole Bible, not isolate texts. We must correlate texts. Those who attribute to the words of Jesus Christ merely symbolic meanings are not correlating, but isolating texts, and doing so inconsistently. The Jews of Jesus' time certainly did not understand Christ to mean symbolic bread. (This has already been explained in the chapter on the Holy Eucharist). Christ meant exactly what He said. Thousands departed because Jesus would give no symbolic meaning to his words. Those who today refuse to accept the reality of the Real Presence of Jesus Christ in the Holy Eucharist are failing in faith, just as the Jews of old did when our Lord was upon earth physically. All things are possible with God, Sacred Scripture teaches. The full explanation is contained in the Gospel accounts of the Last Supper.

> And while they were at supper, Jesus took bread, and blessed, and broke: and gave to His disciples, and said: Take you, and eat. THIS IS MY BODY. And taking the chalice, He gave thanks, and gave to them, saying: Drink you all of this. FOR THIS IS MY BLOOD." (Matt. 26:26-28; Mark 14:22-24; Luke 22:19-20).

Jesus Christ gave us his promise at Capharnaum that he would give us Himself to eat and drink. He fulfilled it at the Last Supper. With great reason did John, who did not want to repeat what Matthew, Mark and Luke had already written, go into great detail on this point in John 6. Trying to convince oneself that John's sixth chapter does not refer to the Holy Eucharist can hardly be based on sincere, objective research.

St. Paul, the great Apostle chosen after Jesus' Ascension, does not mince words in writing on the Holy Eucharist. "The chalice of benediction which we bless, is it not the communion of the blood of Christ? And the bread which we break, is it not the partaking of the body of the Lord?" (1 Cor. 10:16). "But let a man prove himself: and so let him eat of that bread, and drink of the chalice. For he that eats and drinks unworthily, eats and drinks judgment to himself, not discerning the body of the Lord." (1 Cor. 11:28-29).

If there be any lingering suspicions in one's search, seek out also the belief of the primitive Christian Fathers on this point. The immediate successors of the Apostles ought to be qualified for interpretation here. They could not have been subject so quickly to corruption, as some claim in saying that the Catholic Church is indeed the first and ancient Church of Jesus Christ but then in time it became corrupt and the Protestant Reformation had to straighten all that out. Some straightening out, with hundreds of denominations. (The 1980 *Church Book of World Religions* lists over eighteen thousand.)

## WHAT DO THE EARLY FATHERS SAY ABOUT THE HOLY EUCHARIST?

Do the primitive Christian Fathers speak of the subject? Research shows they say a great deal on this central mystery of our faith. The leaders and teachers of the infant Christian Church called the bread and wine consecrated on the altar the "Eucharist." They unanimously maintained that by virtue of the consecration it was no longer common food-stuff, but by the Omnipotent Power of God, through the powers Jesus gave the Apostles, the bread and wine become the true Body and Blood of our Savior.

St. Cyril of Jerusalem, a Father of the fourth century, wrote:

Since then He has declared and said of the bread, "This is My body," who after that will venture to doubt? And seeing that He has affirmed and said, "This is My blood," who will raise a question and say it is not His blood? (See chapter 6 on the Holy Eucharist for more extensive quotes from early Church Fathers).

It has taken the heresy of Modernism, which has infected Christianity to come up with only symbolic or representative interpretations of Jesus' words concerning His Body and Blood received in Holy Communion. Neither Scripture itself nor Christian writings from the first days after the Apostles can be used to justify mere symbolic interpretations.

Where is one led in an extensive, objective search for true and full Christianity? In the Bible, our Lord and Savior Jesus Christ tells us that we need to eat of His Flesh and drink of His Blood in order to have eternal happiness and be with him forever in heaven. In the Bible, the great Apostle Paul tells us that we should prove our faith by discerning the Body and Blood of Jesus Christ in the consecrated bread and wine. There is history where we find the early Church Fathers condemning as heretics all Christians who do not associate themselves with the Real Presence of Jesus in the Holy Eucharist. Where does this leave one without the divine soul-saving Living Bread come down from heaven?

This calls for a positive course of action. It calls for a search for that particular Church which can give us the true and living Jesus Christ in Holy Communion. We can get common everyday bread and wine any place, even the market place, and have it represent anything we desire. Calling upon many Protestant churches one ends up with explanations that offer only "symbols" of Christ's flesh and blood, or at best with "abodes of his Spirit," or with "temples of his sacramental presence" or with "vehicles of his hidden flesh and blood" or with "bread and wine mysteriously merged with his flesh and blood." Some ministers call their communion bread and wine the real body and blood of Jesus, but when pinned down, and asked if "real" meant corporeal, the real living substance of the Body, Blood, Soul and Divinity of Jesus Christ under the appearance of bread and wine, they will answer no. One does not find in Protestant churches that Holy Communion is productive of grace but it is explained in some fashion, differing as widely as there are different Protestant denominations, that the Eucharist is a reflection of the grace already present in the soul through faith. Such explanations, so common outside the Catholic Church, amount to a rejection of the doctrine of the Real Presence. To receive Jesus Christ with worthy dispositions of heart, is to eat his Body and drink his precious Blood, so as to receive real grace, an increase of the divine life. It is not a mere reflection of His grace? Jesus said,

> ... Unless you eat the Flesh of the Son of Man, and drink his Blood, you shall not have life in you. He who eats my Flesh and drinks my Blood has life everlasting and I will raise him up on the last day (John 6:54-56).

It is in the Roman Catholic Church that one finds the glorious fulfillment of Christ's promise.

It is true that various Orthodox churches have preserved the Apostolic Chain but do not have the perfect unity and history in faith under Peter going directly back to Jesus Christ, as does the Catholic Church. The Orthodox surely have far more members than the many Protestant denominations and have retained so much of its traditions. It is remarkable that after more than one thousand years of separation from the Roman Catholic Church, the Orthodox hold to the Real Presence of Jesus in this great Sacrament of the Holy Eucharist.

In the Roman Catholic Church one finds the Manna come down from heaven, the Communion which is truly the Body, Blood, Soul and Divinity of our Lord and Savior, Jesus Christ. There one can find Jesus' Real Divine Presence. True, one must have love and faith to gain grace by this Real Presence but it is not the individual's faith that makes Jesus present. It is the power of the holy priesthood, the power Jesus passed on to His holy Catholic Church two thousand years ago at the Last Supper which brings Jesus Christ to us. Here is faith in the power and integrity of Jesus Christ which He bestowed to His Church, the Catholic Church. Yes, those who end their search and find themselves inside the Roman Catholic Church may have been previously validly baptized in infancy or later. But in coming to the fullness of true faith they are "born again" and discover with a new and far deeper thrill what it means to live in Jesus Christ, to have Jesus Christ live in us.

# CHAPTER 10

# The Pope
# — Did Jesus Put One Man in Charge?

## (The Development of the Church from Apostolic Times)

Among Christians for whom the Pope is not necessary, a purely human invention, or even a threat, many accusations are made regarding the papacy. Popes have been misquoted, and statements taken out of context. Some actually think that it is Catholic teaching that the Pope is the living Christ in person. A Pope Nicholas I is quoted as saying that the Pope, being God, is "judged by no man." Some believe the Catholic Church teaches that the Pope can never sin, can never make a human mistake of any kind, etc. Some outside the Church have considered the Pope the "anti-Christ." Some point to human failings of individual Popes in the attempt to show that the Pope could not possibly be infallible.

For many, the papacy is a symbol not of unity but rather of authoritarianism and crushing uniformity. Protestants generally regard the papacy to be of human origin. Because of the way the papacy is regarded by many Christians outside the Roman Catholic Church, Pope Paul VI himself once said "the Pope ... is undoubtedly the greatest obstacle in the path of ecumenism." The Pope was indicating the fact that it is the greatest difficulty for Christians of many denominations who are searching for unity to recognize the Catholic position that the papacy is the Rock intended by Christ upon which to build His Church and thereby keep it in unity by the guidance of the Holy Spirit. If these separated Christians could accept the position of the Pope as held by the Catholic Church they would become Catholic.

Before taking up an overview of recent scholarly Scriptural studies and dialogues regarding the papacy, let us present some typical questions and objections to the papacy, and the Catholic response.

To the question, "Why do Christians need a Pope?" the shortest answer is because that is the way Jesus Christ set up His Church. To have the fullness of true faith we must accept the Church according to the constitution Jesus gave it, that is, with a hierarchy of Pope, bishops, the Sacraments, etc. Such is the provision Jesus Christ Himself gave us. To say "but Jesus Christ is enough" is again to fail to recognize the divine nature of the Church as the "body of Christ." The Pope is not replacing Jesus Christ but is His chief representative upon earth.

Those who claim that the early Church was without a Pope are not being honest with history. St. Peter was appointed Pope by Jesus Christ Himself. "You are Peter, and upon this rock I will build my Church . . . and I will give to you the keys of the kingdom of heaven" (Matt. 16:18-19).

Those who claim that the Holy Spirit was ruling the early Church and there was no need of the Pope then as now, quote Biblical passages such as Acts 8:29: "And the Spirit said to Philip ..." Acts 15:28. "For the Holy Spirit and we have decided to lay no further burden upon you . . . ." It is true that the Holy Spirit then worked immediately in individual souls and does so now. We are all members of the Church. The Holy Spirit is the Soul of the Church and dwells as in a temple in every Christian in the state of grace. As indicated in a former chapter, Scripture also tells us that while we are all "the body of Christ, member for member," not all have the same gifts. "And God indeed has placed some in the Church, first Apostles, secondly prophets . . . . Are all Apostles? . . . . Do all interpret? Yet strive after the greater gifts" (1 Cor. 12:27-31).

It follows that the Holy Spirit does not work exactly in the same way in every member of the Church. Not all are Apostles, and not all Apostles and their successors are the Rock, successor to St. Peter in whom the Holy Spirit will work in a special manner. That not all are bishops, priests or deacons shall be gradually pointed out in this chapter. There is no case of the Holy Spirit inspiring any man to act against the lawful and highest authority as found in Peter which is identified with the authority of Jesus Christ, which He gave to His Church (Matt. 16:18-19; Matt. 28:16-20). The Holy Spirit is presented as working always in union with the Church.

It is strange that some Christians are willing to attribute to every Christian the guidance of the Holy Spirit in interpreting Sacred Scripture, and the teachings of Jesus Christ. However, they are unwilling to attribute to the successor of St. Peter and the whole Church the same kind of unerring guidance.

St. Paul is pointed to as evidence in the New Testament that we do not need a Pope. But St. Paul did in fact need a Pope, and respected St. Peter. Timothy, who wrote in Scripture that there is one mediator between God and man, Jesus Christ, in no way denies the need for the papacy. The Pope is the representative of Jesus Christ he speaks for Jesus, points to Jesus and declares himself to be Jesus' servant to all Christians.

The idea that we can go directly to Jesus Christ without need of the Church is and over-simplification. We do go the Father through the Mediator Jesus Christ and His Church, which is His body. In "the body of Christ," the Church, we encounter God in, with and through Jesus Christ. The Sacraments are the acts of Jesus Christ extended in time and space. The Sacraments dispense the effects, the grace of the mysteries of Christ. St. Paul wrote, "Let a man so account us, as servants of Christ and stewards of the mysteries of God" (1 Cor. 4:1-2). " ... If I have forgiven anything — I have done for your sakes, in the person of Christ, that we may not be defeated by Satan; for we are not unaware of his devices" (2 Cor. 2:11).

The word "Pope" means simply "father." It is certain from Sacred Scripture, Tradition, and from history, that Christ appointed Peter to be visible head, or spiritual father, of the whole Christian family, and that he died in Rome as did Paul. Jesus Christ conferred the primacy of teaching, governing and sanctifying in the Church to St. Peter in such a way that it would continue after Peter's death. The early Christians obviously so understood, for after his death they selected a successor, and this has been done for two thousand years.

The Pope has to live somewhere. Peter went to Rome and presided over the Church at Rome. The tradition developed that the Bishop of Rome inherits the position of primacy over the universal Church. Jesus did not spell out how a successor to St. Peter would be made. He left practical decisions to His Church to which He gave all His authority. A process of selecting successors to Peter gradually developed. In recent centuries, cardinals, that is, special men who advise the Pope in the government of the Church, elect a new Pope. According to present Church law cardinals must at the same time be bishops, successors to the Apostles.

## EARLY CHRISTIAN RECOGNITION
## OF THE PRIMACY OF PETER

Irenaeus of Lyons, at about the year 180, identified Peter and Paul as the founders of the Church at Rome. This historical record underlines the unique authority of the Church of Rome. "For it is a matter of necessity that every church should agree with this church, on account of its preeminent authority, that is, the faithful everywhere" (*Against Heresies*, III, 3.2).

In 252, Cyprian of Carthage drew attention to Rome's position among the local churches when he referred to Rome as " ... the throne of Peter ... the chief church whence priestly unity has arisen" (Ep. 59:14). His statement transfers to the Roman Church his understanding of Peter's role as the source of episcopal unity.

By the fourth century it is very evident that the Roman primacy of jurisdiction, based on the authority of Peter, which is passed on to his successors, was established as part of the faith of the Church. The first Christians obviously knew this and passed it on. There are historical records of similar claims by a series of Roman bishops, beginning with Damascus (366-384). Its most powerful expression is found in Leo the Great (440-461), who said that Peter continued to preside over the whole Church through the Bishop of Rome. His intervention and decisive authority is seen in the great Christological controversy of the fifth century during which he declared null and void the decisions of a false council. His famous "tome" to Flavian of Constantinople became the basis for the Christological confession of the Council of Chalcedon (451) and was acclaimed by the bishops at the council by saying: "Peter has spoken through Leo."

The human dimension of the papacy is seen in the Middle Ages when it gains great power. The Popes struggled to protect the Church and their office from secular rulers. Unfortunately, at the same time they became caught up in the politics of the West. The fact that human prudential judgements can sometimes be made in management has nothing to do with the doctrine of the Church concerning infallibility, as shall eventually be explained in this chapter.

Christians in the East, after separating from Rome, continued to recognize Rome's primacy of honor, but rejected the principle that Rome had plenary power and could formulate unilateral laws binding on the Church. Relations deteriorated with politics getting involved between the East and the West until the big break came in 1054. (In recent years remarkable advances toward reunion have been made between Orthodox Christians of the East and the papacy with its headquarters in the West). Vatican Council I marked the high point of development of explaining the Catholic position regarding the papacy.

The dogmatic constitution *Pastor Aeternus* (1870) of the Council Fathers declared that Peter received a primacy of jurisdiction over the universal Church from Christ, and that the primacy is passed to whomever succeeds Peter in the Roman See, and that the Roman Pontiff has full and supreme power over the universal Church, not only in regard to faith and morals but also in matters that pertain to the discipline and government of the Church throughout the world, and thus over local churches, pastors, and the faithful.

The Council declared that the Pope when speaking *ex cathedra* "is possessed of that infallibility with which the Divine Redeemer willed that His Church should be endowed for defining doctrine regarding faith or morals." Vatican Council II (1962-1965) continued to develop a collegial understanding of Church authority. This is not to deny the supreme authority of the Pope as chief representative for Christ in the teaching Church but to spell out the authority of bishops as successors to the Apostles who teach in union with the Pope. The Council Fathers (bishops of Vatican II), looked back to the first bishops or Apostles appointed and ordained by Jesus Christ, and said,

> The order of bishops is the successor to the college of the Apostles in teaching authority and pastoral rule; or, rather, in the episcopal order the apostolic body continues without a break. Together with its head, the Roman Pontiff, and never without this head, the episcopal order is the subject of supreme and full power over the universal Church. But this power can be exercised only with the consent of the Roman Pontiff. For our Lord made Simon Peter alone the rock and key-bearer of the Church (cf. Matt. 16:18-19), and appointed him shepherd of the whole flock" (cf. John 21:15ff) (LG n. 22).

Since the Second Vatican Council, which reaffirmed that "the Roman Pontiff has full, supreme, and universal power over the Church" (LG n. 22), also gave more explicit recognition of collegiality with the Catholic bishops of the world, this has served to win greater sympathy from mainline Protestant churches, such as Lutherans, Anglicans, and certainly Orthodox. While it does not describe Protestant fundamentalists, there is a growing awareness among many Christians, other than Catholics, of the necessity of a specific ministry to serve the Church's unity and universal mission. More and more Christians are gradually coming to see that the only viable ministry for Christian unity this could actively involve would be the papacy, which traces itself back to St. Peter appointed by Jesus Christ Himself.

St. Peter is mentioned more often in the New Testament than all the other Apostles collectively. His name always appears first in the listing of the Apostles (Mark 3:16). Peter was known to Jesus and the disciples as Simon. Jesus tells Peter the first time He met him that his name will be changed to Rock. Jesus gave him the name "Peter," which is Greek, or "Cephas," which is the Aramaic equivalent. "Peter" and "Cephas" mean "the rock" (John 1:42). The Gospels of Matt., Mark and Luke place Peter in an inner circle with James and John in relationship to Jesus. St. John's Gospel closely associates Peter with the beloved disciple.

Simon Peter confessed Jesus as the Messiah (Mark 8:29) and the Holy One of God (John 6:69). There is Scriptural evidence that Peter was the first Apostle to whom the risen Jesus manifested Himself (1 Cor. 15:5; Luke 24:34). Peter was the first official apostolic witness to the Resurrection. Note how John waited for Peter to go into the empty tomb first.

In the early Christian community of Jerusalem among the Twelve, Peter predominates. Acts presents him as their spokesman. Galatians 1:11-19 gives testimony to Peter's importance. St. Paul gives evidence of his special recognition of Peter's authority. After recognition that there "were appointed Apostles before me," he said he retired into Arabia, and again returned to Damascus. "Then after three years I went to Jerusalem to see Peter . . . ."

In is generally agreed among Biblical scholars that Peter reached Rome, and like Paul was martyred there around the mid-sixties. The image that becomes apparent in the developing Church is of Peter as the shepherd, or chief pastor. Peter is seen as the shepherd of the sheep (John 21:15-17); as model presbyter (1 Peter 5). St. Matthew's Gospel portrays Peter as the unique leader of the whole Church, the one on whom the Church is founded and to whom Jesus entrusts the power of the keys of the kingdom. Peter is also presented as a Christian martyr (John 21:18-19), and as one who receives special revelation (Acts 10:9-16); the confessor of the true Christian faith against false teaching, interpreting Scriptural prophecies (1 Peter 1:20-21). He is presented correcting the misinterpretations of people who have appealed to the authority of other Apostles, such as Paul (2 Peter 3:15-16).

The Gospels also present the weak human side of Peter so it ought not to surprise us to learn of the weaknesses of Peter's successors, such as five or six Popes throughout history whose personal private lives left much to be desired. In Mark 8:33; 9:5-6; John 13:6-11, Peter is a weak and sinful man who misunderstands Jesus, who denies Him, yet afterwards repents (John 21:15-17) and confirms his brothers and sisters in the faith (Luke 22:32).

While one can look in the New Testament and say that Jesus is not recorded as explicitly saying there should be a continuity of Peter's office, it does not say otherwise either. It is the living Tradition of the first Christians handed down to us, that in fact they did select a successor to Peter. And the Church has done so 264 times.

Since fundamentalists reject Catholic teaching regarding Tradition, it is no wonder that they also reject the tradition of the papacy. They would require it in black and white, literally stated, before they could accept that Jesus intended Peter to have a successor. However, for some of the mainline Protestant denominations which have been in dialogue with the Catholic Church in recent decades, there is a growing appreciation, as stated above, of the petrine office. More are realizing the need of a ministry for unity in the Church. Such dialogues and studies have profound Scriptural scholars involved.

## ONE MAN OR MANY GOVERNING THE CHURCH?

Protestants claim that the Catholic position is that only the Pope is the spokesman for Jesus Christ in the Catholic Church, and that bishops, priests, religious, and laity simply "echo" what one man teaches. But this is not the teaching of the Catholic Church. It is the fruit of those who do not know the Catholic Church and do not love the Catholic Church. Let us consider here the reality of how Jesus established His Church with the three powers: teaching, governing and sanctifying.

Jesus, in building His Church, established a college of bishops and gave the primacy to Peter. All bishops of the world share in the teaching, governing and sanctifying powers Jesus gave to His Church. The college of bishops, as successors to the Apostles, is spoken of as the episcopal order. The bishops share authority with Peter's successor. This is to answer the question "Did Jesus Christ put one man in charge of His Church?" He obviously put the Apostles, the first bishops in charge, with the primacy given to Peter. We shall see that the Apostles, or bishops, shared their powers with priests and deacons.

As quoted above "Together with its head, the Roman Pontiff, and never without this head, the episcopal order is the subject of the supreme and full power over the universal Church" (LG 22). Since the final documents of an ecumenical council, made up of the Pope and the world's bishops, contain official teachings of the Church on the subject of how many govern the Church, it is appropriate to quote further from Vatican Council II:

> It is definite, however, that the power of binding and loosing, which was given to Peter (Matt. 16:19), was granted also to the college of Apostles, joined with their head (Matt. 18:18; 28:16-20).

This college, insofar as it is composed of many, expresses the variety and universality of the People of God, but insofar as it is assembled under one head, it expresses the unity of the flock of Christ. In it, the bishops faithfully recognizing the primacy and pre-eminence of the head, exercise their own authority for the good of their own faithful, and indeed of the whole Church, with the Holy Spirit constantly strengthening its organic structure and inner harmony.

The supreme authority with which this college is empowered over the whole Church is exercised in a solemn way through an ecumenical council. A council is never ecumenical unless it is confirmed or at least accepted as such by the successor of Peter. It is the prerogative of the Roman Pontiff to convoke these councils, to preside over them, and to confirm them. The same collegiate power can be exercised in union with the Pope by the bishops living in all parts of the world, provided that the head of the college calls them to collegiate action, or at least so approves or freely accepts the united action of the dispersed bishops, that it is made a true collegiate act.

This collegial union is apparent also in the mutual relations of the individual bishops with particular churches and with the universal Church. The Roman Pontiff, as the successor of Peter, is the perpetual and visible source and foundation of the unity of the bishops and of the multitude of the faithful. The individual bishop, however, is the visible principle and foundation of unity in his particular church; fashioned after the model of the universal Church. In and from such individual churches there comes into being the one and only Catholic Church. For this reason each individual bishop represents his own church, but all of them together in union with the Pope represent the entire Church joined in the bond of peace, love, and unity.

The individual bishops, who are placed in charge of particular churches, exercise their pastoral government over the portion of the People of God committed to their care, and not over other churches nor over the universal Church. But each of them, as a member of the episcopal college and a legitimate successor of the Apostles, is obliged by Christ's decree and command to be solicitous for the whole Church . . . .

Among the principal duties of bishops, the preaching of the Gospel occupies an eminent place. For bishops are preachers of the faith who lead new disciples to Christ. They are authentic teachers, that is, teachers endowed with the authority of Christ, who preach to the people committed to them the faith they must believe and put into practice. By the light of the Holy Spirit, they make that faith clear, bringing forth from the treasury of revelation new things and old (cf. Matt. 13:52), making faith bear fruit and vigilantly warding off any errors which threaten their flock (cf. 2 Tim. 4:1-4). Bishops, teaching in communion with the Roman Pontiff, are to be respected by all as witnesses to divine and Catholic truth. In matters of faith and morals, the bishops speak in the name of Christ and the faithful are to accept their teaching and adhere to it with a religious assent of soul. This religious submission of will and of mind must be shown in a special way to the authentic teaching authority of the Roman Pontiff, even when he is not speaking *ex cathedra*. That is, must be shown in such a way that his supreme magisterium is acknowledged with reverence, the judgments made by him are sincerely adhered to, according to his manifest mind and will. His mind and will in the matter may be known chiefly either from the character of the documents, from his frequent repetition of the same doctrine, or from his manner of speaking" (*Dogmatic Constitution on the Church*, LG nn. 22-25).

While the above official statements of Catholicism on the Pope and its bishops may not impress a fundamentalist, the statements at least put into proper perspective the teaching authority of Jesus with which He commissioned His Church through the College of Bishops (Apostles). They clarify that Jesus gave authority, according to Catholic doctrine, to more than one man. What about priests and deacons?

## THE APOSTOLIC AGE AND CONTINUITY OF THE FAITH

Did Jesus Christ really intend that His priesthood be shared in the Church only with deacons, priests and bishops? To answer explicitly, according to Sacred Scripture, Jesus intended His royal priesthood to be shared by every baptized member of His Church. All, however, do not share in the priesthood of Jesus Christ to the same degree and in the same manner.

> You, however, are a chosen race, a royal priesthood, a holy nation, a purchased people; that you may proclaim the perfections of Him who has called you out of darkness into His marvelous light. You who in times past were not a people, but are now the people of God; who had not obtained mercy, but now have obtained mercy (1 Peter 2:9-10).

Every baptized person has been baptized in Jesus Christ the High Priest. This participation has various names, "priesthood of the baptized" or "priesthood of the faithful" or "common priesthood" — meaning possessed in common by all who have been baptized into Jesus Christ. This is royal, great, magnificent, and far beyond what we deserve or could ever merit. By Baptism each one of us participates in some manner in Jesus Christ as Priest, Prophet and King.

Christ the Lord, High Priest taken from among men (cf. Heb. 5:1-5), "made a kingdom and priests to God His Father" (Rev. 1:6; cf. 5:9-10) out of this new people. The baptized, by regeneration and the anointing of the Holy Spirit, are consecrated into a spiritual house and a holy priesthood. Thus through all those works befitting Christian men they can offer spiritual sacrifices and proclaim the power of Him who has called them out of darkness into His marvelous light (cf. 1 Peter 2:4-10). Therefore all the disciples of Christ, persevering in prayer and praising God (cf. Acts 2:42-47), should present themselves as a living sacrifice, holy and pleasing to God (cf. (Rom. 12:1). Everywhere on earth they must bear witness to Christ and give an answer to those who seek an account of that hope of eternal life which is in them (cf. 1 Peter 3:15).

Though they differ from one another in essence and not only in degree, the common priesthood of the faithful and the ministerial or hierarchical priesthood are nonetheless interrelated. Each of them in its own special way is a participation in the one priesthood of Christ. The ministerial priest, by the sacred power he enjoys, molds and rules the priestly people. Acting in the person of Christ, he brings about the Eucharistic Sacrifice, and offers it to God in the name of all the people. For their part, the faithful join in the offering of the Eucharist by virtue of their royal priesthood. They likewise exercise the priesthood by receiving the Sacraments, by prayer and thanksgiving, by the witness of a holy life, and by self-denial and active charity.

It is through the Sacraments and the exercise of the virtues that the sacred nature and organic structure of the priestly community is brought into operation. Incorporated into the Church through Baptism, the faithful are consecrated by the Baptismal character to the exercise of the worship of the Christian religion. Reborn as sons of God, they must confess before men the faith which they have received from God through the Church. Bound more intimately to the Church by the Sacrament of Confirmation, they are endowed by the Holy Spirit with special strength. Hence they are more strictly obliged to spread and defend the faith both by word and by deed as true witnesses of Christ (*Dogmatic Constitution on the Church* LG, nn. 10, 11).

Accordingly, every baptized member of the Church, the "body of Christ," is to spread the faith. The Sacrament of Confirmation commissions everyone of the faithful to witness for Jesus Christ before others. The work of spreading the faith is not restricted to the Pope, to bishops, priests or religious. The obligation rests upon all. An important example is that the Church teaches that parents are the first teachers of their children in the faith.

The Catholic Church believes that the priestly powers of Jesus Christ are special in men who have received the Sacrament of Holy Orders. While all the baptized share in the priesthood of Jesus Christ, those of the ministerial priesthood, who have received the Sacrament of Holy Orders, share in Christ's ministerial priesthood, not simply in a greater *degree* but in *essence*. Many Protestant churches would attribute a mere functional difference between the priesthood of the baptized and those in the ministerial priesthood.

According to many Protestants, if the minister was sick on a Sunday morning, anyone with the necessary talent in the pews could come to the front of the congregation and perform the same function as the minister (or priest) with the same effect. The priesthood is believed to be merely functional. All that were baptized would have the same powers as Christ. This has been in opposition to Catholic Church teaching since New Testament times. The Apostolic Chain, which transmits the powers of Christ's priesthood, has been broken within many Protestant churches so that, in fact, their ministers do not have any special priestly powers.

A study of both the New Testament and the sub-apostolic age, which is the development of the Church after the death of the Apostles, indicates the basic structure of the Church with deacons, priests and bishops, as well as the primacy of Peter. There were internal tensions and external challenges faced by the very first Christians. Conflicts and tensions, so common today, are nothing new to Christianity. The problems of holding together the early Christian communities in the face of internal tensions and external challenges had to be dealt with from the time of the Apostles. These problem increased as the apostolic age faded into history. Colossians, Ephesians, Acts, the pastoral letters, Jude, 2 Peter, and the Johannine epistles reflect the concern for the problem of false teachers.

Even early Christian tradition was not inclined to attribute the

Second Epistle of Peter to Petrine authorship. Scholars date it between 110 and 140 AD. It reminds readers of the divine authenticity of Christ's teachings. It takes up the question of the interpretation of Scripture by pointing out that it is possible to misunderstand the Sacred Writings (1, 19-2.1). The structures which mark the post-New Testament great Church are beginning to emerge more clearly.

We cannot expect to pick up the Bible and find therein a modern-day catechism. Jesus Christ presented His teachings, and founded a Church upon the Apostles. He ordained the Apostles bishops, giving them the fullness of His priesthood, with Peter having the primacy. As indicated in an earlier chapter, Jesus founded a Church, not a book. His teachings were not written down in some concise, analytical, scientific manner. The different men who wrote under divine inspiration of the Holy Spirit were not part of some team that one day agreed to write a structured book containing all the teachings of Jesus Christ. Jesus rather built His Church on men, on Apostles, for whom He promised the Spirit. Thus this People of God, with Apostles, were given the Holy Spirit to become the "body of Christ," which could never be destroyed. We need to study the Scriptures as the Word of God. We need, too, to study Tradition — what the early Christians did and taught and how they developed the early Church from the teachings of Jesus Christ under the guidance of the Holy Spirit. To limit all to "the Book" is not Scriptural, but contrary to Sacred Scripture. The Catholic position of Church, Scripture, and Tradition is in harmony with Sacred Scripture itself.

The structure of the Catholic Church we know today can be seen emerging in the late New Testament books. Even non-canonical works from the same period, e.g., 1 Clement (around 90 A.D.) and the letters of Ignatius of Antioch (around 115) harmonize with the teachings and structure of the Catholic Church we know today.

Emphasis in these late New Testament books on Church structure, office, authority, and the apostolic tradition has lead to the expression "early Catholicism." The study of Scripture and historical records point clearly toward the end of the first century as the beginning of the Church, in which structural and institutional aspects were first articulated, and in a manner that characterizes the Catholic tradition to the present day.

The honest scholar of early Christianity finds the traditional threefold ministry of bishops, presbyters and deacons. Evidence is seen in the letters of Antioch's Bishop Ignatius. It was here that the disciples are first called "Christians" and the Church is first described as

"Catholic." Here also, very clearly in place, is the threefold ministry of bishops, priests, and deacons which we know throughout the universal Church through the centuries.

When 1 Corinthians, Romans, Colossians and Ephesians describe the Church as "the body of Christ" the word "Church" is used clearly in a universal sense. 1 Timothy describes the Church as "the pillar and bulwark of truth" (1 Tim. 3:15). We see the Church developing from the teachings of Jesus Christ. Timothy's letter reminds us of an early collection of canon law, with liturgical regulations (2:1-15), qualifications for ministerial priesthood (3:1-13). There are rules for widows (5:3-16); regulations on the payment, discipline, and the installation of presbyters (5:17-22). So what's new? The basic message that a teaching authority belongs to the Church's office is clearly part of Catholic tradition from New Testament times.

The Acts of the Apostles is often called the "Gospel of the Spirit." Therein we read of an early history of the Church, how it grew from the first days of the community of faith in Jerusalem. This book has a great appeal for evangelical Christians and missionaries. If read with objectivity, the concept of Church office in Luke and Acts is a developed one. The Holy Spirit is seen working in a particular way through Church leaders. The foundation of the Church is seen in the ministry of the Apostles, a group which St. Luke restricts almost exclusively to the Twelve (Luke 6:13). He describes the appointment of deacons, the Seven, through the invocation and laying on of hands (Acts 6:1-6). Ministry comes from the Spirit. Paul and Barnabas are chosen by the Spirit for missionary work (13:2). Paul tells the presbyters at Ephesus that the Spirit has made them overseers (20:28). This is in harmony with Catholic doctrine through the centuries. God calls. He uses men in authority in the Church to verify God's call. We see an emphasis on ministers being sent or commissioned by others in authority, in regard to the Apostles themselves (Acts 1:2-8). Evidence of other ministers appointed by the Apostles is seen in Acts 6:6; 14:23. In the context of what is generally recognized as a Eucharist celebration, Paul and Barnabas are given the title "Apostles" only after the Church leaders at Antioch have laid hands on them and commissioned them (Acts 13:1-3).

We notice that the call comes not simply from the assembly of the people, but from God, and in conjunction with a commission given by Church leaders. This is the Catholic teaching today and through the centuries. Every man called to the holy priesthood is believed to have a call from Jesus Christ in the Holy Spirit. It takes the discernment of the bishop to verify the call in order to administer ordination.

The post-apostolic great Church, rooted in Jesus through the original Apostles, emerged. The Greek word *diakonos* (Latin for "minister") originally meant one who served at table — a servant. From early times it became the basic term for those exercising roles of service in the Church. St. Paul described the Apostles as "qualified ministers of a new covenant" (2 Cor. 3:6). While the special office of the diaconate appears later than bishops and priests, from the time of the Apostles it was obviously understood that the ministerial priesthood can be bestowed in three orders: that of bishop, priest, and deacon.

1 Timothy presupposes a well-established Church at Ephesus with a college of presbyters (1 Tim. 5:17). Titus shows a more primitive situation, calling for the establishment of a group of presbyters in each city on Crete (Titus 1:5). Presbyters are commissioned by the laying on of the hands by a successor of the original Apostles. This rite has been essential to the Sacrament of Holy Orders through the centuries.

A primary duty of priest-bishops in the pastoral epistles is the safeguarding of the faith for the entire community. They are to encourage others to follow sound doctrine and refute those who contradict it (Titus 1:5-14). Faith is described in terms of teaching, doctrine, truths handed down — the deposit of faith. Not to be overlooked in harmonizing history with the New Testament or early Church development is the *Didache* (the Teaching of the twelve Apostles). It is a first-century treatise, written before 100 A.D. The *Didache* is divided into three parts: 1) The Two Ways: the way of Life, and the Way of Death. 2) A liturgical manual on Baptism, fasting, Confession, and Holy Communion, and 3) a treatise on the ministry. Doctrinal teaching is presupposed. The Way of Life is the love of God and of neighbor. The Way of Death is a list of vices to be avoided. There is a brief instruction on Baptism, references to Apostles, bishops, and deacons, and an exhortation to watch and be prepared for the coming of Christ. The *Didache* seems to have come from Syria and its writing shows a familiarity with the Matthean traditions. Of bishops and deacons, the *Didache* says: "they, too, conduct (*leitourgousi*) the liturgy of the prophets and teachers." Ignatius of Antioch placed great importance on the role of bishop as a principle of unity. He grounded his office in Jesus Christ and stressed the bishop's right to regulate the Sacraments and the life of the Christian community. "Let no one do anything touching the Church apart from the bishop. Let that celebration of the Eucharist be considered valid which is held under the bishop or anyone to whom he has committed it. Where the bishop appears, there let the people be, just as where Jesus Christ is, there is the Catholic Church. It is not permitted without authorization from the bishop either to baptize or to hold an agape; but whatever he approves is also pleasing to God" (Smyrneans 8:1-2).

The Roman Catholic Church teaches that "by divine institution bishops have succeeded to the place of the Apostles as shepherds of the Church" (LG n. 20). Their authorization proceeds from Christ to the Apostles and from the Apostles to the bishops (LG n. 21). Only bishops, who have the fullness of the priesthood of Jesus Christ, have the power of Jesus Christ in the Spirit to ordain priests and bishops. This teaching is present in the New Testament itself. In Acts, Paul summons the presbyter-bishops of Ephesus for a farewell address. He instructs them to guard the flock against the false teachers who will come after his departure (Acts 20:29-31). 2 Timothy is concerned greatly with handing on the apostolic Tradition. Timothy, having received the laying on of hands from Paul (2 Tim. 1:6), is told to "guard the truth that has been entrusted to you" (2 Tim. 1:14) and to hand it on to those who will teach it to others (2:2).

The responsibility of those who succeeded in the role of guiding the churches falls upon the presbyter-bishops, as seen in 1 Peter 5:1. An author writing in Peter's name as a "fellow-presbyter" to the presbyters of Asia Minor claims for their ministry a continuity with the ministry of the Apostle. Timothy and Titus are delegated by Paul to set up presbyterial colleges in their communities (1 Tim. 5:22; Titus 1:5). The communities to which the *Didache* was addressed were told, "appoint for yourselves bishops and deacons worthy of the Lord" (15:1). When the Protestant reformers of the early sixteenth century denied the special powers of the ministerial priesthood — those in Holy Orders — and claimed that the priesthood was purely functional, there developed in the Catholic Church a stronger emphasis on the clergy to offset this error. There became in the Catholic Church a one-sided emphasis on the special sacramental powers of the priesthood. It is true that the priesthood of those ordained in Holy Orders is a very high dignity and a very grave responsibility. But those who are merely baptized also form a kingly and priestly people. At present there are efforts in the opposite direction, as the Church always struggles with fallen human nature in order to keep its balance. In more recent years, there have been dangers of "clericalizing the laity." There has been an emphasis on liturgical roles of the laity, but this has been met with criticism, since it tends to be done at the expense of the layman's function as the Catholic leaven in the secular world.

## THE INFALLIBILITY OF THE CHURCH

Consider some of the opinions held regarding the Church's teaching on infallibility: "The Pope is head not simply of a religious organization, but of a political state with temporal interests of its own." "The Catholic Church is rich in its papacy and its Holy See and is in it for power, wealth and prestige." "In Romans 11:22, St. Paul wrote to the Church of Rome, telling her to 'abide in goodness, otherwise you also shall be cut off.' Isn't that enough to say the Church of Rome isn't infallible?" "In the lifetime of St. John, the Lord found it necessary to rebuke the seven Churches in Asia for errors (Rev. cc. 1-3)." "Consider the Galileo case when an 'infallible' Pope pronounced Galileo's theory of the revolution of the earth around the sun to be a damnable heresy." "And there have been sinful Popes. How can they be infallible?"

Many more accusations have been thrown at the Catholic Church and the papacy. The above examples should suffice. There have even been accusations that St. Peter, the first Pope, was never at Rome. Modern excavations under St. Peter's Basilica, engaged in by scientists of different religious persuasions, have verified that St. Peter was in Rome and was buried there.

The ancient historian Eusebius wrote,

> Peter the Apostle, the first Pontiff of the Christians when he had first founded the Church at Antioch, proceeds to Rome where, preaching the Gospel, he continues for twenty-five years bishop of that city ... Linus was the first after Peter that obtained the episcopate of the Church of the Romans.

The Protestant Lightfoot wrote of Eusebius,

> To Eusebius we are indebted for almost all that we know of the lost ecclesiastical literature of the second century ... in no instance that we can test, does Eusebius give a doubtful testimony ... I do not join in the vulgar outcry against the dishonesty of Eusebius. Whenever I have been able to investigate this charge, I have found it baseless.

Vatican City covers 108.7 acres and includes the Vatican Palace, St. Peter's Basilica, Vatican Radio Station, and numerous other buildings that serve the Pope and the administration of the universal Church. Ultimate authority over this tiny piece of land, the smallest state in the world, is vested in the Pope but actually administered by the Pontifical Commission for the State of Vatican City. It is a politically neutral State. Only citizens of Vatican City owe allegiance to the Pope as temporal ruler. The Church has to have its administration some place on earth and the first Pope went to Rome. It is really a city state within the greater city of Rome.

The wealth of the Church is a myth. About half of the bishops of the world who came to Vatican Council II could not afford to pay their own expenses. The Vatican itself is in debt and for years has faced financial crises like so many other institutions in the modern world. Its arts treasures are not for the personal wealth of the Pope or anyone else but are preserved by the Church for the privileged enjoyment of the entire world and for historical reasons.

*Infallibility* and *impeccability* are two different things. Infallibility means that the bishops as successors of the Apostles and official teachers of the Church in union with the Pope, are unable, collectively, to define erroneous doctrines as dogmas of faith. Impeccability means that one could not commit sin and fall from grace. Jesus Christ was impeccable. But Christians, including the Pope, are not impeccable. The Pope goes to confession.

Regarding the book of Revelations and the seven Churches in Asia, who were in error, a thorough study reveals no hint that the teaching authority of the Church was guilty of error in doctrine. Infallibility means that the universal Church cannot officially teach false doctrine. But some of her officials can err in their conduct, or grow lax and careless in administration.

Infallibility, while belonging to the whole Church collectively, belongs specifically in its particular exercise to Church teachings, that is, its Magisterium. The Magisterium consists of the bishops who teach in union with the Pope. The Church has never taught that the Pope or bishops are infallible each time any one or all of them together open their mouth to speak on any subject.

The universal Church is infallible only in matters of faith or morals. Also, the Pope must be teaching the *whole* Church, not just an individual audience or country. He must make known he is defining an official position of the universal Church. This is generally done after consultation with the world's bishops. The Pope seldom issues an infallible doctrine. But members of the Church are to listen to the Church in its ordinary day-to-day-teachings.

As defined by the First Vatican Council,

The Roman Pontiff, when he speaks *ex cathedra* — that is, when in discharge of the office of pastor and teacher of all Christians, by virtue of his supreme apostolic authority, he defines a doctrine regarding faith or morals to be held by the universal Church, by the divine assistance promised to him in Blessed Peter, is possessed of that infallibility with which the divine Redeemer willed that His Church should be endowed in defining doctrine regarding faith or morals; and therefore such definitions are irreformable of themselves, and not in virtue of consent of the Church.

The Galileo affair was a matter of science, not religion. It did indirectly concern the Church and spiritual interests because of the circumstances of the time, and Galileo's own indulgence in theological speculations. Galileo would not have clashed with religion had he not interjected his own interpretations of Sacred Scripture regarding what he thought to be a contradiction between the Bible and his scientific discoveries. The Church as Church did not digress from spiritual matters in the Galileo case, as is presented by the Church's enemies. Some at the time ridiculed Scripture regarding the sun, etc. Because of the spiritual implications, the Church was seriously concerned.

There were unfortunate decisions made in connection with the Galileo case but it was not a decision involving the infallibility of the Church. The Church teaches that infallibility involves only matters of faith and morals, not natural science, geography, etc.

Are there Scriptural grounds for the infallibility of the Church? There certainly is, provided we interpret infallibility the way the Church explains it and do not confuse it with impeccability or with every word that comes from the Pope or every statement of the bishops. Read again St. Matthew 16:18-19. Jesus Christ says to Peter:

> I say to you that you are Peter, and upon this rock I will build my Church; and the gates of hell will not prevail against it. And I will give to you the keys of the kingdom of heaven. Whatsoever you shall bind on earth, it shall be bound in heaven; and whatsoever you shall loose on earth, it shall be loosed also in heaven.

Jesus Christ thus constitutes, in promise, Peter as head of the Church, declaring that the office would carry with it the power to act vicariously in the name of God. In St. Luke 22:31, 32, Jesus says,

> Simon, Simon, behold Satan has desired to have you, that he might sift you like wheat. But I have prayed for you, that your faith fail not; and do you, being once converted, confirm your brethren.

St. John 21:15-17 tells how Jesus, after His Resurrection, commissioned St. Peter to feed His lambs, and to feed His sheep, that is, to be shepherd over the whole flock.

There are attempts to explain away these texts, especially that of St. Matthew. But the text is quite clear even if not pleasing to some outside the full Catholic Tradition whose history goes back to the first Christians, back to St. Peter, the first Pope. Christ said, "I am the Light of the World" and in St. Luke 10:15,16; we hear Jesus say, "He who hears you, hears Me; and he who rejects you, rejects Me; and he who rejects Me, rejects Him who sent Me."

If there is no teaching authority of Jesus in the one Church He founded, then we do not have Christ, the Light of the world shining in the darkness. Rather, He has then been defeated and we cannot know His truth but are left to our own sinful resources, contradicting one another. This in fact has happened with thousands of Christian denominations out of full union with the Roman Catholic Church, each claiming to interpret the Bible according to the mind of Jesus. All are supposedly guided by the Holy Spirit, the One Holy Spirit of Truth. This interpretation makes the Holy Spirit, "the Spirit of Truth" contradict Himself on these issues. Truth does not permit contradictions on the same issues. Truth is one. Truth demands the conformity of the mind with reality. The ultimate Reality is God.

The infallibility of the Church, with the Pope as the chief spokesman for Christ, in the teaching Church, does not depend on the wisdom and power of man. Infallibility is not due to the intelligence of man. It is due to the power and wisdom of God. It is due to the Holy Spirit who keeps the Catholic Church in the truth of Jesus Christ. If we do not believe that Jesus promised the Holy Spirit as the "Spirit of Truth" to guide His Church, to keep it in oneness, holiness, and unity until the end of the world, then we cannot be certain in faith of anything we believe. If the one Church Jesus founded no longer is present in the world, Jesus did not keep His promise to abide with us forever.

## SUMMARY OF THE HISTORY OF THE CHURCH

It should be noted that the early Scriptures were written in a hostile world, when even those who considered themselves the People of God under the Old Covenant — especially many of the Jewish leaders — did not want to recognize Jesus Christ as Savior and the long expected Messiah. Also, the early Christians suffered persecutions the first few hundred years. In spite of this, however, the historical resources available on the structure of the Church from Apostolic times is remarkable.

Following is a summary of the high points of Christian history:

About 4 B.C. — Jesus is born in Bethlehem. (Note, it is generally accepted that our modern count of numbering our years since the birth of Jesus, "A.D." is about four years off).

67 A.D. — St. Peter, after establishing the Church in Rome, was martyred by being crucified upside down. His martyrdom, as predicted by Jesus Himself, took place during the first persecution of Christians

under Nero.

303 — the persecutions of Christians in the Roman Empire became severe and many Christians are put to death during the next decade. In 313 the Emperor Constantine issued the Edict of Milan which granted religious toleration to Christianity in the Roman Empire.

325 — the bishops of the Church at the First Council of Nicaea, in what is now northwest Turkey, set forth fundamental Christian beliefs in what is known as the Nicene Creed.

431 — the Council of Ephesus (Turkey's western coast) was held, which declared that Mary is the Virgin Mother of the God-Man Jesus Christ. In 431-461 St. Patrick converted Ireland to Catholicism. In 451 the Council of Chalcedon (in Turkey across the Bosporus Strait from Istanbul) acknowledges the authority of the Pope by accepting the doctrine espoused by Pope Leo I of the two natures, human and divine, of Jesus Christ.

496 — the conversion of Clovis, King of the Franks. The year 589 marks the conversion of the Visigothic King of Spain. 596-604: St. Boniface established the Church in Germany. 732: Charles Martel's victory at Tours checks the Islamic invasion of western Europe.

800 — Pope Leo III crowned Charlemagne emperor of the Holy Roman Empire, successor of the Roman Caesars. 966: the Baptism of Prince Mieczyslaw of Poland. 985: conversion of Geza, the ruler of Hungary, and his son St. Stephen. 988: conversion of Vladimir and the establishment of Christianity as the official religion of Russia.

1054 — the major split between Roman Catholic and Eastern Orthodox branches of the Church. (There has been remarkable progress toward eventual reunion in recent years as we approach the third millennium of Christianity. The Orthodox have long recognized the Pope as successor of St. Peter and "first among equals.") When the Orthodox broke union with Rome they kept their bishops. Thus, they have a valid priesthood with powers that Jesus gave the first Apostles, or bishops of the Church. If the Orthodox recognized the Pope not simply as "first among equals" but the supreme bishop of the Church they would be in complete union with the Catholic Church. They are already united in almost every other area of faith and morals.

1059 — Celibacy for the clergy is strongly enforced.

1066 — William of Normandy invades England and defeats the Anglo-Saxons. William allows the Church to have its own system of canon law.

1095-1291 — Wars known as the Crusades are undertaken by European Christians to recover the holy lands of the Middle East from the Moslems. 1182-1226: St. Francis of Assisi adopted a life of preaching and strict poverty that becomes a model for many Christians.

1215 — King John, under pressure from England's barons and the Church, accepted the Magna Carta, considered a forerunner of the U.S. Bill of Rights and a model for limited government.

1225-1274 — St. Thomas Aquinas applies philosophical principles to Christian theology, teaching that truth can be attained by reason and faith, and that both are gifts of God. There can be no contradiction between right reason and true faith. (This is not to say that true faith comes from reasoning powers, but as St. Paul says in Scripture, "have a reason for the faith that is in you".)

1417 — The Council of Constance (in southern Germany) ends the Great Western Schism, during which rival Popes in Rome, Avignon (southern France) and Pisa (Italy) fought for supremacy in the Church. However, there was never more than one Pope in Christ's Church. There was a time when up to three men claimed to be Pope.

(Such breakages have occurred right through the centuries, beginning already in apostolic times. Simon Magus, of the New Testament, is a forerunner of independent men who set up religions of their own. Christ predicted that such things would happen. "There will arise false Christs and false prophets to seduce if possible even the elect" (Mark 13:22). Some early independent leaders who led Christians into disunity are now only names in textbooks, such as Montanus, Manicheaus, Arius, and Donatus.

In later centuries, from 1054 onwards, we find founders of the Greek Church, Photius and Michael Cerularius, who were influential in breaking Christians of the East from Rome. Politics and an interest in human power became involved in the break of 1054 as it would again at the beginning of the sixteenth century.)

1517 — Martin Luther posted his 95 theses in Germany, beginning the Protestant Reformation, which was to lead to a breakup among Christians in the western world into hundreds of denominations. They are not able to keep united since they deny the authority of the Pope, the successor to St. Peter. Jesus appointed Peter to keep His Church one in the faith.

1534 — King Henry VIII declared himself to be the head of the Church in England, thus separating the country from Rome. To the present day the Queen or King of England has as a title, head of the Church of England.

1545-1552 — St. Francis Xavier does missionary work in India, Malaysia, Indonesia and Japan.

1545-1563 — The Council of Trent (in northern Italy) meets to bring about a reform, where needed, among Catholics. It was a counter-reformation to bring the members of the Church more into line with the Gospels, the teachings of Jesus. This was the kind of reform needed, not the founding of new churches. Men must be changed by religion, not religion by men. The Protestant Reform (Revolt) led to many churches. One important change by the council was the setting up of seminaries for a proper formation and education for future priests. The council also spelled out the doctrines of the Church in harmony with the Scriptures to offset misunderstandings and misinterpretations.

1790 — John Carroll of Baltimore was consecrated as the first Catholic bishop of the United States.

1870 — The First Vatican Council defined the Church's teaching on infallibility.

1950 — Pope Pius XII, exercising this infallibility, after consulting all the bishops of the world as to the faith of the people, issued the infallible dogma of faith that the Blessed Virgin Mary was bodily assumed into heaven.

1962-1965 — The Second Vatican Council was called by Pope John XXIII and was continued by Pope Paul VI. It spelled out more precisely the collegiality of bishops with the Pope, and the role of laity in the Church. It allowed the Sacrifice of the Mass and Sacraments to be administered in the language of the people. It sought dialogue with other religions to bring about the unity of all religions in Jesus Christ. It condemned anti-Semitism.

1978 — Karol Joseph Wojtyla of Poland became the first non-Italian Pope in 456 years. He took the name Pope John Paul II.

A complete history of the Church during its first two thousand years would require many volumes. No history of the Church can be presented with any objectivity if Peter and his successors, the Popes, are ignored.

---

For a more extensive treatment of Church history, readers are encouraged to obtain the book by the same author of this volume titled, *A Catechism Of The Catholic Church — 2,000 Years Of Faith And Tradition.* Franciscan Herald Press, 1434 West 51st. St., Chicago, Ill. 60609.

"I say to you that you are Peter,
and upon this rock I will build My Church . . . ."
(Matt. 16:18)

"This is the Bread which has come down from heaven . . . ."
(John 6:59)

# CHAPTER 11

# The Born-Again Catholic

"Born-again Christian" is an expression frequently heard today and ascribed to certain people. "Are you a born-again Christian?" people ask. In the strict sense, every Christian has been born again. Less often heard is the subject of this chapter: "born-again Catholic."

Words and phrases are easily and flippantly thrown around today. We read of eighth graders taking "theology classes." We read of anybody and everybody studying the Scriptures without any guides or Church authority to help them in interpretation. Religious words and expressions are used without regard to their exact meaning. Everybody becomes an authority on the Word of God. The Bible becomes everybody's book and everybody is its authority. The Church is not needed and even what the Church is has often been forgotten. Consequently we hear of religious confusion.

There is a sense in which the author will use the term "born-again Catholic" in this chapter. First, it is important that we get a precise understanding of the Sacrament of Baptism, wherein one is "born again" in the sense in which Jesus spoke and which cannot be repeated. While many "born-again Christians" today get caught up in great emotional displays of the faith, and God bless them for zeal, yet, it is important that we have some exact understanding of our faith and what it means to be "born again" lest we fail to discern spirits and are led by evil spirits.

We begin then with a summary of the Church's teaching on Baptism.

Baptism is the Sacrament given the Church by Jesus Christ for spiritual rebirth. This Sacrament, in which Jesus Himself acts, cleanses a person of all sin and incorporates one into Jesus Christ. The Prophet

Ezekiel foretold it: "I shall pour clean water over you and you will be cleansed; I shall cleanse you of all your defilement and all your idols. I shall give you a new heart, and put a new spirit in you" (Ezek. 36:25-26).

The word "Baptism" means immersion in the sense of dipping under water. It also means to bathe or to wash clean. Every Sacrament which Jesus gave His Church has an outward sign. The sign of Baptism whereby we can know that Jesus is acting, is the external pouring of the water or immersion into water, along with the invocation of the Holy Trinity. The meaning of the Baptismal sign is that the person is reborn in Jesus Christ.

Baptism removes all guilt of sin from the soul and all punishment due to sin. It confers the grace of regeneration and the infused virtues. It incorporates a person into Jesus Christ and His Church. One baptized receives the baptismal character of Jesus Christ on his soul for all eternity, and grace which gives one the right to heaven. St. Paul writes in the Scriptures: "It was for no reason except His own compassion that He saved us, by means of the cleansing water of rebirth" (Titus 3:5). That grace of regeneration that is infused into our souls at Baptism is that supernatural life, that sharing in the life of God, which Jesus Christ merited for us by His death and Resurrection. It is the new birth, that being "born again" of which Jesus spoke to Nicodemus (John 3:3). It is that new creation described by St. Paul (2 Cor. 5:17).

Baptism infuses the virtues of faith, hope and charity into the soul. Baptism gives the soul the supernatural power to believe in God, to believe the teachings of Jesus Christ as contained in the deposit of faith of His Church. Faith is activated under the influence of the will, which requires the assistance of grace in order to believe. For example, one cannot believe that Jesus Christ is present Body, Blood, Soul and Divinity under the appearances of bread and wine in the Holy Eucharist except by the power of God, the supernatural virtue of faith. So divine faith, while in harmony with reason and the use of the intellect, is not simply an intellectual act of the soul. The act of faith is the assent of the mind to what God has revealed.

Baptism infuses into the soul the supernatural power to trustfully expect to possess God in heaven for all eternity. It belongs to the will and enables a person to desire eternal life, the heavenly vision of God whereby in heaven we will see God "face to face, even as He is." The Apostle wrote:

> We see now through a mirror in an obscure manner, but then face to face. Now I know in part, but then I shall know even as I have

been known. So there abide faith, hope and charity, these three, but the greatest of these is charity (1 Cor. 12-13).

Hope is confident that what is desired will certainly be attained. It too is not merely a natural act. It is God's power in us enabling us to trust Him for things divine. Baptism infuses into the soul the supernatural power of charity. It is not natural but a supernatural virtue by which a person loves God above all things for His own sake, and loves others for the sake of God. It cannot be acquired by mere human effort. It is conferred only with divine or sanctifying grace. One who falls into mortal sin loses the supernatural virtue of charity although he may still possess the virtues of hope and faith.

One who is baptized is incorporated into the crucified and glorified Christ and is reborn to a sharing of the life of God. St. Paul the Apostle wrote, "For you were buried together with Him in Baptism, and in Him also rose again through faith in the working of God who raised Him from the dead" (Rom. 6:4). St. Paul also spoke of being grafted into Jesus Christ, like the branch of a tree is grafted onto another and becomes one with it (Rom. 11:16-20). We, natural beings, through Baptism are grafted into Jesus and His divine life flows into our souls and we become one with Him.

Jesus said,
I am the vine, you are the branches. He who abides in Me, and I in him, he bears much fruit; for without Me you can do nothing. If anyone does not abide in Me, he shall be cast outside as the branch and wither; and they shall gather them up and cast them into the fire, and they shall burn. If you abide in Me, and if my words abide in you, ask whatever you will and its shall be done to you. In this is my Father glorified, that you may bear very much fruit, and become my disciples. As the Father has loved Me, I also have loved you. Abide in my love. If you keep my commandments, you will abide in my love, as I also have kept my Father's commandments, and abide in His love. These things I have spoken to you that my joy may be in you, and that your joy may be made full (John 15: 5-10).

Note that all that Jesus thus speaks about comes through Baptism, bringing a life that must be lived and grow, nourished by Himself in the Holy Eucharist. The love He is speaking of is the divine act of love, not possible by human power alone. The joy He speaks of is supernatural also. Among the gifts of grace infused at holy Baptism are the peace and joy of the Holy Spirit, which makes possible the practice of the Beatitudes. All baptized persons belong to the Church of Jesus

Christ. In some sense all baptized persons, even though not baptized by a priest, but if baptized validly, that is, with proper form and matter, proper intention, using water with the words, "I baptize you in the name of the Father, and of the Son, and of the Holy Spirit," — all belong to the Church. Vatican II states,

> It remains true that all who have been justified by faith in Baptism are incorporated into Christ; they therefore have a right to be called Christians, and with good reason are accepted as brothers by the children of the Catholic Church" (*Decree on Ecumenism*).

The indelible character of Jesus Christ which is sealed in the soul is thrilling and breathtaking to contemplate. By this indelible mark of Christ one receives a likeness to the priesthood of Jesus Christ. Even if one lost the virtue of faith, or lost even one's soul by dying unrepentant of mortal sin, the indelible character of Christ would remain upon the soul for all eternity. Scriptures picture Christ Jesus being ashamed of the soul that departs into eternal fire, in the abode of the damned, separated from God forever. Why? Because it takes with it the indelible seal of Jesus on its soul.

> If anyone wishes to come after Me, let him deny himself, and take up his cross, and follow Me. For he who would save his life will lose it; but he who loses his life for my sake and for the Gospel's sake will save it. For what does it profit a man, if he gain the whole world, but suffer the loss of his own soul? Or what will a man give in exchange for his soul? For whoever is ashamed of Me and of my words in this adulterous and sinful generation, of him will the Son of Man will also be ashamed when He comes with the holy angels in the glory of His Father (Mark 8:34-38).

The person baptized will remain for all eternity a Christian because the indelible character gives the soul a permanent relationship with Jesus Christ.

Old time Catholics (and there are no other kind of authentic Catholic), used to say, "Once a Catholic, always a Catholic." Is that true if a Catholic loses his faith? Yes. Once a Catholic a person will always remain a Catholic in the fundamental sense of possessing the indelible character of Baptism that can never be wiped away. One cannot stop being a Catholic because, once baptized, he cannot have the Baptism undone. The indelible seal of Baptism will remain on the soul for all eternity.

Baptism restores the one baptized to the state in which Adam and Eve were created. In fact, it does more in the spiritual sense; it gives the soul an even greater potential in Christ than when Adam and Eve lived in the state of original justice. It does not, however, give back the special gifts, called preternatural, possessed by our first parents. "To all who did accept Him He gave power to become children of God" (John 1:12). The person baptized still has the consequences of original sin: concupiscence or weakness of the flesh, darkness of the intellect and weakness of will, suffering, and the necessity of physically dying.

Baptism, however, gives one the supernatural helps to cope with sufferings; it supernaturalizes them by uniting them to the sufferings of Jesus Christ. Baptism promises a person bodily immortality and Resurrection at the end of the world. Sufficient grace is promised to resist temptations of the flesh and to grow in holiness. Baptism infuses the virtues of faith, hope, and love once possessed by our first parents, and the sharing in the life of God, commonly called "sanctifying grace."

The Holy Spirit comes even more actively into the soul when one receives the Sacrament of Confirmation. Confirmation brings a spiritual strengthening. The Holy Spirit is received in a new and special way, strengthening the person in grace and giving him special help to witness Jesus Christ to others. It completes the grace of Baptism. A person must first be regenerated by Baptism in order to be introduced to maturation in the life of grace through Confirmation, as well as through the effects of these two Sacraments throughout our life in Christ upon earth.

There is evidence in the New Testament that Jesus Christ instituted Confirmation. It was prophesied in the Old Testament when the outpouring of the Spirit of God over the whole of mankind was foretold as a sign of the Age of the Messiah (Joel 3:1, Is. 44:3-5, Ezek. 39:29). Jesus also promised His Apostles and all faithful of the future that He would send them the Holy Spirit (John 14:16, Luke 24:49, Acts 1:5, John 7:38). We read what happened on the feast of Pentecost (Acts 2:4). Later the Apostles communicated the Holy Spirit in the rite or outward sign of the imposition of hands on the baptized (Acts 8:14-17). St. Paul did the same to some twelve disciples in Ephesus after they were baptized (Acts 19:6). In Hebrews 6:2, four early converts from Judaism were told that the imposition of hands brings the communication of the Holy Spirit and belongs to the foundation of the Christian religion.

The above may all seem very intellectual to one who is captivated by the emotionalism of certain fundamentalists but it is all very Scriptural and part of two thousand years of Christianity. Meditating on these sublime truths will truly touch the heart and set one aflame with divine love. The heart is very important in Christian living. So is the head. The intellect and the will, the highest faculties of the soul, must both be involved in cooperating in the divine acts of faith, hope and love which accompany sanctifying grace.

This brings us to the term, "born-again Catholic." Is it possible? It is possible in the sense of coming alive to the reality of our faith in Jesus Christ. It is possible in the sense of rediscovering a deeper reality of our faith, our life in Jesus Christ. It is possible in the sense of coming, by cooperation with divine grace, from a dead faith to a living faith. It is possible therefore in the sense of developing a personal relationship in Jesus Christ, coming alive in the Spirit, and truly becoming conscious of the indwelling of the Blessed Trinity in the soul. We need but study the lives of the saints of the Catholic Church to see how far many people fall from reaching the potential that is ours if we but cooperate with grace.

How often does it happen that young people growing up do not appreciate all that their parents have provided for them? Sometimes they do not discover and appreciate their natural gifts until late in their teens, or into young adulthood, or even until they are parents themselves and must provide for their own children.

As the born-again Catholic, who discovers more deeply the reality of his faith as a child of God and member of the one true Church, launches out into the deep for a catch as Jesus Christ commanded, and drinks of the deep waters of divine faith, he will come to live with Christ in God. There is a death-dealing spirit of the world so widespread today with all the secular media about us. There is need to be open to the vivifying Spirit of Christ to bring about a spiritual renewal of the world. That must begin with each one of us, within our inner souls. Each of us must co-operate with the Divine Spirit in our souls.

The purely intellectual, the lukewarm, the activist, or the worldly-minded, will hardly be "born again" in the sense in which we speak. They will remain blind to the supernatural world available all around them, and within them. The deeper development of the interior life demands more than an intellectual pursuit of more theological or Scriptural knowledge. There must yet be the surrender of self to Jesus Christ in God. It is a language the world cannot understand. "Having eyes, they see not, having ears, they hear not ... ."

Love should be the response to knowledge. We ought not pray for more knowledge than love. The knowledge may remain simply on the natural level. Faith is on the divine, the supernatural level. Let us ask God, "Give me as much love as knowledge, and not more knowledge than love. I wish to know You more so that I may love You more intensely."

Yes, we can read Scripture and see the words "In Him we live and move and have our being" (Acts 17:28). And yet we could remain blind to Jesus Christ. St. Paul wrote, "It is now the hour for us to rise from sleep and put on the armor of light" (Rom. 13:11, 12). How few there are who experience their faith as God would have it, a faith that recognizes His presence everywhere and is within us by grace. To realize in childlike faith that God is within me and I am in Him; to know by faith and love intensely the reality that begins with Baptism, and intensifies with Confirmation. We become the temples of God.

How we complain about sufferings and fail to supernaturalize them by joining them to the sufferings of Jesus Christ to thereby make them of eternal value. Eternity is for uninterrupted enjoyment and delight of the beatific vision, of seeing "God face to face, even as He is." We have only this brief earthly span for pain and suffering wherein we can give glory to God, and do reparation for the salvation of souls — if we but join them to the sufferings of Jesus, which make our sufferings have spiritual value. "For I reckon that the sufferings of the present time are not worthy to be compared with the glory to come that will be revealed in us" (Rom. 8: 18).

Is this strange language? Is it meaningless? Tasteless? Then, "taste and see that the Lord is sweet" (Ps. 33:9). Perfection does not consist in uninterrupted interior and exterior peace, an exuberant joy that wants spontaneously to shout at every moment "Alleluia." Jesus said, "Shall I not drink the cup that the Father has given Me?" (John 18:11). Also, "My soul is sorrowful, even unto death" (Mark 14:34). How far from true religion are those who really mean what they ask, "If God really exists, why does He permit suffering?"

In Me, Jesus Christ says, you shall have peace; in the world you shall have distress (John 16:33). Now, does not the average Christian, be he Catholic or otherwise, find it difficult to understand how one could simultaneously have peace and be in distress? But as one drinks more deeply of divine realities he sees that hardships and sufferings actually become a means toward a more intimate and vital union with God. They are actually offered as a holocaust to the Divine Indwelling of the Blessed Trinity reigning in the depths of the soul. One comes, as did the Apostle Paul, to rejoice at suffering for the love of God in Jesus Christ.

Ah! but these are such profound spiritual realities, too deep, too complex for the likes of me, the reader may think. Maybe so, for now.

Perhaps you still pray as did St. Augustine on the way to his not-yet-completed conversion, "Lord, make me pure, but not yet." The Christian life ought to be a life of new beginnings. We should grow and never stand still in the spiritual life. Open to the divine workings in the human heart, we should, we can, we must — if we take our faith and our goal of eternal life seriously — come to something of more than a fourth-grade understanding of the faith. God leaves us upon the earth for a certain number of years. He expects us to grow in knowledge, and correspondingly love, and give Him greater service through the years.

But let us return to basic things that are the theme of this book. Even the basics of our holy faith serve us in our quest for holiness, since the divine truths about the Person we love were revealed in order to lead us to a personal relationship with Jesus Christ, Son of God, Savior. Abstract doctrines, and perfect knowledge of them, however accurate, are insufficient. They must become alive, truths about the Person Whom we love.

Jesus is our mediator with the Father in the unity of the Holy Spirit. Let us be honest with ourselves: are even the basics of the true faith animated in our consciousness through which we see and embrace Jesus Christ, and thereby the Father?

How many a Christian has come to the fullness of Catholic faith and has thrilled at the realities of Catholicism to discover there divine realities they thought not possible, not existing or available upon this earth? The author has known of no sincere entrance of a Protestant Christian into the fullness of Catholic faith that ever complained of having had to give up anything precious to him or her in their former church. Each one confessed that all of the former faith was kept.

Everything precious was still believed and breathed in one's daily spiritual life. Like a flower formerly a bud, now, with the profession of the fullness of Catholic faith, the bud has grown, bloomed into a magnificent flower never before beheld. In this newfound fuller faith there is so much more — such an abundance never dreamt possible. Now one has access to divine life "more abundantly."

Many a Catholic is born and baptized into Catholicism at a tender age when the "born again" process begins. Somehow the faith became stagnant, lifeless. Then there is a reawakening to grace and its realities. The interior life is discovered. The exterior life in the world loses it flavor, and one becomes concerned about treasures which neither rust nor moth consumes (Matt. 6:20).

In the Bible passage mentioned above, Jesus went on to explain about spiritual treasures:

For where your treasure is, there your heart also will be. The lamp of the body is the eye. If your eye be sound, your whole body will be full of light. But if your eye be evil, your whole body will be full of darkness. Therefore if the light that is in you is darkness, how great is the darkness itself! No man can serve two masters; for either he will hate the one and love the other, or else he will stand by the one and despise the other. You cannot serve God and mammon (Matt. 6:21-24).

Jesus went on to speak of trust in God. And what do we do? We fear in giving our all to God that He will not give us happiness, fulfillment in return. What fools! And so we remain on the borderline of Catholicism, forgetting that if we give our all, He gives His all. We stay on the shoreline. We never launch out into the deep where the really big fish are to be found. Jesus says to us,

Therefore I say to you, do not be anxious for your life, what you shall eat; nor yet for your body, what you shall put on. Is not the life a greater thing than the food, and the body than the clothing? Look at the birds of the air; they do not sow, or reap, or gather into barns; yet your heavenly Father feeds them. Are not you of much more value than they? But which of you by being anxious about it can add to his stature a single cubit? .... .

Your Father knows that you need all these things. But seek first the kingdom of God and His justice, and all these things shall be given you besides. Therefore do not be anxious about tomorrow; for tomorrow will have anxieties of its own. Sufficient for the day is its own trouble (Matt. 6:25-34).

The "born-again Catholic" discovers his treasure and trusts God. He begins to see what he would look at previously and not behold. He begins to listen and hears the same sounds with his ears that were heard before but now there is meaning — deep, beautiful, other-worldly eternal meanings that thrill the heart. It is like a person whose hearing is impaired — he cannot hear certain pitches that give beauty and harmony to the musical masterpiece. But now they are first heard.

The Mass is no longer a begrudging obligation for him. It is a supernatural joy and privilege. It is the Sacrifice of the Cross perpetuated wherein he joins himself to Jesus Christ, the eternal Son of God made flesh. Together with, through and in Christ he offers God the Father in the unity of the Spirit, an infinite Gift. It is not simply a doctrine but a truth lived and put into conscious action at each Mass. The infinite Gift is Jesus Christ Himself to whom he is joined by faith and grace. The Mass is not an obligation consisting of putting in time to hear readings, songs off or on key, and listening to particular priest whose personality may not blend with our own. The Mass is a divine reality, a spiritual treasure house of the infinite, wedded to human activity — of more value than all our prayers and sacrifices in the world until the end of time. It is God offering God to us, with and through Jesus Christ. No matter the particular priest who offers this particular Mass, he beholds in faith Christ the High Priest at every Mass and in every Sacrament.

How is this possible? Now, one can grasp in divine faith, in complete trust, in divine charity that the Mass is Christ perpetuating His Sacrifice of the Cross which redeemed the world. Only now, extended in time and space, the born-again Catholic is there. He is part of it. He offers his very self in union with Christ the divine Gift offered to the Father. He lives and he offers in the Spirit. It is a reality, a loving reality, an embrace divine in the one mediator.

And after this unique and infinite gift of Christ and self to the Father in the Spirit, the Father has a return-Gift. He gives you the Body, Blood, Soul and Divinity of Jesus Christ so that you become one in Christ Jesus. You grow in the sharing of His divine life. You know what He means when He says:

> He who eats my flesh and drinks my blood has life everlasting and I will raise him up on the last day. For my flesh is food indeed, and my blood is drink indeed. He who eats my flesh, and drinks my blood, abides in Me and I in him. As the living Father has sent Me, and as I live because of the Father, so he who eats Me, he also shall live because of Me ... (John 6:55-58).

The "born-again Catholic" begins to actively gather the fruits of Calvary. Now he appreciates how the Apostle could say, "Have this mind in you which was also in Christ Jesus ... " (Phil. 2:5). He has emptied self of self so as to be filled with Christ Jesus. The vessel which is emptied more has room for more liquid to be poured therein. It is true of our souls. The more detached we are from things temporal, emptied of self and natural cravings which tie us to the world and worldly ways, the more is there the capability for the Divine One to come in "and dine with us."

How beautiful to be a "born-again Catholic" and to thirst after the living God. "I found Him whom my soul loves and I will not let Him go" (Cant. 3:4). Such a Catholic discovers that the kingdom of God is within him. Jesus said to the Samaritan woman, "If you did know the gift of God, and Who it is who says to you, 'Give Me to drink,' you perhaps would have asked of Him, and He would have given you living water." The Jerusalem Bible has this translation: "If you only knew what God is offering . . . " Jesus gives us a hint of the reality of sanctifying grace when He says to the Samaritan woman, "The water that I shall give will turn into a spring inside him, welling up to eternal life."

Sanctifying grace is a sharing in the life of God. A short sentence, easily spoken. But what divine and thrilling realities it means to one who grasps the meaning of "to share in the life of God." How much more beautiful and communicative of the divine truth of what the supernatural gift of grace is if we have grown accustomed to thinking and calling grace what it is: "a sharing in the life of God," rather than simply to speak of being in "the state of grace."

Grace is not stationary. We must grow in it. The very word "mortal," on the other hand, implies death to something. It is death to our sharing in the life of God. Mortal sin does not bring death to the soul itself, which is immortal (it can never die). It does bring an absence of any share in God's life. In the absence of "eternal life" we then lose our right to heaven.

The "born-again Catholic" has come to meditate on the beautiful divine reality of grace as a "sharing in the life of God." He comes to appreciate more deeply what Jesus Christ meant, "I have come so that they may have life and have it more abundantly" (John 10:10). Jesus did not come for mere human fulfillment of a better human life. Mankind had human life, physical life, before Jesus came. Jesus came to give us divine life. This is a life above our nature as humans. We share in God's life.

Human life is a beautiful gift but at birth we are still only creatures of God, made in His own image and likeness, possessing only natural human life. Before Baptism we do not partake of God's divine nature. We do not share in His divine life. We have only human life. We hear some speak of "Baptism in the Holy Spirit." We were all baptized in the Holy Spirit in that Sacrament which initiated us into the life of Jesus and again more profoundly at Confirmation. In discovering by spiritual experience in divine faith and love the gift of "what God is offering," we will be renewed in the Light that is Jesus Christ.

Sacred Scripture informs us that we are "children of God." That is not just a pious expression but a divine reality. We really are God's children. The Apostle John said it would have been a grand and glorious condescension for God only to have called us His children, even if we actually were not. But think of it. God has actually *made* us His children.

Sacred Scripture speaks of us as the adopted children of God. But

it is something more than the legal sense of adoption. We really are, in
the divine sense, children of God:

> But to as many as received Him He gave the power of becoming
> sons of God; to those who believe in His name: who were born
> not of blood, nor of the will of the flesh, nor of the will of man, but
> of God" (John 1:12-13).

> See what love the Father has bestowed on us in letting us be
> called children of God! Yet that is what we are (1 John 3:1).

We are children of our parents in the natural sense because we
have a natural human life like theirs and we got it from them. We are
children of God because we share in the divine nature as St. Peter said.
We have a share in God's life and we got it from God.

> For indeed His divine power has granted us all things pertaining
> to life and piety through the knowledge of Him who has called us
> by His own glory and power — through which He has granted us
> the very great and precious promises, so that through them you
> may become partakers of the divine nature ... (2 Peter 1:3-4).

The born-again Catholic has meditated on the beautiful divine reality of grace as a "sharing in the life of God," or as 2 Peter puts it,
"partakers of the divine nature." Perhaps the Catholic Christian who
has come alive in Christ Jesus had recited the words "sharing in the
life of God" or "partakers of the divine nature" as a child, even as a
teenager, but without listening, without realizing what was read or
said. But then, launching out into the deep, drinking of that living water, the profound, the real, something of the divine was discovered in
finding the life of Jesus in unity with the Holy Spirit and within oneself
with a hunger to share it and see it in all around. Then like Saint John,
he thinks: what a marvelous thing if God had only *called* me His child,
but marvelous still more, I really *am* the child of God. I have His divine life in me. For the person who is in the state of sanctifying grace,
the entire Blessed Trinity dwells in his soul. Blessed Elizabeth of the
Trinity, the Carmelite nun of our own times who had such a devotion
to the divine indwelling, would say, "I have found my heaven upon
earth, for heaven is where God is and God is in my soul."

One does not find in Scripture Jesus speaking of "grace," using
that word. But Jesus frequently speaks of "life." The born-again Catholic sees "life" again and again in the Scriptures, coming forth from
God. This is something new in his experience. Jesus wants to give each
of us His divine life to the full (John 14:6). "So the Son gives life to anyone He chooses" (John 5:21). "But if you wish to enter into life, keep
the commandments" (Matt. 19:17). "But the Author of life you killed

(Acts 3:15). "If it is certain that death reigned over everyone as the consequence of one man's fall, it is even more certain that one man, Jesus Christ, will cause everyone to reign in life who receives the free gift that he does not deserve, of being made righteous" (Rom. 5:17). "I am the Resurrection and the life .... Unless you eat the flesh of the Son of Man you shall not have life in you ... ," etc.

Sacred Scripture abounds in reminders that when we are in grace, we are in Jesus, that is, share in the life of God. It speaks of "eternal life," "everlasting life." For the born- again Catholic it is wonderful to behold that eternal life has begun in us now. We do not have to wait for physical death of the body. A new life in Jesus Christ begins not at physical death but at Baptism. That is why Jesus spoke of it as being "born again." Heaven is a continuation of the life of God in which we share even now. Death of the body is but a lifting back of the curtains, the dark glass through which we now see and behold God now only vaguely, but then "face to face, even as He is." When the soul departs the body and we enter heaven it will be the opening up, the blossoming into a full realization of the eternal life which has been ours upon earth.

No wonder the Apostle Paul of the Bible could happily exclaim, "It is now no longer I who live, but Christ who lives in me." He also wrote: "For me to live is Christ, to die is gain." We lose not our identity. We are specially created persons, made in God's own image and likeness, transformed, engrafted into Christ Jesus, the Son of God made man. We become one in Christ, living in Him and He is us. We become branches of the Vine, Christ. With all due respect to some in the charismatic movement, we must not get so naturally enthusiastic and carried away with emotion that we forget the fullness of Divine Revelation regarding our life still upon earth. A true disciple of Jesus Christ must die on the cross and be tried in the furnace to purify His love from what is of earth. There is the cross of pain, trials, of misunderstandings at every turn. What matters is accepting the cross in the right spirit in union with Jesus Christ. This is why saints have regarded themselves as a block of marble to be chiseled and hammered into a shapely column, into copies of Jesus Christ.

God will permit the trials to test us in the furnace. If we are truly to be a "born-again Catholic," we must endure the blows of reviling and persecution. These come in the way we least expect. The danger is in not recognizing them when they come — then we fail to embrace the crucified Christ in our lives and thus could miss the resurrected Christ.

What kind of trials are we talking about? The uncharitable judgments of others, the misinterpretation of our best intentions. For some there are bodily pains, years of suffering, even a lifetime of physical pains. For others mental worries. Jesus suffered more in His soul then in His body: "My soul is sorrowful even unto death." In some mysterious way great growth comes about through the dark night of spiritual anguish, which has been called "the dark night of the soul." "My God, my God, why have you forsaken Me?" Jesus called out to the Father from the Cross. He does this in us if we are open to grace. All this is in a foreign language not understood by the one who may live a long life upon earth, looking only from the shorelines, perhaps even back from the shoreline, afraid to dip into the living waters. The life of the sea is thus never experienced.

An enlightened soul, however, avails itself of all adversities and hardships to grow more into the likeness of Christ Jesus. On the other hand, what sacrifices are so often made to obtain the good will of the world? Some risk even their lives for worldly crowns. As St. Paul said, all run the race, but only one receives the crown of the world, which only perishes. In the life of Christ we all indeed run the race and each one of us can win the eternal reward, life in Christ, living in the Blessed Trinity forevermore. We cannot grow in perfection without accepting our daily crosses at the hand of God and from the Heart of Jesus.

For the beginner, God nourishes the soul with lights and delights of faith. Then God deprives the soul of the exquisite transports of joy. Faith may be tested in the midst of darkness and holy seclusion (Lam. 3:2, 6) but we can still behold the Light shining in the darkness. It is a suffering without light, while believing the Light is still there.

One can feel alone in this suffering. Even the great saints have experienced it. Then one must seek the God of consolations and not simply the consolations of God. It is at times like these that the soul's inerrant fidelity is more meritorious than when it is flooded with light. When God supports us, we are not appalled by an army in array (Ps. 27:3).

No one can be born again in the sense that is used in this chapter without entering into the innermost recesses of one's being. God is there and wants our love and adoration. God takes up His abode in our soul which He created in such wise that it is capable of loving and knowing Him. Why do not more come to relish here below the delights of faith in the sweetness of God's embrace? It must be that they are not willing to embrace the crucified Christ, to unite their sufferings to Him.

Why do so many neglect the Divine Son? It is because of dissipation and attachment to material things. It can hardly be possible when the soul is fed with the modern media. So much on television, the cinema, secular magazines is pagan, even pornographic. God's word is clear: lusting after worldly pleasures closes the mind to the divine realities. Listen to many a modern talk show. The Catholic Church is ridiculed. "It is not up to the times." Some people call themselves "Catholic" and appear before the public media declaring themselves "devout" or "good Catholics," but talk destructively about the Catholic Church. Not only are these people not Catholic; they are not Christian.

But even though we live in a "liberated" society, violent protests are raised when one speaks with such candor and truth about nominal Catholics. It is said, "How dare anyone protest their right to think and live, and believe as they please and still consider themselves Catholic?" The answer is simple. Whoever gives God's Word and divine reality a different meaning than that revealed by Truth Itself and that which is guarded by His Church, through the power of the Holy Spirit, is not a true Catholic.

It is a marvelous grace to find God after having known Him so weakly or having forgotten Him. The born-again Catholic can pray with St. Augustine, "Too late have I known you, too late have I loved you, you ancient yet ever-new beauty! Behold, you were in my heart and I sought you without!"

The Catholic who comes into the House of God where the Eucharistic Lord abides can pray as did Jacob, "Indeed the Lord is in this place, and I knew it not. How terrible is this place! This is no other but the house of God and the gate of heaven" (Gen. 28:16). If this was true under the Old Covenant, how vastly more profound the divine reality under the New Covenant in which we live, God become man in Jesus Christ and dwelling in our midst:

> I write of what was from the beginning, what we have heard, what we have seen with our eyes, what we have looked upon and our hands have handled: of the Word of Life. And the Life was made known and we have seen, and now testify and announce to you, the Life Eternal which was with the Father, and has appeared to us. What we have seen and have heard we announce to you, in order that you also may have fellowship with us, and that our fellowship may be with the Father, and with His Son Jesus Christ. And these things we write to you that you may rejoice, and our joy may be full.
>
> And the message which we have heard from Him and announce to you, is this: that God is light, and in Him is no

darkness. If we say that we have fellowship with Him, and walk in darkness, we lie, and are not practicing the truth. But if we walk in the light as He also is in the light, we have fellowship with one another, and the blood of Jesus Christ, His Son, cleanses us from all sin (1 John 1-7).

And we have seen, and do testify, that the Father has sent His Son to be Savior of the world. Whoever confesses that Jesus is the Son of God, God abides in Him and he in God. And we have come to know, and have believed, the love that God has in our behalf. God is love, and he who abides in love abides in God, and God in him (1 John 4:14-16).

What a difference the Sacrifice of the Mass will make in the living faith of the born-again Catholic. No longer will the Mass be merely Scriptural readings, homilies (sermons), songs, prayers. It will be a striking anew of the New Covenant first struck by Jesus Christ on the Cross of Calvary. The foremost fruit of Holy Communion will be to dwell in the purest and closest intimacy with Jesus. This "bread of angels," this heavenly food, will cause the soul to take on the semblance of Christ. The movements and mysteries of Christ's life will be completely in God. One will be divinized. One's inclinations will be sanctified. One will radiate Christ-love, Christ-life.

The born-again Catholic ponders the Mass, the Holy Eucharist as the Mystery of Love. "If any man love not our Lord Jesus Christ, let him be anathema" (1 Cor. 16:22). Love for the Eucharist is love for Jesus Christ and must spring from the heart and be ever alive in one. Not only does the born-again Catholic exercise the head, he exercises the heart. The heart must be exercised to love the true living God, to long for "the Author of Life" (Acts 3:15).

Great saints have contemplated the passion and death of Jesus Christ, Love poured out for our salvation. The born-again Catholic knows that each Mass he participates in is an active participation in the Sacrifice of the Cross participated. Holy Communion is the loftiest point of exercising one's love. The consuming flames from the Heart of Jesus Christ unite with the heart of a mere creature. St. Gemma Galgani asked that she would become "a flaming ball afire with love" for Jesus.

Another saint, St. Therese of the Child Jesus, became very ill. She dragged herself with great effort to Church to participate in the Sacrifice of the Mass and to receive Jesus in Holy Communion. One morning after Holy Communion, exhausted in her cell, one of the other sisters remarked that she should not exert herself so much. Saint Therese replied, "Oh, what are these sufferings to Me in comparison with one Holy Communion?"

We all may not have the graces of a Saint Paul, a St. Therese or a modern Padre Pio, the late stigmatist priest of Pietrelcina, Italy. All of us can launch out, however, to drink much deeper of the living waters of grace. We can study the lives of the great saints and even modern mystics to inspire us. Padre Pio, who died in 1968, had the bleeding wound marks of Christ's Crucifixion for fifty years. People came from all over the world to participate in the Sacrifice of the Mass offered by Padre Pio and confess their sins to him. Seeing his bleeding hands and experiencing the sweet perfume from his body, was a wonder to behold. To see Padre Pio look upon the consecrated bread, the host, now the Body and Blood of Jesus Christ, to adore Jesus before receiving Him in Holy Communion, was an experience that challenged one to greater faith and deeper love.

Once Padre Pio said of the people to whom he was a confessor, "I torment their souls and a fire devours them." Through his stigmata, people were given a glimpse of Christ's Passion, of how they were redeemed through Christ's Blood. Padre Pio brought us back to, "Take up your Cross . . . ."

A chef at the Home for the Relief of the Suffering, Laurino Costi, went into the confessional one day to confess to Padre Pio. Looking through the grille, he discovered he was face to face with the Passion of Christ in a particularly disturbing sense. Padre Pio's face was covered in blood that ran down from a cross-shaped wound on his forehead. "I began to cry," the man recalled. I went on crying for three days and three nights. I kept seeing him before my eyes as I had seen him in the confessional . . . . I could not sleep. I could not eat. I wept continuously. I thought I was losing my mind." No, Laurino Costi was not losing his mind. He was in the process of becoming more deeply a "born-again Catholic." Lest the reader think the late Padre Pio is mere history fading into legend, thousands the world over who experienced similar unexplainable events concerning this holy priest are alive today.

We have contemplated the loving and deeper meanings of God's Word and the thrill of the reality of being in grace, "sharing in the life of God." But ah! for that you must be free of mortal sin. How can I know that my sins of a lifetime which I've committed since Baptism are forgiven? Again, the loving mercy of Jesus Christ is available, giving us certain knowledge. We have the Sacrament of Mercy, the confession of our sins to a duly authorized priest who will grant us absolution. Thereby we can know with certainty from God that Jesus Christ, His divine Son, forgives us and grants us His divine life.

How sad for a Christian who does not appreciate the place of the Blessed Virgin Mary in the life of the Church and for each one of us. Christianity without a mother is an abstraction. No wonder there are so few "born-again" people and those who flippantly speak of being a "born-again Christian" have not yet claimed their spiritual Mother. They still are missing so much. They may think they have it all but they are not open to Mary to show them her All.

The born-again Catholic who develops a personal relationship with the Mother of the Church comes to a deeper and more personal relationship with her Son, Jesus Christ, our Lord, God and Savior. Mary is no challenge to a deeper faith and love of Jesus Christ. Her goal is to lead us to her Son and say, "Do whatever He tells you." She herself is our model of faith and love for and in Jesus Christ.

Neither are the angels, especially the Guardian Angel of each of us, in competition with Jesus Christ, the one Mediator. Those Christians not open to the good holy angels will also miss much in the spiritual life. The angels behold Christ Jesus as their King together with us as they do Mary their Queen. So, too, do the saints of heaven who enjoy the beatific vision. This Communion of Saints is a grand and glorious family to live in the midst of; it is a doctrine come alive, a reality made present to us in Jesus Christ.

How much upon this earth a person misses who has only part of the true faith, or although born into its fullness, becomes dead or remains lukewarm in it!

> I would that you were cold or hot. But because you are lukewarm, and neither cold nor hot, I am about to vomit you out of my mouth; because you say, 'I am rich and have grown wealthy and have need of nothing,' and do not know that you are the wretched and miserable and poor and blind and naked one. I counsel you to buy of Me gold refined by fire, that you may become rich, and may be clothed in white garments, and that the shame of your nakedness may not appear, and to anoint your eyes with eye salve that you may see. As for Me, those whom I love I rebuke and chastise. Be earnest therefore and repent. Behold, I stand at the door and knock. If any man listens to my voice and opens the door to Me, I will come into him and will sup with him, and he with Me. He who overcomes, I will permit him to sit with Me

upon my throne; as I also have overcome and have sat with my Father on His throne. He who has an ear, let him hear what the Spirit says ... (Rev. 3:16-22).

# CHAPTER 12

# Questions & Answers Commonly Asked About The Catholic Faith

1. WHY DOES THE CATHOLIC CHURCH BAPTIZE IN-FANTS? THERE IS NOTHING IN THE BIBLE ABOUT BAPTIZING BABIES. THE CHURCH SHOULD WAIT UNTIL THEY ARE ADULTS OR CAN DECIDE FOR THEMSELVES. ISN'T IT RIDIC-ULOUS TO CLAIM THAT A LITTLE BABY WILL BE CON-DEMNED TO HELL FOREVER WHEN IT DIES WITHOUT BAP-TISM THROUGH NO FAULT OF ITS OWN?

There is much in Sacred Scripture to substantiate the practice of the Church from the earliest centuries in the Baptism of infants. While it is true that Scripture speaks of the call of adults to faith and subsequently Baptism, we must remember that the first converts to Christianity were adults. While the New Testament may not speak so clearly as does present Canon Law about the Baptism of infants, it does repeatedly speak of the Apostles baptizing whole families.

The Acts of the Apostles tells of an earthquake where the Apostle Paul was miraculously freed and the jailer asks, "Men, what must I do to be saved?" The result was that "He and his whole household were baptized. He joyfully celebrated with his whole family his newfound faith in God" (Acts 16:30-34).

Other entire households baptized by the Apostles are mentioned in Acts 11:14; 16:14-15; 18:8 and also in 1 Cor. 1:16.

The Greek term of the Bible translated "household" encompasses everyone living together in a home, immediate family members, relatives, slaves, servants and children. This fits well with the New Covenant being a fulfillment of the Old where infants were circumcised into the People of God. Baptism was called Christian circumcision (See Col. 2:11). God's covenants extended not just to an individual but to whole families. Parents could make spiritual commitments for their children. For example, Joshua declared: "for me and my house, we will serve the Lord (Joshua 24:15). Biblical scholars call this "family solidarity."

This concept of family solidarity continues in the New Testament. Peter on Pentecost calls to the crowd: "You must reform and be baptized every one of you, ir the name of Jesus Christ, that your sins may be forgiven; then you will receive the gift of the Holy Spirit. It was to you and your children that the promise was made, and to all those still far off whom the Lord our God calls" (Acts 3:38-39).

Origin, writing at about 230 A.D., spoke of "a tradition of the Church from the Apostles" to baptize babies. A manual of Church teaching written in Rome at about 215 A.D. speaks of Baptism for infants "too young to speak." Jesus Himself said, "Let the children come to Me and do not hinder them. It is to just such as these that the kingdom of God belongs" (Mark 10:14).

Some of those "liberal" or modernist "Catholics" who would delay Baptism would be surprised to find themselves in the fundamentalist conservative camp of separated brethren who insist that only those old enough to make a personal profession of faith should be baptized. Today, in harmony with the practice from the time of the Apostles, Roman Catholics, Eastern Orthodox and most major Protestant denominations follow the ancient practice of baptizing infants.

While the Church has never condemned unbaptized infants to hell, its theologians have spoken of limbo. Some speculate that Baptism of desire on the part of the parents or Church could suffice for the removal of original sin; yet it is only sacramental Baptism which confers the indelible character of Jesus Christ on the soul for all eternity. It would be a terrible responsibility for any one of us to take into eternity the responsibility for having had the opportunity to have baptized a dying infant but refused to do so.

## 2. HOW CAN THE CATHOLIC CHURCH BAPTIZE WITHOUT IMMERSION? THAT'S THE WAY BAPTISM IS SUPPOSED TO BE PERFORMED.

The Catholic Church recognizes and permits immersion but does not require it for a valid Baptism. Either immersion or the pouring of water over the head is correct. Nothing in the New Testament requires that Baptism must be conferred only by immersion. On the occasion of St. Peter's first sermon, three thousand converts in Jerusalem were baptized in one day, hardly by immersion. Research has shown that there was no sufficient water supply available in the city at the time to make it possible. When St. Paul baptized his jailer in prison, there was hardly a river flowing through the jail. It could only have occurred by pouring. There are bedridden invalids and the dying who desire Baptism. Water poured on their foreheads would retain the significance of grace washing their souls as the water washed their bodies. Each Sacrament has a sign. For Baptism it is the washing of the water and the speaking of the words. Baptism washes away sin and gives the divine life of grace. Water is a sign of washing and life.

Jesus acts in each of the Sacraments. The sign is sufficient along with the proper intention of the one administering and the proper words to make the Sacrament valid. Again, we are blessed with the authority Jesus Christ gave his Church to answer these practical questions that arise. We do not have to depend on each one's private interpretation of Scripture to know what is necessary for a true Baptism. The authority of Jesus, speaking in His Church, tells us that what is sufficient is the pouring of water over the forehead, along with the simultaneous action of saying the words, "I baptize you in the Name of the Father, and of the Son, and of the Holy Spirit." There is evidence in the New Testament and in the constant tradition of the Church that from the time of the Apostles, Baptism has been administered either by immersion or by pouring water on the person to be baptized.

### 3. INFANTS CAN'T BE BAPTIZED BECAUSE THEY ARE NOT YET CAPABLE OF MAKING THEIR OWN DECISIONS AND THEIR OWN ACT OF FAITH TO ACCEPT BAPTISM. THEY ARE NOT EVEN AWARE OF BEING BAPTIZED.

It is true that infants are not aware of being baptized. Neither are they aware of receiving their natural life — but they are not prevented from receiving it. God created Adam and Eve in grace without asking them if they wanted to be so created. God created all the angels in grace. We know that Adam and Eve, and the angels in some cases, later rejected grace. Jesus Christ can surely baptize through his Church and put the souls of infants in grace and remove original sin from their souls without the knowledge or free consent of the infant. The consent of the parents who thus promise to educate and form the child in the faith suffices.

For many Protestants, Baptism is merely an external act associating the person baptized with their church and implying a profession of

Christian faith. Many do not think it actually gives a new principle of divine life interiorly.

Jesus Christ is God who came down to our level by becoming our brother. He became a man while remaining true God, the second Person of the Blessed Trinity. He took our human life. He gives us His divine life. He gives it first by baptismal regeneration. This is when we are born again. It gives us the supernatural life required to live the life of heaven. The baby born, although created in God's image and likeness, does not share in the God-life until it is baptized. The first is a natural birth. It is being born to natural physical life, even though the soul has an intellect and will like unto God in spiritual powers. Yet, the soul's life at its creation is merely human, not divine. The soul of the infant is capable of receiving a share in God's life and that requires Baptism.

The faith of the parents is sufficient when they desire that their children share the divine life. The parents desire to have their child become "born again" and share the faith they have. Later the child will know and be able to accept for himself the wisdom of the parent's choice and make it his own. God will give that child sufficient grace if it freely cooperates according to God's loving will. God will not force Himself on the child to continue to accept his love.

## 4. WHAT ABOUT LIMBO? I UNDERSTAND THE CATHOLIC CHURCH TEACHES THAT UNBAPTIZED BABIES GO TO LIMBO AND WILL NEVER SEE GOD. WHY SHOULD AN INNOCENT BABY BE PUNISHED?

No innocent baby will ever be punished by God by an eternity in hell or any place else. Limbo is not a place of punishment, but of perfect natural happiness. Limbo is the abode of souls excluded from the full blessedness of the beatific vision, that is, in seeing God face to face, even as He is. Souls there do not suffer any punishment. They enjoy the happiness that would have been our human destiny if humans had not sinned in Adam and Eve or had never been elevated to the supernatural order.

God does not owe us His divine life. The life of sanctifying grace is not due the nature of man. Catholic theology distinguishes two kinds of limbo: 1) The limbo of the Fathers, a place where the saints of the Old Testament remained until Jesus' coming to redeem the world, and 2) the limbo of infants, the permanent state of those who die in original sin but are innocent of any personal guilt.

Jesus said, "Unless a man be born again of water and the Holy Spirit, he cannot enter the kingdom of God" (John 3:5). This raises practical questions about infants who die without Baptism, or those who never have the use of the soul's faculties and die without Baptism. Regarding the limbo of infants, those who die without Baptism and for whom the want of Baptism had not been supplied in some other way, cannot enter heaven. It is possible that God might supply the want of Baptism by some other means. St. Bernard suggested that such infants could reach heaven because of the faith of their parents.

The great majority of theologians, whose study on this subject is approved by the Church, teach that infants who die in original sin, that is, without Baptism, suffer no "pain of sense." They are simply excluded from the beatific vision. They do not grieve because they are deprived of heaven because the pain of punishment is proportional to personal guilt, which does not exist here. Rather, as St. Thomas Aquinas said, "They rejoice because they share in God's goodness and in many natural perfections" (*De Malo*, V, 3). Souls in limbo know and love God intensely by the use of their natural powers. They enjoy perfect natural happiness. They are perfectly happy on the natural level.

A study of our previous chapter dealing with grace explained that the life of heaven is a state of happiness and life above our nature as human beings. It is *supernatural* happiness. Limbo is a place of perfect *natural* happiness. So to speak of punishment in limbo is to fail to comprehend its meaning. While the Church has never defined limbo as a dogma of faith, yet there is strong support for it in the teachings of the Church.

Among those who have denied the existence of limbo were the Jansenists, whose theory of selective predestination excluded the need for any mediatorial source of grace, including Baptism. At stake in the traditional belief regarding limbo is the revealed doctrine that heaven is a pure gift of God's goodness and that Baptism of water or desire is necessary to enter heaven. The phrase was used by the Church Fathers. In the Apostles' Creed when it is said about Christ, "He descended into hell" — that is a reference to limbo, the place where the just souls remained before Christ redeemed us on the Cross and ascended into heaven. The soul of Jesus Christ was in limbo after His death until His Resurrection, announcing to them their salvation. There is strong Scriptural basis, then, for this belief in limbo.


## 5. IT DOES NOT REALLY MAKE ANY DIFFERENCE WHAT CHURCH WE BELONG TO. THERE IS NO LACK OF THE

ESSENTIAL UNITY JESUS REQUIRED IN HIS CHURCH, FOR ALL DENOMINATIONS TOGETHER FORM THE ONE TRUE CHURCH, RIGHT? THE IMPORTANT THING IS TO HAVE FAITH IN JESUS CHRIST AS LORD, GOD AND SAVIOR, NOT MEMBERSHIP IN A CHURCH.

It is essential to have faith in Jesus Christ as Lord, God and Savior. It is also important to have true faith, not mixed with error. As quoted in this book more than once, the Word of God calls for "One Lord, one faith, one Baptism." Jesus prayed for unity in His followers but we have hundreds of conflicting answers which are attempts at explanations of the various points of the faith. That is not what Jesus prayed for and called for in his priestly prayer for unity (John 17).

Hundreds of conflicting churches are not unity in Christ. The claims that the Church of Rome is the "Whore of Babylon" (John 17:5) is an example of an uncharitableness that has too often existed between Christians in the name of religion. This is not of God and is not faith in the "One Lord, one faith, one Baptism" which describes the "body of Christ," which is the Church.

6. DID NOT ST. PAUL WRITING IN THE BIBLE ACKNOWLEDGE THAT THERE WERE VARIOUS INDIVIDUAL CHURCHES ALREADY IN HIS TIME?

St. Paul was not writing about different religious denominations. He was writing about different local churches, or the communities of faith in different areas. The Catholic Church still speaks of local churches under bishops in union with the Pope, and with Jesus Christ. In St. Paul's time they were as much united as are Catholics today in New York who are sincere with sincere believing Catholics in Berlin, Australia, Rome or any other part of the world. Each bishop is over a local church and the Catholic bishops of the world are united with the Bishop of Rome, the Pope. It was in this sense that St. Paul spoke of individual churches, not different faiths.

7. WHY IS IT SO IMPORTANT TO HAVE ONE SUPER-CHURCH? GO INTO ANY CHRISTIAN CHURCH AND YOU WILL HEAR JESUS CHRIST PROCLAIMED AS SAVIOR. THEY REALLY ALL BELIEVE ESSENTIALLY THE SAME.

Would that all Christian denominations did believe essentially the same. If you question some who claim to be Christian closely you will even discover that their faith in Jesus does not consists in believing Him to be true God and true Man, the Second Person of the Blessed Trinity made flesh, who died on the Cross for our salvation, rose again from the dead and ascended into heaven to be with the Father, Who prepared a place for us and sent the Holy Spirit to keep us in the truth. You will find some very peculiar explanations even of who Jesus Christ is among people who claim to be Christian.

It is true that there is some truth in the many Protestant churches. But Jesus commanded his Apostles to go forth and teach "all" that He had commissioned them to teach. He gave them His authority, and His priestly powers as found in the Sacraments, which have been largely lost within Protestant churches.

Jesus said, "And if he refuses to hear them, appeal to the Church, but if he refuses to hear even the Church, let him be to you as the heathen and the publican ... " (Matt. 18:17). Which Church? Jesus, in giving chief authority to Peter, spoke of only one Church.

In many hundreds of Christian denominations one hears now one, then another doctrine. They contradict each other, even on essential matters like Baptism and the Eucharist.

### 8. IN THE CATHOLIC CHURCH IT SEEMS THAT BISHOPS AROUND THE WORLD ARE JUST AGENTS FOR THE POPE.

There has never been any teaching of the Church to verify your assumption. The bishops are successors of the Apostles. Each bishop has governing, teaching and sanctifying authority within his local church (diocese) and also over the universal Church in communion with other bishops and the successor of St. Peter, the Pope. Vatican II said in its decree on the bishops,

> Sharing in solicitude for all the churches, bishops exercise this episcopal office of theirs, received through episcopal consecration, in communion with and under the authority of the Supreme Pontiff. All are united in a college or body with respect to teaching the universal Church of God and governing her as shepherds. They exercise this office individually over the portions of the Lord's flock assigned to them, each one taking care of the particular church committed to him (*Decree Concerning the Pastoral Office of Bishops in the Church*, n. 3).

### 9. WHAT ABOUT THE INQUISITION IN WHICH THE CATHOLIC CHURCH PUT TO DEATH PEOPLE WHO DID NOT

AGREE WITH ITS TEACHINGS? THAT SURELY PROVES THE CATHOLIC CHURCH CANNOT BE THE TRUE CHURCH, DOESN'T IT?

Fundamentalists have frequently used and abused the Inquisition story in the attempt to disprove the Catholic Church. Not all is rosy about the Inquisition. There have been abuses among Christians and it is not restricted to Catholics. Protestantism has its witch-hunting of which it is not proud. At the time of the Protestant Revolt their were abuses on both sides, wars, etc. The Inquisition was the special court or tribunal appointed by the Catholic Church to discover or to suppress heresy and to punish heretics. The Inquisition extended over six centuries. The Roman Inquisition of the middle twelfth century arose during the ravages of the anti-social Albigensian sect. Its doctrines and practices were destructive both of faith and of Christian morality and public order. While Church authorities would condemn a person found guilty of heresy it was not the Church which inflicted punishment. That was done by civil power. The first thing the Church desired was the reformation of the heretic. By exhortations and minor punishment he was encouraged to give up his false beliefs. Many did so. The relapsed heretics who were found guilty were turned over to the civil government for punishment required under civil law.

We must understand all history in the light of the times. The fact that secular law prescribed death at times must be understood in light of those days, when heresy was anarchy and treason and leniency in criminal codes was unknown. Institutions with human characters give room for abuses to creep in.

King Ferdinand and Queen Isabella set up the Spanish Inquisition in 1478 and it was empowered by Pope Sixtus IV. It was directed against the lapsed converts from Judaism, crypto-Jews, and other apostates whose secret activities were dangerous to both Church and state. The civil government had great power in the administration of this Inquisition. The Spanish ecclesiastical tribunal, which is accused of scandalous cruelty, must admittedly share its condemnations with them. The latter worked in those days, however, in defiance of the Holy See which frequently condemned inquisitors because of their cruelties.

While there were abuses, these abuses have been grossly exaggerated. Good was accomplished in saving the Latin countries from anarchy. Much falsity in modern minds surrounds the events of this period which must, as said, be judged by standards of the times, not by modern ideas of the human person and religious freedom in which much has been learned about the dangers of union of Church and state.

To give an example of the problems of the times, in Spain both Jews and Moors had pretended to be Christians, had received Baptism but not in good faith, and sometimes even worked their way into bishoprics, their intention being to undermine both the nation and its Catholic religion. The Inquisition detected such false pretenses. The Church finally expelled them from her communion while the state dealt with them as traitors. We see from this that attempts by enemies to infiltrate the Church, as is sometimes attributed to Marxist Communism in our own times, is nothing new in history.

Authorities at the time of the Inquisitions were well aware that they could not make any man interiorly change his views against his will or interiorly accept the teachings of the Church if he did not desire to. But they could compel individuals to keep their private opinions to themselves and to cease to publicly propagate their errors that were judged disruptive to both Church and State.

There is much dispute among honest historians regarding how many deaths occurred under the Spanish Inquisition. Some say there were fewer than three thousand death sentences, others put it higher. Histories of the Inquisition have been written by people filled with prejudice and hatred for the Catholic Church. An authentic historian, however, should always be objective, even when the truth hurts. The track record of the Catholic Church is to be honest and open, even when in some cases there have been abuses among some of its members in certain parts of the world.

The Catholic Church is certainly not proud of abuses that took place. "The end does not justify the means." The Inquisition, however, was a consequence of the times. In evaluating the Inquisition the times must be kept clearly in mind, which requires some profound knowledge of history, and we should be careful of much that is claimed which is only the fruit of fundamentalist slander. Many fundamentalists, reading anti-Catholic literature, actually believe that more people died under the Inquisition than in any war or plague in history.

If the fundamentalist who brings up the subject of the Inquisition is attempting to prove that the Church has had sinners, he is right. If he is trying to prove that the Church is false because of abuses of some of its members he is no more right than disproving Jesus Christ because of the denials of Peter or the betrayal of Judas. A study of Protestantism will also demonstrate great abuses at times among its membership.

Sir James Stephens, a historian of English criminal law, writes that there were eight hundred executions a year during the early post-Reformation period in England. The Inquisition never operated in England. Many Catholics were put to death for remaining loyal to the papacy. The burning of alleged witches was a practice almost unknown in Catholic countries. Yet, in Britain thirty thousand went to the stake for witchcraft. In Protestant Germany the figure was one hundred thousand. These details do not justify abuses in the Spanish executions but point out that severity in punishment was not due to Catholicism but to the general character of the times.

The Catholic Church does not try to cover up the Inquisition. It asks that it be put in perspective.

## 10. IT DOES NOT MAKE ANY DIFFERENCE WHAT PARTICULAR FAITH ONE HAS, JUST SO YOU HAVE SOME FAITH. GOOD INTENTIONS ARE WHAT COUNTS, NOT WHAT CHURCH YOU BELONG TO.

It is not just any faith, true or false, that will assist you in getting to heaven and giving God the proper glory He deserves from us. Only true faith can do that. Jesus did not say it made no difference what people believe. He did not tell the Apostles to go out and preach just any faith. He promised them the Holy Spirit, the "Spirit of Truth" to keep them in truth and remain with His Church until the end of the world. False faith is no help to heaven and what is not right in a faith does not give glory to God, Who is infinite Truth itself.

Christians who do not have the fullness of true faith may get to heaven if they are sincere and do the best they know how — if it is through no fault of theirs that they do not have the fullness of true faith. That, however, does not say that one faith is a good as another or that all that is important is that one have some kind of faith. Each one of us has the obligation to seek the whole truth as Jesus Christ intended and then to live that fullness of true faith with the help of God's grace. To say that one faith is as good as another is the same as saying false faith is as good as true faith.

## 11. WE ALL BELIEVE IN THE SAME GOD AND ALL ARE STRIVING TO GET TO THE SAME HEAVEN. SO WHAT DIFFERENCE DOES IT MAKE WHICH CHURCH YOU BELONG TO?

We all should believe in the one God. We should all believe truths about God. Insofar as we are deprived of the fullness of true faith we are deprived of a fuller knowledge about God that He intended for us to have upon this earth. The early Christians who believed in Jesus as Lord, God and Savior spoke of themselves as followers of the "Way." Jesus had said, "I am the Way, the Truth and the Life." He did not give us many ways to the Father, but one Way. He is the Way. The Catholic Church is the Mystical Body of Christ. The Catholic Church is the Way as it is identified with Jesus the Way. It is the Way to go, not any way of our choosing, not another way.

## 12. I KNOW SOME PROTESTANTS WHO LIVE A BETTER CHRISTIAN LIFE THAN SOME CATHOLICS.

So do I. Jesus said that those to whom more has been given more will be expected. The Catholic with the fullness of true faith and the fullness of the priestly powers of Jesus Christ has the greatest opportunities for giving adoration to God and obtaining the grace of Jesus Christ for salvation. Some "Catholics" are nominal and do not really possess the faith. It is more of a cultural inheritance. Others know the faith but do not live it. Some Protestants avail themselves to better use their part of the true faith than some Catholics. Those who have been given the faith in any degree and use it poorly, Catholic or Protestant, will have to answer to God for the way they used the gifts, the talents He gave them according to the measure He gave them.

## 13. YOU CATHOLICS ARE NOT UNITED. I ONCE HEARD A PRIEST IN A NEWMAN CENTER CALL BENEDICTION, OR ADORATION OF THE HOLY EUCHARIST "BREAD WORSHIP." HE SAID YOUR HOLY FATHER, THE POPE, WAS NOT TOO IN-TELLIGENT. HE ALSO SAID SOME MAKE MARY OUT TO BE A WORSHIP GODDESS, ETC.

I could add to your list of such statements by unloyal members, be they priest or otherwise. As a priest and Catholic journalist for many years, working in national apostolates as well as serving as a pastor, I've heard from people in every part of the United States. I've received considerable letters from other countries. I believe what you wrote is true and that you did hear some priest say these things. Many Catholics, shocked, have reported hearing similar things. Such persons who call themselves "Catholic" and are not united with the official Catholic Church in its faith if they know the Catholic teachings are not living honestly.

There have been incidents in the two-thousand-year history of the

Catholic Church in which priests have disagreed with its teachings, left the Church, and in some cases, started new denominations. The Church that Jesus Christ founded and built upon the Rock of the papacy goes on and will do so until the end of the world, despite attacks from without and betrayals from within.

Yes, there is disunity among some who call themselves "Catholic." Many have abused and misconstrued what Vatican II said. One will find nothing in the sixteen documents of the Second Vatican Council (1962-1965) to substantiate the many weird inroads that modernists have been attempting in order to infiltrate the Catholic Church. It is sad, and unfortunately, as has been brought out in this book, that this situation has prevented a considerable number of young people born of Catholic parents, even baptized into Catholicism, to be educated and formed in true Catholicism. One of the goals of this book is that it will be read by some baptized Catholics who were validly baptized into the Church, but were poorly educated or led astray as to what is true Catholicism. If they have discontinued active membership in the Church or fallen into Fundamentalism, it is hoped that a careful study of this entire book will bring them to a discovery of what the Church really teaches and thus bring them back to the fullness of true faith like a new rebirth. If a priest misrepresents the true teachings of the Church than we should go to a loyal priest of the Church.

It has been mentioned more than once in this book that some young Catholics never recognize the true face of Catholicism. Just as many outside the Catholic Church do not recognize it, it is so among some not educated and formed in the basics of Catholicism. Some years ago the Vatican became concerned and required an investigation of Catholic seminaries in the United States so that future priests would be formed and educated in loyalty to true Catholicism.

The Catholic Church is still united. This does not mean that every one who wears the label "Catholic" possesses the Catholic faith. Jesus said to Peter that after his conversion he should confirm his brethren in the faith. Catholic bishops who teach in unity with the Pope make up the Magisterium, or "Teaching Church." It is this united faith under the Magisterium that determines what is true Catholicism, and not individuals, who say other than what the universal Church teaches.

14. I AM NOT A FUNDAMENTALIST BUT I THINK I AM MORE TOLERANT THAN ROMAN CATHOLICISM. MY CHURCH DOES NOT CLAIM TO BE RIGHT LIKE YOURS. I BELIEVE IN BELIEVING AS ONE IS INCLINED TO OR DESIRES TO BELIEVE AND TO HAVE A RESPECT FOR THE FAITH OF

OTHERS WITHOUT CRITICISM. ISN'T THAT A BETTER AP-
PROACH? ISN'T THAT FREEDOM OF RELIGION?

We have to give credit to fundamentalists for believing in most
cases that they are right. If you say that you or your church does not
claim to be right you are really saying that you have no definite
grounds for what you believe. How can you have faith in what you
claim does not have to be right? You are really saying that freedom of
religion should also mean religious indifference to the truth.

In America our mentality has been so affected by democratic ideas that in religion we may get the idea that religious faith and practices
are determined by the vote of the people. Truth is from above. God is
Truth. What is true in faith does not have its source in man but in God.
Your position amounts to saying that you believe in believing in error.
Is that why Jesus came to earth? Jesus came that people might have divine life through true faith; He said, "I am the Truth." He commanded
people to give up beliefs that were not true and to accept what He
taught in order to save their souls.

The Catholic Church believes in freedom of religion. We should
be charitable and respect the faith of others. We ought not to criticize
uncharitably. But to claim that no one can know or hold that they have
true faith is really, unwittingly at least, to insult Jesus Christ who promised to found His Church, and preserve it in true faith until the end of
the world through the Spirit of Truth. Jesus said, "I am the Light of the
World." If you can't have true faith or claim to believe in the truth, is
that light?

15. I STILL SAY IT REALLY DOES NOT MAKE ANY DIF-
FERENCE WHAT YOU BELIEVE BECAUSE RELIGION IS A
MATTER OF CONSCIENCE.

You are then saying again it makes no difference if what you believe is true or false. We do have an obligation to follow our conscience
but we also have the obligation to form our consciences *correctly*. There
are right consciences and false consciences. There is such a thing as
*culpable ignorance*, ignorance for which we are to be blamed. God gave
us intelligence. Intelligence tells us that a contradiction of a point of
faith cannot be true.

Some believe that Jesus, who said He was the "living bread come
down from heaven" was only speaking symbolically when He spoke
over and over again, as found in John 6, that He was giving us
His Body to eat and His Blood to drink. The hundreds of different

Protestant denominations have countless of different interpretations for the same teaching of Jesus Christ on the Eucharist. Contradictions on the same teaching cannot be all true. It *does* make a difference whether it is truly and substantially the living Body, Blood, Soul and Divinity of Jesus Christ, the Word made Flesh, or merely the substance of bread and wine that represents Jesus. Whether there are three Persons or one Person in the Godhead makes a difference; whether Baptism is necessary for salvation makes a difference, and so on. Why treat the teachings from God that involve our eternal destiny so flippantly? You would not do this with mathematics or scientific teachings.

God expects us to pray for guidance, to be open to the Holy Spirit, and to use our intelligence in seeking the truth under divine guidance. He has given us the Church, His Mystical Body with the Holy Spirit as the Soul of this "Body of Christ" which makes up the People of God. Our guide to a true conscience should be to follow the means Jesus Christ Himself gave us, the one true Church. "He who hears you, hears Me" (Luke 10).

## 16. ARE YOU SAYING THAT IF I KNOW THAT THE CATHOLIC CHURCH IS THE CHURCH THAT WAS FOUNDED BY JESUS CHRIST AND IS HIS TRUE CHURCH I CANNOT BE SAVED UNLESS I JOIN IT AND LIVE ACCORDING TO ITS TEACHINGS?

Exactly. That is the teaching of the Roman Catholic Church and it was repeated in the document of the Second Vatican Council in its *Dogmatic Constitution on the Church, Lumen Gentium.*

If you believe the Catholic Church has the fullness of true faith, that it is the Church which Jesus Christ founded and placed upon the earth until the end of time with the Pope as the visible head, while Jesus Christ Himself is the invisible head of the Church and the Holy Spirit keeps this one Church in truth, then to refuse to join this Church, or to refuse to remain in it is to reject the will of God as you know it. How can you do the will of God if you refuse to accept what you believe to be true? You would have to go to the judgment and say to God, "I knew the Catholic Church was your Church. I knew you placed the Catholic Church upon earth, built it upon Peter and kept it in truth through the Holy Spirit. Still, I refused to join it to live according to its teachings, which were therefore Your teachings." That would be the same as saying, "I refused to do your will."

17. BUT IF SINCERE PROTESTANTS HAVE PART OF THE TRUE FAITH AND CAN BE SAVED BY LIVING AS GOOD PROTESTANTS BELIEVING IN JESUS CHRIST AS LORD, GOD AND SAVIOR, WHAT DIFFERENCE DOES IT MAKE? YOU END UP IN HEAVEN ANYWAY, WHETHER YOU BE PROTESTANT OR CATHOLIC, PROVIDED YOU LIVED THE FAITH SINCERELY.

An important part of your question is "provided you lived the faith sincerely." One who refuses to join or remain in what he or she knows is the true Church of Jesus Christ is not sincere. We are obligated to seek to live not just any faith but the true faith. You must consider not only what you are deprived of outside the fullness of true faith but what you deprive God of in the glory you could have given Him through the Mass and the Sacraments and the profession of the fullness of true faith. If you have the Catholic faith in the essence of what the Mass is, then you believe that the Eucharistic Sacrifice perpetuates the Sacrifice of the Cross which gives infinite adoration to God the Father, in, with and through Jesus Christ in the unity of the Holy Spirit. The Mass is the Sacrifice of the Cross perpetuated. It is Jesus Christ the High Priest, Himself, giving perfect adoration to the Father. You are one with Him in doing so. This is not possible in the Protestant denominations. Also, in the various Protestant denominations where the Apostolic Chain has been broken — that is, where the powers Jesus Christ given to the Apostles as the first bishops of the Church have been lost because they separated from the Catholic Church, the power to ordain other bishops and priests has been lost.

Being separated from the powers of Christ, which are found through the Apostolic Chain, means that you will never be able to receive our Divine and loving Lord Jesus Christ Himself in Holy Communion. If you are a Protestant minister, you will never be able to offer the infinite Sacrifice of the Cross, the perfect adoration in, with and through the priesthood of Jesus Christ in the manner He intended through the Holy Eucharist. You will not have a valid priesthood to forgive you your sins in the Name of Jesus Christ in the Sacrament of Penance. You will be deprived of the many graces that could be yours in the fullness of true faith and its practice. It does make a big difference.

18. WHEN ONE FOR YEARS HAS HEARD ACCUSATIONS AGAINST THE ROMAN CATHOLIC CHURCH, EVEN HEARING IT CALLED "THE WHORE OF BABYLON"; THAT SAINT

PETER NEVER WAS IN ROME; THAT ITS POPES HAVE BEEN POWER AND WEALTH-HUNGRY, ETC., IT BECOMES EMOTIONALLY DIFFICULT FOR ONE TO ACCEPT THAT THE ROMAN CATHOLIC CHURCH COULD BE THE TRUE CHURCH OF JESUS CHRIST. THERE ARE TIMES WHEN ALL WHAT YOU HAVE SAID SEEMS TO FIT TOGETHER AND THEN THE FEAR COMES OVER ME THAT THE CATHOLIC CHURCH COULD BE THE ANTI-CHRIST. CAN ONE BE HELPED IN SUCH DIFFICULTIES?

The above is an excellent and honest observation and question. It is what keeps many out of the Catholic Church. Even after some intellectually come to the realization of the fullness of true faith of Catholicism, they hesitate for years because of having been formed in other Christian traditions, the pressure of others, and their own emotions, which sometimes for decades have been nursed in opposition to Catholicism. One can arrive at the point where the intellect says, "Yes, the Catholic Church is the one true Church" but the emotions keep nagging at one's will to hold back. It is often difficult to conquer feelings. Here is where humility and strength of will are needed in accepting the grace of God. You must pray intensely for courage, for strength.

It takes more then mere intellectual conviction to be converted to the fullness of Catholic faith. It requires a grace from God and a humble and free acceptance of that grace. Consider for a moment the great giant of an intellectual, John Henry Newman. He had risen to a leading position in the Church in England and came to realize the truth of Catholicism. He wrote his memorable poem, "Lead Kindly Light." Later he wrote, "From the time I became a Catholic, I have been at perfect peace and contentment. It was like coming into port after a rough sea." After becoming a Catholic he eventually became a bishop and cardinal of the Church. Today his cause for canonization is promoted.

Robert Hugh Benson, the convert son of the Anglican Archbishop of Canterbury, wrote, "The Church promises a great deal, but my experience is that she gives ten times more. The Catholic Church is supremely what she promises to be. She is the priceless pearl for which the greatest sacrifice is not too great."

Prayer is important. One taking a course of Catholic instructions should pray to God to guide himself into the fullness of true faith. While at the beginning of one's investigation there can hardly be a readiness to pray explicitly to become a Catholic, since one is not yet convinced. One ought to pray, "Dear Lord and Savior, Jesus Christ, I beg you, lead me to fullness of true faith according to your will, wherever it is to be found." Once you have joined the Church, and are able to believe that your sins are forgiven, that you are joined intimately to Jesus Christ, especially at the Mass and in the reception of our Divine and loving Savior in Holy Communion, and can participate in offering the Father the Sacrifice of Jesus in infinite worship, the joy that will be yours will far outweigh all the sacrifice involved. Jesus said, "Unless you take up your cross and follow Me . . . . " Peace will then be yours. Is not that what Jesus said when he gave His Church the power to forgive sins: "Peace be to you."

### 19. WHAT WILL I SAY TO FRIENDS WHO CLAIM THAT IN JOINING THE CATHOLIC CHURCH ONE IS JOINING AN EXCLUSIVE DENOMINATION WITH A CLOSED PULPIT AND A CLOSED COMMUNION THAT CONSIDERS ITSELF SUPERIOR?

The Catholic Church is not a denomination. It is the Church of Jesus Christ. Whatever may be meant by a "closed pulpit," it is true that the priest or deacon preaching is expected to preach only the faith of the Catholic Church. If he preaches otherwise he is preaching himself, not Jesus Christ. The Catholic Church believes in ecumenism — the working for Christian unity — but not at the expense of compromise of the true faith. An honest seeking for unity cannot come about in dishonesty, of compromising the truth. Under supervision of the bishop, there has sometimes been exchange of pulpits for the cause of understanding and promoting unity through knowledge of one another. This is not done at the official worship of the Mass. It is not to be indiscriminately done. The Catholic Church believes it has the commission of Jesus Christ to keep the faith intact and free of corruption.

As for "closed Communion," it is true that only those baptized and professing the fullness of the Catholic faith, and who are free of mortal sin are permitted by the Church to receive Holy Communion in the Catholic Church. Those whose conscience accuses them of serious sin must first make a good confession in sorrow with a firm intention to change from their sin and receive absolution of the priest before they may receive. Other Christians who are not in full union with the Catholic Church may not receive.

The Catholic Church welcomes those Christians who are not fully united with the Church to the celebration (not reception) of the Eucharist. It is a consequence of the sad divisions in Christianity that we cannot extend to them a general invitation to receive Holy

Communion. Catholics believe that the Eucharist is an action of the celebrating community signifying a oneness in faith, life, and worship of the community. Reception of the Eucharist by Christians not fully united with the Church would imply a oneness in Jesus Christ which does not yet exist, and for which all should pray. The Holy Eucharist is the Sacrament of unity and it would be a lie to admit to this Sacrament those who do not profess the faith of the Catholic Church which consecrates and administers this Blessed Sacrament of the Lord's Body and Blood.

## 20. CATHOLICS CALL THEIR PRIESTS "FATHER." JESUS SAID CALL NO MAN YOUR FATHER UPON EARTH (MATT. 23:9).

Jesus also said at the same time to avoid being called "teachers." We ought not then speak of teachers in our schools or speak of an earthly parent as father. Yet God has commanded us to "honor your father and your mother." Jesus is using hyperbolic speech typical of the time. Jesus is not rejecting authority in principle, but authoritarianism. He is not rejecting the use of titles, but the failure to acknowledge that authority exists to serve God, His anointed One (Jesus), and one's neighbor. Jesus is saying that we must recognize that all fatherhood is of God; we owe Him our being, all that we are and have, including our earthly father. Jesus, in the Hebrew fashion, is saying that no earthly father must be held in greater respect than God, the one supreme Father of all.

Catholics do not call a priest "Father" in the same way that they call God their Father. A priest by the authority of God is a spiritual father. By administering Baptism he is an instrument of Jesus Christ in bringing grace, in bestowing a sharing in the life of God, to the soul for the first time. Through the Sacraments, especially the Holy Eucharist, the priest nourishes the spiritual life of the soul. In the Bible, St. Paul speaks of himself as a spiritual father.

I am writing you in this way not to shame you but to admonish you as my beloved children. Granted you have ten thousand guardians in Christ, you have only one father. It was I who begot you in Christ Jesus through my preaching of the Gospel" (1 Cor. 4:14-15).

## 21. THE CATHOLIC CHURCH HAS HISTORICAL EVIDENCE OF BEING THE FIRST CHURCH OF JESUS CHRIST. YET, THERE IS ALSO EVIDENCE THAT IT BECAME THE TOOL

OF THE STATE. EMPERORS CONVENED THE ECUMENICAL
COUNCILS BEFORE THE GREEK OR ORTHODOX SCHISM.
HOW COULD THIS BE IF THE POPE WAS ALWAYS CONSID-
ERED THE SUPREME BISHOP OR VISIBLE HEAD OF THE
CATHOLIC CHURCH?

It is correct that early Councils were convened by the emperors after the conversion of Constantine. But this did not mean that the
Church considered that the emperors had Church authority or could
replace the Pope. The Pope alone had the authority to give the character of an ecumenical council to the gathering of the bishops. No council of the Church has ever had ecumenical value without the ratifica-
tion of the Pope as successor of St. Peter.

You are speaking of a time when there was a very close relationship between the Church and the State. Heresies in those times were
considered to greatly disturb social peace. When there were disrup-
tions over the faith the emperors wanted questions of faith and order
in the Church straightened out for the good of the empire. The emperors knew that questions of faith were subject to the authority of the
Pope. The emperor had no authority in making the decisions of these
Councils.

22. THE CATHOLIC CHURCH HAS LAWS WHICH I CAN-
NOT FIND IN THE BIBLE. HOW COME? ISN'T GOD'S WORD
ENOUGH?

Jesus Christ certainly gave authority to his Church to make laws
for the good of our souls when he said, "Whatever you bind upon
earth, is bound in heaven." The necessity of obedience to the Church is
also seen in these words of Christ: "He who hears you, hears Me; and
he who despises you despises Me ... " (Luke 10:16). There is certainly
evidence in the Bible that St. Paul made regulations according to his
discretion, and insisted upon obedience to them.

St. Matthew ends his Gospel with the words of Christ: "Full authority has been given to Me both in heaven and on earth; go, therefore, and make disciples of all the nations ... ." It is obvious that Jesus, before his Ascension, is sharing his authority with the Apostles,
the first bishops.

23. THE CATHOLIC CHURCH CLAIMS TO BE THE ONE
TRUE CHURCH GOING BACK TO THE TIME OF JESUS
CHRIST'S PHYSICAL PRESENCE UPON EARTH, AND THAT

## THE CHURCH'S TRUTH DOES NOT CHANGE. YET, I'VE KNOWN IN MY OWN LIFETIME THAT THE CATHOLIC CHURCH HAS CHANGED SOME OF ITS LAWS. HOW CAN THE CATHOLIC CHURCH BE THE TRUE CHURCH IF TRUTH CHANGES?

You are failing to distinguish between *doctrine* and *discipline*. The dogmas of faith — that is, the solemnly defined doctrines of the Church — do not change. An example of divine law is the Ten Commandments, which come directly from God. Discipline, on the other hand, is Church law, made by the Church itself, and can change.

Jesus Christ gave His Church the power to make laws and to change them or loose us from them, and he said heaven would so respect them. Jesus spoke of this power for His Church at the very time He was declaring the primacy of Peter as the Rock:

> And I will give you the keys of the kingdom of heaven; and whatever you shall bind on earth shall be bound in heaven, and whatever you shall loose on earth shall be loosed in heaven (Matt. 16:19-20).

Jesus set up his Church in such a way that it had authority and could adapt its own laws for the good of souls and the glory of God according to the needs and challenges of the time. The Church is the living body of Christ, not a dead, stagnant, ungrowing or unmoving body that is locked in dry, dead, printed pages of history. It is the very life of the Church that gives living spirit to the Word of God. Or, better put, it is the Holy Spirit that brings within the Church, Christ's own Mystical Body, life to the Word of God in the hearts of men in each age.

To use but a few examples of change in the Catholic Church which did not involve changes of divine law or teachings: The Second Vatican Council (1962-1965) permitted the Divine Liturgy, the Mass and Sacraments, to be said in the language of the people. It also permitted some of the ceremonies to change. Still, the essence of the Mass as perpetuating the Sacrifice of the Cross and bringing us the Sacrament of the Holy Eucharist, which is the Body, Blood, Soul and Divinity of Jesus Christ, remains the faith of the Church without alteration. Any changes in ceremonies in the administration of the Sacraments did not involve a change in sign or in the essential words as given to the Church by Jesus. The law of abstinence from meat on the Fridays of the year were changed to make it possible to do other kinds of penance. That involves a human or Church Law based on divine teaching. While retaining the ancient practice of Friday as a special day of penance in memory of the day Jesus Christ died on the Cross for our sins, the Church said that other forms of penance were possible, but gave preference to abstinence from meat. (It retained abstinence from meat, however, for Ash Wednesday and Fridays of Lent.) While Jesus did not specify exactly the kind of penance we should do, He did make it clear that it is divine law that we must do penance of some kind to be saved. The Church cannot thus dispense us from all forms of penance.

To sum it up, there have been no changes in the Church in dogmas of faith or divine law.

24. WHEN I ATTEND CHURCHES OF THE FUNDAMENTALISTS I CONSTANTLY HEAR THAT "JESUS CHRIST IS LORD, GOD, SAVIOR; THAT HE DIED FOR US TO SAVE US." I'VE GONE TO A CATHOLIC CHURCH WHERE THE PRIEST SEEMS TO TALK MUCH ABOUT THE SOCIAL ISSUES, HELPING OUR NEIGHBOR, THE POOR, ETC.

Don't knock these doctrines you've heard in the Catholic Church. They are part of the teachings of Jesus Christ. Jesus was strong on the social issues for the purpose of our going to heaven. Read his account on the Last Judgment, in St. Matthew 25:31-46. "Amen I say to you, as long as you did it, (or did not do it) for one of these the least of my brethren you did it (or did not do it) for me." Anyone who preaches a constant single theme is not preaching the whole Gospel. Before as-  cending into heaven, Jesus told the Apostles to go and teach all nations "to observe all [not part] that I have commanded you" (Matt. 28:20).

Teaching "all" must include the basic teaching of Jesus Christ as Lord, God, Savior; the Holy Eucharist as Sacrifice and Sacrament; the authority of Christ vested in Peter and the Apostles and their successors; the social issues, etc. Admittedly, not every priest ideally presents the fullness of true faith in his preaching. But the deposit of faith, given to us in its completion by our Divine Lord by the time of the death of the last Apostle, is full and complete and preserved within the teachings of the Catholic Church until the present day and will be so until the end of the world.

25. THERE IS NO MENTION OR ROOM IN THE BIBLE FOR A PLACE CALLED "PURGATORY." THE BIBLE MENTIONS ONLY HEAVEN AND HELL. GIVING PRIESTS MONEY FOR MASSES FOR THE DEAD IS SIMPLY ANOTHER WAY FOR THE CHURCH AND ITS PRIESTS TO MAKE MONEY AND GET RICH.

Lest we be talking about different things, it is best to begin with the Catholic explanation of the meaning of purgatory. It is the place or condition in which the souls of the just are purified after the death of the body before they can enter heaven. It is not a third possible permanent place. It is temporary. Souls that enter purgatory will eventually be admitted into heaven and enjoy the beatific vision, namely to be perfectly happy while seeing God "face to face even as He is" for all eternity. Souls admitted to purgatory are those that died in God's grace but are not in a state of perfection. They may be purified there of the guilt of their small, or venial, sins for which they did not repent in this life. Souls go to purgatory for two reasons: 1) unforgiven venial sins, 2) not having done sufficient penance in this world for their forgiven sins, mortal or venial.

The word purgatory is taken from the Latin word, *purgatio*, which means a place of cleansing, or purifying. God in His mercy permits souls that died in grace but not in perfection to become completely purified in a place of temporary cleansing after they leave this earthly life. There, the souls are purified by atoning for the temporal punishments due to sin by the willing acceptance of suffering imposed by God. The sufferings in purgatory are not the same for all but are proportioned to each person's degree of sinfulness.

The sufferings in purgatory can be lessened in duration and intensity through the prayers and good works of the faithful on earth when directed to such an intention. Since the souls there are part of the Communion of Saints and since the Church upon earth is still in a state of merit, we can gain merit for them. That is, we can help do the penance for them for that which they failed to do upon this earth.

In common language Catholics speak of the "fires of purgatory" to express purification that is undergone there; we speak of the cleansing fires of purgatory. This does not mean they are in fire such as we know it upon earth. One must remember that the soul is spiritual and would not be subject to natural fire. Their suffering involves their being deprived of God's immediate presence when they believe in Him and love Him sufficiently to have died in the state of sanctifying grace. That is, their bodies died when their souls were participating in the divine life, in the virtues of faith, hope and love. They suffer intensely at being deprived of the perfect union of vision with the God they love.

The pains of purgatory are not incompatible with great peace and joy, for these poor souls deeply love God and are certain they will reach heaven. As members of the Church Suffering, they can intercede for persons on earth. Catholics still living in this world are encouraged to invoke the aid of the poor souls through their good works and prayers of penance, especially by participating in the Sacrifice of the Mass for their intentions. Purgatory is a temporary place, for it will not continue after the general judgment. Its duration for any particular soul continues until it is free from all guilt and punishment due to forgiven sin. The soul is assumed into heaven immediately upon achieving perfect purification.

While many Protestant denominations do not accept as divinely inspired the two books of Machabees, which complete the Old Testament, they cannot deny that these are historical books going back to the time before the coming of Jesus Christ. The books testify to the faith of God's people then. Thus, we read in 2 Machabees 12:46: "It is therefore a holy and wholesome thought to pray for the dead, that they may be loosed from sins."

Reading the whole account of Judas Machabaeus we are informed that soldiers were punished by God for small sins. They could be released from sin by the sacrifices of the people, which included almsgiving, which was in conformity with Old Testament worship.

Read also 1 Corinthians 3:13-15:

> Every man's work shall be manifest. For the day of the Lord shall declare it, because it shall be revealed in fire. And the fire shall try every man's work, of what sort it is. If any man's work abide, which he has built thereupon, he shall receive a reward. If any man's work burn, he shall suffer loss: but he himself shall be saved, yet so as by fire.

Ecclesiasticus (Sirach, in some Bibles) 5:5 says, "Be not without fear about sin forgiven: and add not sin upon sin." Why does Sacred Scripture tell us to fear even sin forgiven? Obviously because of God's justice. God's justice requires a perfect balancing of the scales even after the sin is forgiven. Every sin is an offence against God. We were made to know, love and serve God. Every sin goes against that purpose. When we are sorry and receive forgiveness in God's mercy, there is still His justice which requires that we make up for the wrong done for the glory we took from Him by offending Him with deliberate sin.

There is a divine order to things, to all of creation. The will of God will eventually be perfectly accomplished, even though man's sinfulness gets in the way. Scripture is clear that nothing defiled shall enter heaven. Only when the will of the soul is perfectly attuned to God's all-holy and good will is the soul ready for the beatific vision. If a soul were to be placed in the presence of the Almighty God in all His glory with even only a small stain of sin upon it, it would surely want to cast itself into the cleansing purgatorial fires. A soul could not bear to be in God's presence — where angels sing, "Holy, holy, holy . . . " and saints fall down in adoration — if the soul had the slightest sin or stain of temporal punishment due from sin still upon its soul. "There shall not enter into it anything defiled or that works abomination or makes a lie, but they that are written in the book of life of the lamb" (Apoc. 21:27).

In 1 Peter 3:18-19 we read what Christ did after His death: "He was brought to life in the spirit, in which also He preached to those spirits that were in prison." This is proof of a third or middle place possible for those who would claim that the Bible mentions only heaven and hell. Christ went to preach, after His death, to souls who were not in heaven or hell. Heaven is no prison. Christ did not preach to the damned in hell. While this verse of 1 Peter can obviously be applied to the limbo of the Fathers, its Scriptural record shows that a third temporary state is not contrary to Scripture. Fundamentalists ought to be well aware of King David and his mortal sin of adultery from which he repented. God sent the prophet Nathan with the message: "The Lord on his part has forgiven your sin: you shall not die. But since you have utterly spurned the Lord by this deed, the child born to you must surely die . . . " (2 Sam. 12:14). Through the prophet, God announced that David's sin was forgiven because of his repentance but he still had to do penance for it. God's mercy does not cancel out his justice.

Jesus says clearly in the Bible, "Unless you take up your cross daily and follow me, you are not worthy of me . . . " "Unless you do penance, you shall all likewise perish." Many do not do sufficient penance in this life, in order to draw from the infinite merits of the redeeming penance Jesus did for us all. Most assuredly Jesus Christ has redeemed us all by his Precious Blood. The Bible does not teach that because Jesus did perfect penance of infinite value we have no need of expiation. It teaches the opposite.

Catholics do not "buy souls" out of Purgatory as is sometimes said in regard to stipends which Catholics may give a priest when they request that the Sacrifice of the Mass be offered for a soul departed. An offering given when they request a Mass for the poor souls is not "buying" forgiveness of sin or the passage of anyone into heaven. The writer of this book can assure readers that no priest gets rich on Mass stipends. When I was ordained, the usual stipend was $1 per Mass. During most of my priesthood the average stipend has been $2 and for some years now such donations have gone into the parish treasury for the good of the Church, as is the case in many dioceses. In other areas of the Church the offering depends upon the means of the people.

The one making the offering is simply contributing in some small way to the support of the Church. The amount from Mass stipends is but a token compared to the needs of the Church. The poor are not required to make any offering. The Bible approves of almsgiving and there is no question of "buying one's way" into heaven. Those making the offering are simply giving something of themselves when they desire to help the poor souls by prayers and penances.

While the value of the Mass is infinite, our participation in the Mass, the merits of Jesus Christ which we draw from Jesus' Sacrifice of the Cross which each Mass perpetuates, depends upon our faith and the good dispositions of our soul. One Mass in which one participates with great faith and love while still upon this earth can be of far greater value in application to one's soul than many Masses someone else may request for us after death. The difference of value is not in Jesus Christ and his redemptive death but in our faith and love.

How quickly a soul enters heaven does not depend then simply on numbers of Masses. If some wealthy person were to order many Masses said for the repose of his soul — a claim some fundamentalists use to show that wealthy Catholics can "buy" their way into heaven — the fact remains that if a soul is in hell we cannot help that soul. All the Masses in the world would not remove a soul from hell. If one were to request Masses in one's will in some selfish and pride-oriented manner, to be offered after death, the value received for oneself would still depend, not on the death of Jesus Christ, for that value is infinite, but on the spirit of faith and charity in which the request was made and the sacrifice involved. It is possible that such a request was made for reasons of pride. A materialistic intent for prestige and without sacrifice would not be of value. Jesus Christ can apply the value of His holy Sacrifice where He desires according to the good dispositions of one's soul.

I have been a priest for nearly thirty-five years and have never run into the imaginary cases that some fundamentalists and others present.

Belief in purgatory is not restricted to Catholics. When one has some realization of the omnipotence of the all-holy and good God and appreciates both His mercy and His justice, common sense tells us of the need for purgatory. How many readers, if they have any sense of sin, think they are so perfect at this moment that should they now die they would immediately enter into God's presence in heaven and see him "face to face even as He is." Since the state of perfection, in which the soul must have not even the slightest defilement, is necessary to get to heaven, how many persons could hope to gain heaven if absolute perfection was required at the moment of death? The existence of purgatory, then, is the fruit of God's mercy and the requirement of His justice. It is mentioned in Sacred Scripture as well as in Tradition, although the Bible does not explicitly use the word.

St. Augustine, who lived in the fifth century, said, "The fire of purgatory is more terrible than all that man can suffer in this life." The souls there, however, suffer in love. In hell they suffer in hatred, without hope, knowing they will never get out.

We have already shown that the belief in purgatory existed before the coming of Christ, even though the Bible does not use the word "purgatory" explicitly, just as it does not use the word "Incarnation" or "Christmas" explicitly but in which Christians in general believe. Tradition and the constant teaching and practice of the Church through the centuries is proof of a purgatory.

To believe in purgatory is not a recent Catholic practice or invention, but an ancient practice with roots in the Old Testament. Not to believe in purgatory is a recent practice among Protestant Christians. When fundamentalists claim that belief in purgatory is a Catholic invention they are at a loss to prove when it was invented. Faith in the existence of a third place of purification extending back to Old Testament times leaves the fundamentalist at a loss to substantiate his claims on this issue as on many others.

Early Christian writers of the second and third centuries spoke of praying for the dead. Tertullian, who lived about 200 A.D., wrote: "The faithful widow prays for the soul of her husband and begs for his repose" (*De Moang*, 10).

In *The City of God*, St. Augustine wrote: "Temporary punishments are suffered by some in this life only, by others after death, by others both now and then; but all of them before that last and strictest judgment." Many Christians outside the Catholic Church have little or no concept of the life of a soul after the death of the body and before the Last Judgment and Resurrection. Many of them think the souls of those who have died in past centuries are totally unaware of their existence. They may use the word "sleeping," but consider them not to be conscious of anything.

The Catholic Church speaks of the "Particular" Judgment, that which occurs for each of us immediately after death and determines our place in eternity. This judgment is irrevocable.

The "General" Judgment refers to the Universal Judgment of the human race at the final resurrection of the dead at the end of the world. All of the early creeds of the Church speak of it in saying that Christ "sits at the right hand of God the Father Almighty, from where

He shall come to judge the living and the dead." Jesus shall then judge the just and the wicked. This general judgment at the end of the world will manifest to everyone who has ever lived God's justice in condemning unrepentent sinners to hell, and His mercy for those who are saved. The final Judgment will reveal not only all sin each one committed but also the merits each one drew from the infinite merits of Jesus Christ by cooperating with divine grace.

So the problem that fundamentalists have in making their objections to Catholic beliefs and practices lies in their misunderstanding of life after death before the final judgment and general resurrection. The Catholic position is an encouraging and joyful doctrine and in harmony with both Tradition and Sacred Scripture. I find the belief of those who think people who have died are unconscious of their existence and merely awaiting the end of the world, which could be many thousands, if not millions of years away, a distressful and depressing lack of the fullness of true faith.

26. THE CATHOLIC CHURCH IS ALWAYS CHANGING ITS DOCTRINES OR ADDING ON TO THEM. THE CATHOLIC CHURCH TEACHES MANY THINGS TODAY THAT WERE NOT BELIEVED BY THE FIRST CHRISTIANS. HOW CAN YOU POSSIBLY JUSTIFY THAT? THE ORIGINAL CHRISTIAN CHURCH WAS DOCTRINALLY THE SAME AS FUNDAMENTALIST CHURCHES TODAY BECAUSE WE USE THE BIBLE ALONE AS THE GUIDE TO OUR FAITH.

In answering this question it should become clear why fundamentalist writers do not want to discuss or objectively research Church history. The Catholic Church does not change its doctrines nor does it add new doctrines. This question confuses such changes in doctrine with *growth* in the Church's understanding of the truths of Divine Revelation. The Church speaks of the "development of doctrine," "dogmatic progress," or "dogmatic development." The infinite mind of God is behind all public Divine Revelation. Man must meditate on the Word of God as long as he exists upon the earth to come to a fuller understanding of God's message. In future centuries God's people should come to an even deeper understanding of God's Word. And yet, the timeless beliefs of the Church will not be contradicted.

There is a gradual unfolding of the meaning of what God has revealed. The substantial truth of a revealed mystery of God, however, remains unchanged. What changes or advances is man's subjective grasp of the revealed truth. The source of the progressive understanding is the prayerful reflection of the faithful, notably of the Church's saints and mystics. There is also the study and research by scholars and theologians and the practical experience of living the faith among the faithful. There is the Magisterium, which is the collective wisdom and teaching of the Church's hierarchy under the Bishop of Rome. The Pope is the successor of St. Peter whom Jesus appointed to be the visible head of His Church after He ascended into heaven from where He, with the Father, sent the Holy Spirit, the "Spirit of Truth."

There is implicit in the development of doctrine the understanding that it is the will of God that the faithful not only assent to what God revealed but also grow in the depth, clarity, and certitude of their appropriation, appreciation and understanding of divine faith. There is no changing of the faith or adding on to what God has revealed; there is a growth in understanding what God had revealed by the time of the death of the last of the original Apostles.

It is a dry and lifeless position which would hold that each generation may not profit from past generations in understanding more deeply the faith contained in divine revelation but must constantly start anew since all is contained in a written book. On the contrary, God promised the Holy Spirit, "Spirit of Truth" not merely to the men whom He used to write the Bible, but to his Church until the end of time as He would always abide by and in his Church, which is as St. Paul describes, "the Body of Christ."

Fundamentalist churches take a very simplistic view of history and of course would deny the development of doctrine. They would say that when Emperor Constantine, the first Christian emperor, issued the Edict of Milan, 313 A.D., making it possible for Christians to worship in freedom, that pagans flocked to the Catholic Church in great numbers hoping to get preferential treatment from the state. The Church could not take in so many so quickly, they argue, so it compromised its principles and became corrupted by adopting pagan beliefs and practices.

Thus there came, say the fundamentalists, the doctrines with which yet today the Catholic Church is identified. Those who apostacized from true doctrine as contained in the Bible supposedly became the Catholic Church. The true Christians, namely the fundamentalists, did not change their faith and were forced to remain in hiding until freedom was granted them with the Protestant Reformation.

The above argument of the fundamentalists is simplistic; it has no scholarship behind it and has absolutely no history to back it up. It is an attempt to deny the unbroken line of faith and practices of the Catholic Church which goes back to Jesus Christ and his Apostles.

The priesthood, the teaching authority of the papacy and bishops in union with the Pope, the Sacraments, the Mass as the perpetuation of the Sacrifice of the Cross, purgatory, (as shown in the answer to the question above), honor and intercession of Mary and the saints, salvation by faith in Jesus Christ accompanied by good works, etc., can be shown in historical research as part of Catholic faith before Constantine gave religious freedom in the early fourth century.

There are historical records of the underground Church before Constantine, namely the Catholic Church of the catacombs of the Christians of the first centuries. But there are no historical records of an underground fundamentalist church after freedom of religion was granted. There are records of heresies and schisms, most of which disappeared with time. Today's fundamentalists cannot find any missing link to date themselves back to the first Christians. There is no unbroken line for the fundamentalists that would support their chief doctrines: Bible alone, salvation by faith alone, an invisible church, etc.

Jesus intended his one Church to have visible qualities. It would be like a city on a mountain for all to see (Matt. 5:14). A church only in the hearts of believers is not visible. A visible Church would need an earthly head; an authority to which Christians could turn for a final answer to questions of faith and morals. The Bible itself as well as two thousand years of historical records are quite clear that Jesus gave that authority to Peter and his successors (Matt. 16:18).

The fundamentalists say that Jesus was simply recognizing Peter's great faith when He said "You are Peter, (Rock) and on this Rock I will build my Church." (Peter's profession of faith is recorded a few sentences earlier.) The word "rock" cannot refer to Christ Himself for He is described by the metaphor "the cornerstone" (Eph. 2:20, 1 Peter 2:4-8).

Only the Roman Catholic Church can historically demonstrate an unbroken line back to the Church of the New Testament of the Bible. Catholic bishops and the Pope, as chief bishop and successor of Peter, can be traced back to Jesus and his Apostles.

The great John Henry Newman, a leader in the Oxford movement originating around 1833 at Oxford University in England, proved the present day fundamentalist's position wrong long ago. The movement was begun by Dr. Keble at Oxford and was an attempt at a restoration in faith and worship within the Anglican church, with an insistence on its alleged Catholic character but without any reference to union with Rome. Others who carried on the movement were Edward Pusey,

Richard Foude, Frederick Faber, Isaac Williams, Charles Marriott, Bernard Dalgairns and William Ward. Some of these became Roman Catholics as the fruit of their study and prayer. John Henry Newman was interested in the development of Christian doctrine. He studied Christian faith through the centuries. Writing in 1844, he worked backward century by century to discover if any Catholic beliefs existing at a given time could be traced to beliefs existing a century earlier. His research took him back until finally he arrived at New Testament times. What John Henry Newman proved is the unbroken line of Apostolic succession and continuity of beliefs that have existed in the Catholic Church from the days of Jesus founding his one Church on Peter as the Rock. John Henry Newman was not a Catholic when he started to write his book but he was converted to Roman Catholicism by the time the book was submitted for printing. He was eventually ordained and made a cardinal in the Roman Catholic Church.

When a fundamentalist goes on the theory of "Bible only," he disregards the benefits of almost two thousand years of study and meditation on the Word of God by fellow Christians and the promise Jesus gave his Church to have the Holy Spirit as the "Spirit of Truth" to keep his Church from being destroyed and always in true faith. He is also deprived of many of the powers and graces of Jesus Christ contained in the Sacraments of the one true Church.

## 27. WELL, ALL THE GOOD WORKS THE CATHOLIC CHURCH PRESCRIBES DO NOT SAVE A PERSON. ONLY JESUS CHRIST SAVES. THE ACTS OF PENANCE, MASSES AND ROSARIES, ETC., DO NOT SAVE. THE BIBLE IS VERY CLEAR THAT THE ONLY THING THAT WILL SAVE US IS THE BLOOD OF JESUS CHRIST.

The Catholic Church teaches that Jesus Christ is our Savior, the one Savior for all mankind. There is no other Savior. Jesus shed his precious blood for the redemption of the world. Here is what the Church teaches:

> Besides, as the Church has always held and continues to hold, Christ in his boundless love freely underwent his passion and death because of the sins of all men, so that all might attain salvation. It is, therefore, the duty of the Church's preaching to proclaim the Cross of Christ as the sign of God's all-embracing love and as the fountain from which every grace flows (Vatican II).

No one can save us except Jesus Christ. We must believe that Jesus Christ, the Second Person of the Blessed Trinity, the Son of God become Man, died on the Cross, shedding his precious blood for our salvation, and rose again from the dead and ascended to the Father after which, together with the Father, He sent the Holy Spirit upon the Church.

It is true — JESUS SAVES. The Church has labored for nearly two thousand years to bring men to faith in Jesus as Lord, God and Savior. We need to respond to that faith in Jesus with works of charity toward God and neighbor. The Rosary will not save us in itself. But if you understood the Rosary or any other approved Catholic devotion properly you would see that they are rooted in the life, death and resurrection of Jesus Christ. The Church calls the Rosary, properly prayed, a "Gospel prayer." Properly prayed, it leads us in faith to the mysteries of Jesus Christ.

## 28. THE CATHOLIC CHURCH BELIEVES IN CONFESSION OF SIN TO A PRIEST. I JUST CAN'T SEE HOW A MERE MAN CAN FORGIVE SIN. ONLY GOD CAN FORGIVE SIN. HOW CAN CATHOLICS BELIEVE IN CONFESSION?

The Catholic Church does not teach or believe that "a mere man can forgive sin." The Church teaches that Christ is always present in His Church and acts in her liturgical celebrations, in the Mass and the Sacraments. The Sacraments are the acts of Jesus Christ extended in his Mystical Body, the Church, in time and space. It is Jesus Christ who baptizes, who forgives our sins when we go to Confession, etc.

The priest acts in the person of Jesus Christ in the Sacrifice of the Mass and in administration of all of the Sacraments. Most Protestant Christians believe that Baptism takes away sin for the first time in a person's life; that is, original sin inherited from Adam and Eve, and any other personal sins if Baptism is received later in life. They therefore believe that God uses a man for the forgiveness of sin in the administration of Baptism. If God can use a man to forgive sin at Baptism, why can he not do so for sins which we may commit after Baptism and for which we are sorry? God can do all things. Has not God in fact shared with men, successors to the Apostles, the power to forgive sins in His name, as He gave them the power to forgive sins for the first time at Baptism?

St. John, in chapter 20:19-23 of his Gospel, tells us of Christ's Easter gift to His Church. "Peace be to you! As the Father has sent me, I also send you." When He had said this, He breathed upon them, and said to them, "Receive the Holy Spirit; whose sins you shall forgive, they are forgiven them; and whose sins you shall retain, they are retained."

St. Matthew in chapter 16 tells us that Jesus Christ promised to give the keys of the kingdom of heaven to the Church, the power of binding and loosing to his Apostles and the Church. To appreciate the Sacrament of Reconciliation, also called the Sacrament of "Penance," or commonly called "Confession," and how God forgives sin through His Church, we must remember the very nature of the Church as the Mystical Body of Christ. Then we can better appreciate that Jesus lives and acts in his Church through His divine Word of the Scriptures, in the Divine Liturgy, the Mass and the Sacraments. Then we will see that it is not a mere man, but the God-Man, Jesus Christ, Son of God and Savior who is forgiving sin when one is sorrowful and properly disposed to amend one's life.

The reason Catholics go to confession is because this is the way Jesus Christ ordained.

## 29. SOME OF THE WRITINGS OF MODERN BIBLICAL SCHOLARS ARE CONFUSING AND DISTURBING. SOME OF THEIR INTERPRETATIONS EVEN TOUCH BASIC CHRISTIAN BELIEFS SUCH AS THE RESURRECTION AND VIRGIN BIRTH. I CAN'T ACCEPT ALL OF THESE MODERN BIBLICAL INTERPRETATIONS.

Neither can the Catholic Church. Joseph Cardinal Ratzinger, prefect for the Vatican's Congregation for the Doctrine of the Faith, spoke in New York recently and expressed concern for some modern trends in Biblical scholarship, singling out for criticism the methods of Martin Dibelius and Rudolf Bultmann. While historical research is both necessary and valuable for the study of Scripture, said Cardinal Ratzinger, Catholic theologians cannot reduce divine Revelation to an account of merely human events.

> No one can really be surprised that this procedure leads to the sprouting of ever more numerous hypotheses until finally they turn into a jungle of contradictions. In the end, one no longer learns what the texts says, but what it should have said.

Obviously the cardinal was referring to Biblical interpreters who attempt to make the Bible fit their own conceptions, which are at conflict with teachings of the Church from the time of the Apostles and through the centuries.

Since the Enlightenment, explained Cardinal Ratzinger, Church doctrine has come to be viewed as "one of the real impediments to a correct understanding of the Bible" instead of the indispensable key to its interpretation. Ratzinger proposed a return to the approach of St. Thomas Aquinas, who said, "The duty of every good interpreter is to contemplate not the words, but the sense of the words." Cardinal Ratzinger also said,

> In the last one hundred years, exegesis [Biblical interpretation] has had many great achievements, but it has brought forth great errors as well. These latter, moreover, have in some measure grown to the stature of 'academic dogmas'. To criticize them at all would be taken by many as tantamount to sacrilege, especially if it were to be done by a non-exegete.

The Cardinal in these words was critical of those who consider their modern Biblical interpretations above the authority of the Magisterium.

The Church is concerned if Bible scholars come up with new interpretations at variance with Church doctrine and forget that they are not the Magisterium, the teaching Church. The same is true of certain theologians who present opinions as if they were doctrine and forget they are not the teaching Church. Jesus Christ foresaw such divisions and prayed for unity among Christians. The New Testament repeatedly warns against dissenters and those who do not preach sound doctrine:

> For there will come a time when they will not endure the sound doctrine; but having itching ears, will heap up to themselves teachers according to their own lusts, and they will turn away their hearing from the truth and turn aside rather to fables (2 Tim. 4:3-5).

Cardinal Ratzinger warned against two opposite but equally dangerous errors in the interpretations of the Bible. The first is a naive fundamentalism which is "understandable" in the face of theological confusion, but which is based on a false understanding of Divine Revelation. The second stems from an abuse of the historical-critical method. This error is rampant not only in exegesis, but also in catechetics and systematic theology. The Cardinal gave as an example the portrayal of Jesus by some liberation theologians as a political rebel rather than as the Son of God. Speaking on defending orthodox Catholic teachings on the Virgin Birth and the Resurrection as crucial, the Cardinal said,

> We must understand that God is active in the world and in history: otherwise, He would not be much of a God. He would become merely a God of ideas which often turns out to be merely the idea of God.

There are some who speak of a "cosmic" Christ as distinguished from the Redemptive Christ. There have been exegetes of the Bible who have attempted to explain away the historical Resurrection of the body of Jesus, the same body which was crucified and later ascended into heaven. The Resurrection is crucial to faith in Jesus Christ as Son of God, Savior. The Virgin Birth is essential for the same reason. In the official teachings of the Catholic Church the rising from the dead of Christ on the third day after His death and burial is a basic truth of Christianity. It is expressed in all the creeds and in all rules of faith of the ancient Church until the present and will be until the end of the world since Jesus promised that the gates of hell shall never prevail against the Church He would build on Peter.

Jesus rose through His own power. The source of the power of Jesus' Resurrection was the *hypostatic union*, that is, the union of the human and divine natures of Jesus in the one Divine Person of Jesus Christ. The principal cause was the Word of God, together with the Father and the Holy Spirit. All forms of rationalism in ancient and modern times, in terms of various hypotheses — that of deceit, of His apparent death, of vision, of symbolism — all deny Christ's historical Resurrection. Nothing is more central in the faith as attested by Peter's sermon on Pentecost Sunday and as defended by the Church ever since, in its most solemn teaching authority. In order to be a Catholic, one must believe that the same body of Jesus, born of the Virgin Mary and which was crucified on the Cross, died and was buried, rose again, and later ascended into heaven. The physical risen body of Jesus was in a state of glory. This is evident from circumstances of the appearances recorded in the Gospels and Acts. Christ's supremacy over the limitations of space and time is presented. The risen Christ retained the wounds in his transfigured body as tokens of his triumph over death (John 20:27) and as evidence that His risen body was the same body that was crucified.

In all the distortions of Christian doctrine in interpreting the Bible, we can see the importance of the authority Jesus gave His Church, which St. Paul repeatedly calls in Scripture "the body of Christ" and which Scripture tells us has the Holy Spirit as Soul and the "Spirit of Truth." Even some Biblical scholars can come to some ridiculous conclusions. While the Church encourages theological studies and Biblical studies of scholars, their conclusions hold no validity in speaking for Jesus Christ without official Church endorsement. Jesus founded a Church to which He and the Father gave His authority and the Holy Spirit. This points out the wisdom of God in giving his Church the papacy. With many and varied interpretations of the

Scriptures, if there was not a primacy of authority speaking for Christ in the Church the result would be that each man would interpret for himself. Separation from the papacy, the See of Peter, has certainly resulted in hundreds of religious denominations. One's objections should be of help in understanding why the authority of the Church, which is the authority of Christ, is more important than individual interpretations of the Bible. It should help you understand that while the Bible is truly the inspired Word of God, we need the Church as the official guardian and interpreter of it.

# *If You Liked*
# Protestant Fundamentalism
# and the Born-Again Catholic

## Fatima Family Messenger — $13 per year
## $25 for 2 yrs. / $35 for 3 yrs. (please note: 1990 prices)
### Foreign: $18 per year (US funds please)

## A quarterly publication / edited by Father Robert J. Fox

### PAYMENT MUST ACCOMPANY ORDER
Order now/RENEW NOW for next issue.
Allow 3 months for first issue.

Bulk prices: $8 *each,* per year, in bulk of 10 or more sent to same address.

## Fatima Family Messenger
FD

Name

Street; RR

City                    State     Zip

Mail payment, name & address to:
*FFA Subscription Dept., New Hope, Ky. 40052*

# *. . . you'll love*
# Fatima Family Messenger

# ABOUT THE AUTHOR

Father Robert J. Fox was ordained a priest in 1955 for the Diocese of Sioux Falls in South Dakota. Since ordination, he has been assigned to various parishes over the years. His "parish" has extended throughout the United States and beyond because of his many writings and extensive youth work.

The author has written more than twenty books, hundreds of articles, and has produced educational audio cassettes and albums pertaining to the Catholic faith. His thirty-nine television shows have been broadcast repeatedly on Eternal Word Television Network.

For years Father Fox was a weekly columnist for the *National Catholic Register* and a frequent contributor to *Our Sunday Visitor* and other nationally-known publications.

Years ago, this priest-author started the Fatima Youth Apostolate and presently is director of the Fatima Family Apostolate. He is editor of the *Fatima Family Messenger*. For many years he has taken Catholic teenagers and young adults to Europe during the summer in order to allow them to experience more deeply their Catholic roots and traditions.

In addition to his writings and apostolates, Father Fox serves as pastor of St. Mary of Mercy Parish in Alexandria, South Dakota, where each June at the Fatima Family Shrine a National Marian Congress is held. The congress features guest speakers of international fame.